State Children's Health Insurance Program (SCHIP)

Mary T. Ewing
Editor

Nova Science Publishers, Inc.
New York

For permission to use material from this book please contact us:
Telephone 631-231-7269; Fax 631-231-8175
Web Site: http://www.novapublishers.com

LIBRARY OF CONGRESS CATALOGING-IN-PUBLICATION DATA

State Children's Health Insurance Program (SCHIP) / Mary T. Ewing (editor)
p.; cm.
Includes index.
ISBN: 978-1-60456-333-7 (hardcover)
1. State Children's Health Insurance Program (U.S.) 2. Child health services--United States--Finance. 3. Insurance, Health--Government policy--United States. 4. Medicaid. I. Ewing, Mary T.
[DNLM: 1. State Children's Health Insurance Program (U.S.) 2. Insurance, Health--economics--United States. 3. Child Health Services--United States. 4. Financing, Government--economics--United States. 5. Health Policy--United States. 6. Medicaid. 7. Medicare. W 250 AA1 S7967 2008]
RA413.7.U53S73 2008
362.198'92000973—dc22

2007050799

Published by Nova Science Publishers, Inc. ✣ New York

CONTENTS

PREFACE

The State Children's Health Insurance Program (SCHIP) offers federal matching funds for states and territories to provide health insurance to uninsured, low-income children in families whose annual incomes are too high to qualify for Medicaid. Unlike Medicaid, which operates as an individual entitlement, SCHIP operates as a capped grant program. Allotment of funds among states is determined by a formula set in law. Once a state depletes a given year's original allotment, other than funds from prior years made available through redistribution, no additional federal funds will be made available to that state for that year. States have the flexibility to design their programs to operate within these funding constraints. The allotment and redistribution methods under current law have been incompatible with state spending patterns to date.

Chapter 1 - The House and Senate approved the conference report (H.Rept. 109-62) on H.Con.Res. 95, the Concurrent Resolution on the FY2006 Budget, on April 28, 2005. The Senate Committee on Finance was instructed to meet a budget reconciliation target of $10 billion in direct spending savings over a five-year period, FY2006-FY2010. On October 25, 2005, the Senate Finance Committee reported its reconciliation proposal to the Senate Budget Committee, which subsequently incorporated the proposal into S. 1932, The Deficit Reduction Omnibus Reconciliation Act of 2005. In the House, the Committee on Energy and Commerce had budget reconciliation instructions that specified a mandatory savings target of $14.734 billion between FY2006 and FY2010. The Committee's recommendations were incorporated into the House Budget Committee's bill, The Deficit Reduction Act of 2005. The House passed its version of the bill on November 18, 2005.

The Senate bill proposes changes to Medicaid, the State Children's Health Insurance program (SCHIP), and Medicare. Based on Congressional Budget Office (CBO) estimates, the largest Medicaid savings amounts are the result of changes in the reimbursement of outpatient prescription drugs. Other areas of Medicaid savings include changes to some asset transfer rules for Medicaid-eligible individuals applying for long-term care services and changes to the Medicaid program designed to combat fraud, waste, and abuse. Increases in Medicaid spending would largely result from temporary federal medical assistance percentage (FMAP) increases targeted to help Medicaid recipients from selected Louisiana parishes and counties in Alabama and Mississippi devastated by Hurricane Katrina, and also from the limiting of any FY2006-FY2007 FMAP decrease to Alaska and the re-computation of FMAPs for FY2006. The bill includes a number of Medicaid demonstration projects and some benefit and eligibility expansions. The proposal would alter the method for redistribution of SCHIP funds to the states. Medicare savings would result from changes in Medicare's Part C (Medicare Advantage) and the establishment of variations in provider payments that reflect quality differences (value-based purchasing, or "pay for performance"). The proposal would also provide for a 1% Medicare payment update for physicians in 2006.

The House bill's health program provisions are largely limited to changes in the Medicaid program. The House bill achieves its largest savings with cost-sharing and benefit changes. The bill also foresees savings from changes in prescription drug reimbursement and asset transfer rules. Increased spending provisions are focused on long-term care service benefits, the establishment of health opportunity account demonstrations, and Hurricane Katrina health program relief.

On December 19, 2006 the House agreed to a conference report on S. 1932. However, the Senate amended the report. The amended agreement passed the Senate on December 21, 2006, and was returned to the House for further action. It is expected that the agreement will be taken up in the early part of the session.

Chapter 2 - Each year, the President is required to submit a comprehensive federal budget proposal to Congress no later than the first Monday in February. The House and Senate Budget Committees then develop their respective budget resolutions. Differences between the houses are supposed to be resolved by April 15, but this deadline is rarely met. Although it is not binding, the resolution provides a framework for subsequent legislative action.

The President's FY2008 budget contains a number of proposals that would affect Medicaid and the State Children's Health Insurance Program (SCHIP). While certain proposals would require legislative action, others would be implemented administratively (e.g., via regulatory changes, issuance of program guidance, or other possible methods). The President's budget also contains a number of proposals that would affect health insurance.

On May 17, the House and Senate adopted a conference agreement on the budget resolution (H.Rept. 110-153 accompanying S.Con.Res. 21). The FY2008 budget resolution provides a reserve fund of up to $50 billion for SCHIP legislation that is deficit-neutral in the Senate and deficit/surplus-neutral in the House, a variety of other deficit-neutral reserve funds, up to $383 million for health care fraud and abuse control, and two "sense of the Congress" provisions regarding health care cost growth and affordable health coverage.

To date, a number of Medicaid and SCHIP issues have seen legislative action in the 110th Congress. A war supplemental appropriations bill enacted on May 25 (H.R. 2206, P.L. 110-28) contains SCHIP funding, delays implementation of certain Medicaid administrative proposals, requires the use of tamper-resistant pads for Medicaid prescriptions, and provides a Medicaid Pharmacy Plus waiver extension. Legislation was also enacted to temporarily extend Medicaid transitional medical assistance (TMA) through September 30, 2007 (S. 1701, P.L. 110-48). Another bill to extend TMA and the QI-1 program through December 31, 2007, apply an asset verification pilot to Medicaid for five years, and delay implementation of the new Medicaid tamper-resistant prescription pad requirement for six months (H.R. 3668, P.L. 110-90) was enacted at the end of September.

On the issue of SCHIP reauthorization, numerous bills have been introduced, including the Senate-passed Children's Health Insurance Program Reauthorization Act of 2007 (S. 1893/H.R. 976) and the House-passed Children's Health and Medicare Protection Act of 2007 (H.R. 3162). A bicameral agreement on SCHIP reauthorization passed the House on September 25 and the Senate on September 27 as an amendment to H.R. 976. President Bush vetoed the legislation on October 3. A continuing resolution that contains short-term funding for SCHIP (H.J.Res. 52, P.L. 110-92) was enacted at the end of September.

Chapter 3 - The Balanced Budget Act of 1997 (BBA 97; P.L. 105-33) established the State Children's Health Insurance Program (SCHIP) under a new Title XXI of the Social Security Act. In general, this program allows states to cover targeted low-income children with no health insurance in families with income that is above Medicaid eligibility levels. As of August 2007, the highest upper income eligibility limit under SCHIP was 350% of the federal poverty level, in one state, New Jersey.

Under SCHIP, states may enroll targeted low-income children in an SCHIP-financed expansion of Medicaid, create a new separate state SCHIP program, or devise a combination of both approaches. States choosing the Medicaid option must provide all Medicaid mandatory benefits and all optional services covered under the state plan, and must follow the nominal Medicaid cost-sharing rules. In general, separate state programs must follow certain coverage and benefit options outlined in SCHIP law. While some cost-sharing provisions vary by family income, the total annual aggregate cost-sharing (including premiums, copayments, and other similar charges) for a family may not exceed 5% of total income in a year. Preventive services are exempt from cost-sharing.

Nearly $40 billion was appropriated for SCHIP for FY1998 through FY2007. Annual allotments among the states are determined by a formula that is based on a combination of the number of low-income children and low-income uninsured children in the state, adjusted by a cost factor that reflects the average health service industry wages in the state compared to the national average. Like Medicaid, SCHIP is a federal-state matching program. While the Medicaid federal medical assistance percentage (FMAP) ranged from 50% to 75.89% in FY2007, the enhanced SCHIP FMAP ranged from 65% to 83.12% across states.

All states, the District of Columbia, and five territories have SCHIP programs. As of June 2007, 15 use Medicaid expansions, 18 use separate state programs, and 23 use a combination approach. At the national level, approximately 6.7 million children were enrolled in SCHIP during FY2006 (latest official data). In addition, 12 states reported enrolling about 701,000 adults in SCHIP through program waivers.

Spending was slow in the early years of SCHIP, but that trend changed in more recent years and has led some states to exhaust their federal SCHIP funds. The Deficit Reduction Act of 2005 (DRA; P.L. 109-171) provided a new appropriation of $283 million to address anticipated FY2006 shortfalls in federal SCHIP funding, although two states (Illinois and Massachusetts) still experienced shortfalls. The NIH Reform Act of 2006 (P.L. 109-482) included provisions to delay FY2007 shortfalls until the first part of May. Under P.L. 110-28, Congress appropriated up to $650 million to cover shortfalls in 12 states in FY2007. Before the August recess, Congress passed legislation (H.R. 3162 in the House and S. 1893/H.R. 976 in the Senate) that would provide additional funding for SCHIP for FY2008 and additional years, and would make a number of other changes to both SCHIP and Medicaid.

The Balanced Budget Act of 1997 (BBA 97; P.L. 105-33) established the State Children's Health Insurance Program (SCHIP) under a new Title XXI of the Social Security Act. The program offers federal matching funds to states and territories to provide health insurance to certain low-income children. Although specific requirements apply to eligibility, benefits, and beneficiary cost-sharing, as described below, these rules can be modified via waiver authority provided in Section 1115 of the Social Security Act.[1]

Chapter 4 - Each year, the President is required to submit a comprehensive federal budget proposal to Congress no later than the first Monday in February. Once it is submitted, the Congressional Budget Office (CBO) analyzes the proposal using its own economic assumptions and estimation techniques. Then, the House and Senate Budget Committees each develop a budget resolution after reviewing the President's budget, the views of other committees, and information from CBO. Differences between the houses are supposed to be resolved by April 15, but this deadline is rarely met. Although it is not binding, the resolution provides a framework for subsequent legislative action on the budget (e.g., annual appropriations bills).

The President's FY2007 budget contains a number of proposals that would affect Medicaid and the State Children's Health Insurance Program (SCHIP). Some are program expansions, and others are designed to reduce federal spending. While certain proposals would require legislative action, others would be implemented administratively (e.g., via regulatory changes, issuance of program guidance, etc.).

On March 9, 2006, the Senate Budget Committee reported a budget resolution, S.Con.Res. 83, which was subsequently amended and passed by the Senate on March 16. The resolution did not include reconciliation instructions for the Senate Finance Committee, which has jurisdiction over Medicaid and SCHIP. It did include a deficit-neutral reserve fund for the uninsured and funding for four of the President's Medicaid and SCHIP proposals.

On March 29, 2006, the House Budget Committee reported its own budget resolution, H.Con.Res. 376, which was subsequently amended and passed by the House on May 18. The resolution did not include reconciliation instructions for the House Energy and Commerce Committee, which has jurisdiction over Medicaid and SCHIP. Its spending levels for Medicaid and SCHIP are based on CBO's baseline projections under current law and policies, with no reduction in Medicaid assumed.

Although no agreement was reached by the House and Senate on a FY2007 budget resolution, current law spending for Medicaid and SCHIP is unaffected. As entitlement programs, their spending levels are based on the underlying benefit and eligibility criteria established in law (in the case of SCHIP, these criteria include a statutory annual funding cap). However, legislation that would increase Medicaid or SCHIP spending above current law could encounter procedural roadblocks in the House or Senate if funding is not assumed in a budget resolution or in a "deeming resolution." The annual appropriations process also provides an opportunity for Congress to place limitations on the availability of federal funds for specified Medicaid and SCHIP activities.

Before the 109th Congress adjourned, it passed two bills — H.R. 6111 and H.R. 6164 — that addressed a variety of Medicaid and SCHIP issues, including some of the proposals in the President's FY2007 budget.

Chapter 5 - The Balanced Budget Act of 1997 created the State Children's Health Insurance Program (SCHIP) and provided nearly $40 billion in appropriations over the 10-year period FY1998 to FY2007. Legislative action would be necessary to provide new funds for SCHIP for FY2008 and beyond, but SCHIP's statutory provisions do not need to be reauthorized as they will remain on the books unless Congress expressly repeals the current law. In the absence of an FY2008 SCHIP allotment, states with unexpended FY2006 and FY2007 federal SCHIP balances could continue to operate their programs with those funds in FY2008. Fourteen states and the District of Columbia are projected to be able to cover all of their federal FY2008 SCHIP spending even without an FY2008 SCHIP allotment. Among the

36 states projected to exhaust their federal SCHIP funds in FY2008, some may be able to access Medicaid funding, though at a reduced matching rate compared to SCHIP. However, 13 states would be in shortfall immediately, entering FY2008 with no prior-year SCHIP balances. An amount equal to approximately 18 days of these states' federal SCHIP expenditures is projected to be available from the redistribution of unspent FY2005 allotments. This report may be updated in December 2007 with states' more recent projections.

Chapter 6 - The State Children's Health Insurance Program (SCHIP) is a federal-state matching program providing health insurance to targeted low-income children (and some adults) in families with income above Medicaid eligibility levels. Because SCHIP is a capped-grant program, it is possible for states to exhaust all of the federal SCHIP funds available to them in a given year. According to data available in late December 2006, 14 states are projected to exhaust their federal SCHIP funds in FY2007 (i.e., have a federal SCHIP shortfall). On January 15, 2007, the President signed into law H.R. 6164 (National Institutes of Health Reform Act of 2006, P.L. 109-482). The SCHIP provisions of H.R. 6164 require a redistribution of certain unspent FY2004 and FY2005 SCHIP original allotments to shortfall states in FY2007. The goal is to delay as long as possible the date in FY2007 on which any state faces a shortfall. Congress may address the remaining FY2007 shortfalls as part of reauthorization that provides SCHIP with appropriations needed beginning in FY2008. The SCHIP provisions of H.R. 6164 delay shortfalls to the first part of May 2007, according to current CRS projections. Although the provisions redistribute an additional $124 million for projected FY2007 shortfalls, the shortfalls remaining for the rest of the fiscal year are projected at $745 million. This report summarizes the SCHIP provisions of H.R. 6164 and their impact on SCHIP financing in FY2007.

Chapter 7 - The President vetoed legislation (H.R. 976) that would have provided new federal funding for the State Children's Health Insurance Program (SCHIP) in FY2008 through FY2012. On September 29, 2007, the President signed a continuing resolution that contains a temporary FY2008 appropriation for allotments for SCHIP (H.J.Res. 52, P.L. 110-92). Under this extension, SCHIP is appropriated the same amount for FY2008 that was appropriated for FY2007 ($5 billion), with the current-law formula used to allot these funds among the states and territories. The current continuing resolution makes the FY2008 allotments available only through November 16, 2007. The FY2008 allotments can be available past November 16 only if new legislation is enacted. Based on states' projections, if the current FY2008 allotments were available through the end of FY2008, 21 states would exhaust all available federal SCHIP funds during the fiscal year, with the first states experiencing shortfalls in March 2008. This report provides projections of those states' shortfalls as well as projections of states' FY2008 allotments as would occur under the vetoed H.R. 976 and new SCHIP legislation approved by the House, H.R. 3963, which is identical to the vetoed H.R. 976 in terms of the appropriations and formulas for SCHIP allotments.

Chapter 8 - Health insurance is an important support for individuals receiving, leaving or diverted from the Temporary Assistance for Needy Families (TANF) welfare or cash assistance program for low-income families. Medicaid and SCHIP (State Children's Health Insurance Program) are key vehicles for providing such coverage. While there is no formal link between TANF and either Medicaid or SCHIP, some TANF-eligibles, especially children, are likely to qualify for one of these programs. But state eligibility rules can be complex and often differ for parents versus children, leaving some parents, in particular, without coverage. Finally, six to 12 months of transitional medical assistance (TMA) for families losing Medicaid coverage for work-related reasons expired on December 31, 2005, but was reinstated retroactively to this date, and extended through 2006 under the Deficit Reduction Act of 2005 (P.L. 109-171).

In: State Children's Health Insurance Program (SCHIP) ISBN: 978-1-60456-333-7
Editor: Mary T. Ewing, pp. 1-56

Chapter 1

BUDGET RECONCILIATION FY2006: MEDICAID, MEDICARE, AND STATE CHILDREN'S HEALTH INSURANCE PROGRAM (SCHIP) PROVISIONS*

Evelyne P. Baumrucker, Hinda Chaikind, April Grady, Jim Hahn, Jean Hearne, Elicia J. Herz, Bob Lyke, Paulette C. Morgan, Jennifer O'Sullivan, Richard Rimkunas, Julie Stone, Sibyl Tilson and Karen Tritz

ABSTRACT

The House and Senate approved the conference report (H.Rept. 109-62) on H.Con.Res. 95, the Concurrent Resolution on the FY2006 Budget, on April 28, 2005. The Senate Committee on Finance was instructed to meet a budget reconciliation target of $10 billion in direct spending savings over a five-year period, FY2006-FY2010. On October 25, 2005, the Senate Finance Committee reported its reconciliation proposal to the Senate Budget Committee, which subsequently incorporated the proposal into S. 1932, The Deficit Reduction Omnibus Reconciliation Act of 2005. In the House, the Committee on Energy and Commerce had budget reconciliation instructions that specified a mandatory savings target of $14.734 billion between FY2006 and FY2010. The Committee's recommendations were incorporated into the House Budget Committee's bill, The Deficit Reduction Act of 2005. The House passed its version of the bill on November 18, 2005.

The Senate bill proposes changes to Medicaid, the State Children's Health Insurance program (SCHIP), and Medicare. Based on Congressional Budget Office (CBO) estimates, the largest Medicaid savings amounts are the result of changes in the reimbursement of outpatient prescription drugs. Other areas of Medicaid savings include changes to some asset transfer rules for Medicaid-eligible individuals applying for long-

* Excerpted from CRS Report RL331, dated January 26, 2006.

term care services and changes to the Medicaid program designed to combat fraud, waste, and abuse. Increases in Medicaid spending would largely result from temporary federal medical assistance percentage (FMAP) increases targeted to help Medicaid recipients from selected Louisiana parishes and counties in Alabama and Mississippi devastated by Hurricane Katrina, and also from the limiting of any FY2006-FY2007 FMAP decrease to Alaska and the re-computation of FMAPs for FY2006. The bill includes a number of Medicaid demonstration projects and some benefit and eligibility expansions. The proposal would alter the method for redistribution of SCHIP funds to the states. Medicare savings would result from changes in Medicare's Part C (Medicare Advantage) and the establishment of variations in provider payments that reflect quality differences (value-based purchasing, or "pay for performance"). The proposal would also provide for a 1% Medicare payment update for physicians in 2006.

The House bill's health program provisions are largely limited to changes in the Medicaid program. The House bill achieves its largest savings with cost-sharing and benefit changes. The bill also foresees savings from changes in prescription drug reimbursement and asset transfer rules. Increased spending provisions are focused on long-term care service benefits, the establishment of health opportunity account demonstrations, and Hurricane Katrina health program relief.

On December 19, 2006 the House agreed to a conference report on S. 1932. However, the Senate amended the report. The amended agreement passed the Senate on December 21, 2006, and was returned to the House for further action. It is expected that the agreement will be taken up in the early part of the session.

FY2006 Budget Reconciliation Targets

The House and Senate approved the conference report (H.Rept. 109-62) on H.Con.Res. 95, the Concurrent Resolution on the FY2006 Budget, on April 28, 2005. The annual concurrent resolution on the budget sets forth the congressional budget. When the federal deficit is expected to be large, budget resolutions often require reductions in mandatory spending. In such instances, the budget resolution includes reconciliation instructions that require authorizing committees to report changes to legislation to reduce spending on mandatory programs under their jurisdictions. The FY2006 budget resolution includes reconciliation instructions that direct authorizing committees to report legislation to reduce mandatory spending for the FY2006-FY2010 period. Subsequently, these proposals are to be combined in a single reconciliation bill by each of the House and Senate Budget Committees.

The Senate Committee on Finance was instructed to meet a budget reconciliation target of $10 billion in mandatory spending savings over the five-year period. On October 25, 2005, the Senate Finance Committee reported its reconciliation proposal to the Senate Budget Committee, which subsequently incorporated the proposal into S. 1932, The Deficit Reduction Omnibus Reconciliation Act of 2005. The Finance Committee met its reconciliation instruction by making changes in Medicaid, Medicare, and the State Children's Health Insurance program (SCHIP). In the House, the Committee on Energy and Commerce had budget reconciliation instructions specifying a mandatory savings target of $14.734 billion between FY2006 and FY2010. The Energy and Commerce Committee mark-up took place on October 27, 2005. In the health care area, its recommendations resulted in changes in Medicaid. The Committee's recommendations were incorporated into the House Budget

Committee bill, H.R. 4241, the Deficit Reduction Act of 2005, and reported on November 7, 2005.

A budget reconciliation conference agreement on S. 1932 was filed on December 19, 2005. The House agreed to the report by a vote of 212-206 that day. On December 21, the Senate removed extraneous provisions form the legislation pursuant to a point of order raised under the "Byrd rule," passed the amended agreement and returned the measure to the House. Final action on the conference agreement is expected when the House reconvenes later this month.

SENATE BILL

Like a number of Senate committees, the Senate Committee on Finance achieves its reconciliation instruction budget mark through recommended program changes that result in both direct spending increases and decreases. The Committee's Medicaid saving proposals include (a) changes in the payment methods for prescription drugs; (b) changes in eligibility and benefit rules for long-term care services; (c) changes in the program's approach to limit fraud; and, (d) changes in some components of state Medicaid financing. The Finance Committee also recommended a number of changes that would result in Medicaid spending increases. These proposals include (a) temporary financial relief for Medicaid costs of individuals who resided prior to Hurricane Katrina in selected parishes in Louisiana and counties in Alabama and Mississippi, and a provision not to allow Alaska's federal medical assistance percentage to fall below its FY2005 level; (b) an increase in the disproportionate share hospital payment allotment in the District of Columbia; and (c) a number of demonstrations and program expansions.

The legislation also contains several provisions that affect the State Children's Health Insurance Program (SCHIP), including (1) provisions to redistribute unspent FY2003-through-FY2005 original allotments to states that fully spent their original allotments, and (2) to prohibit additional states from using SCHIP funds to cover childless adults. The Medicare provisions include both direct spending savings and increases. The three major areas of Committee recommendations include (a) changes to the Medicare Advantage component of Medicare; (b) the development of value-based reimbursement for Medicare providers; and (c) a 1% update for physician reimbursement rates in 2006. The Finance Committee provisions include a number of other Medicare-related provisions.

Based on Congressional Budget Office (CBO) estimates, changes in the Medicare program would amount to $5.7 billion in savings from FY2006 to FY2010; changes in the Medicaid and the SCHIP program would amount to $4.3 billion in savings over the period.[1] The change in Medicare's payment for physician services would result in a $10.8 billion increase over the five-year period. But this would be offset by $12 billion in Medicare Advantage plan savings, and an additional $4.5 billion in savings from value-based purchasing. A temporary increase in federal medical assistance percentage (FMAP) payment rates for individuals in selected Louisiana parishes and counties in Alabama and Mississippi affected by Hurricane Katrina would increase Medicaid spending by $1.8 billion. The largest Medicaid savings proposal is the result of changes in the reimbursement for outpatient prescription drugs. The Finance Committee proposals result in a $6.3 billion reduction over the five-year period.

The health provisions in the Senate Finance Committee proposal were modified by several floor amendments. The amendments included changes that (1) would require that FY2006 FMAPs would be recalculated, and it would limit any reductions in a State's FY2006 FMAP rate. The estimated increased cost of this provision would be offset by extending outpatient prescription drug rebates to most managed care organizations. Other amendments would 1) authorize the continued provision of certain adult day health care services or medical adult day care services under a State Medicaid plan; (2) exclude discounts provided to mail order and nursing facility pharmacies from the determination of average manufacturer price and to extend the discounts offered under fee-for-service Medicaid for prescription drugs to managed care organizations; (3) amend Medicare to make a technical correction regarding purchase agreements for powerdriven wheelchairs, provide for coverage of ultrasound screening for abdominal aortic aneurysms under part B, improve patient access to, and utilization of, the colorectal cancer screening benefit, and provide for the coverage of marriage and family therapist services and mental health counselor services under part B of such title; (4) modify the quality measurement system defined in the Medicare value-based purchasing section of the proposal; (5) provide for a Medicaid demonstration project for low-income HIV-infected individuals; and (6) modify the Federal Upper Payment limit for independent pharmacies located in rural and frontier areas. Information on these amendments are incorporated in the Senate bill provision descriptions.

MEDICAID

Medicaid Outpatient Prescription Drugs

The major Medicaid outpatient prescription drug provisions alter the upper limits that apply to federal reimbursement of state spending on prescription drugs, alter the formulas for calculating the rebates that prescription drug manufacturers are required to pay to states, and establish special reporting requirements for the prices of certain "authorized" generic drugs and certain outpatient drugs administered in physicians' offices.

Federal Upper Limits

Under current law, state Medicaid programs set the prices paid to pharmacies for Medicaid outpatient drugs. Federal reimbursements for those drugs, however, are limited to a federal upper limit (FUL). The FUL that applies to drugs available from multiple sources (generic drugs, for the most part) is calculated by the Centers for Medicare and Medicaid Services (CMS) to be equal to 150% of the lowest published average wholesale price (AWP) for the least costly therapeutic equivalent. The upper limit that applies to brand-name and other drugs is equal to the acquisition cost as estimated by the states.

The Senate bill would replace the current FUL requirement so that state payments for single source drugs provided in pharmacies that are not critical access pharmacies would qualify for federal reimbursement up to 105% of the average manufacturer price (AMP) as reported to CMS by the manufacturers. FULs for multiple source drugs provided in pharmacies that are not critical access pharmacies would be equal to 115% of the weighted AMP for those drugs. State payments for single source drugs provided in critical access retail pharmacies would qualify for federal reimbursement up to the lesser of 108% of the AMP or the wholesale acquisition cost for the drug. FULs for multiple source drugs provided in critical access pharmacies would qualify for federal reimbursement up to the lesser of 140% of the AMP or the wholesale acquisition cost for the drug. Critical access retail pharmacies are defined as those retail pharmacies that are not within 20 miles of any other retail pharmacy. In addition, the bill includes interim upper payment limits that would apply during calendar year 2006, before the new FULs become effective..

In addition, this section of the bill would modify the definitions of the prices that manufacturers are currently required to provide to CMS. The definition of AMP, an important price point for calculating Medicaid drug rebates and for the proposed FULs, would become more specified than under current law. For example, one of the new specifications would direct manufacturers to include cash and volume discounts in the computation of AMP. The bill would also define weighted AMP for the purpose of calculating FULs for multiple source drugs, and would establish that dispensing fees for multiple source drugs may be higher than those for single source drugs.

Rebates

Under current law, prescription drug manufacturers that participate in the Medicaid program are required to pay rebates to states for drugs provided to Medicaid beneficiaries for which fee for service payments are required. The rebates are calculated based on a formula in statute. For single source and "innovator" multiple source drugs (those drugs that had formerly been sold under a patent, but are now off patent) basic rebates are equal to the greater of 15.1% of the AMP or the difference between the reported AMP and the best price for each drug. The rebate for all other multiple source drugs is equal to 11% of the AMP. The Senate bill makes two major changes to Medicaid rebate policy. The bill would require manufacturers to begin paying rebates for drugs provided to Medicaid beneficiaries who are enrolled in most managed care organizations and would raise the rebate percentages for all drugs. The basic rebate for single source and innovator multiple source drugs would be raised to the greater of 18.1% of the AMP or the difference between the reported AMP and the best price for each drug. The rebate for all other multiple source drugs would be raised to 17% of the AMP. States would have the option of collecting rebates from pharmaceutical manufacturers for those drugs provided to enrollees of MCOs, or alternatively, allowing the MCOs to collect the rebates in exchange for reduced MCO payment rates.

Authorized Generics and Physician-Administered Drugs

Authorized generic drugs are generics that are produced by the same manufacturer that produces the brand-name version of the drug; or by a different manufacturer with the authorization of the manufacturer that holds the patent on the brand-name version. The Senate bill would establish a requirement that a manufacturer reporting the AMP and best price for a brand-name product must also include the prices at which authorized generic versions are sold. This provision is estimated to increase rebates that result in savings to the Medicaid program, since authorized generic drugs are generally less expensive than brand-name versions of the same drug. In addition, the bill would require states to provide utilization and coding information to CMS for physician-administered outpatient drugs. This would improve the ability of CMS to ensure manufacturers pay rebates for those drugs.

Long-Term Care under Medicaid

Medicaid is a means-tested program. Current law regarding eligibility, asset transfers, and estate recovery are designed to restrict access to Medicaid's long-term care services to people who are poor or have very high medical or long-term care expenses, and who apply their income and assets toward the cost of their care. Under current law, states must impose penalties on individuals applying for Medicaid who transfer assets (all income and resources of the individual and of the individual's spouse) for less than fair-market value (an estimate of the value of an asset if sold at the prevailing price at the time it was actually transferred). Specifically, states must delay Medicaid eligibility for individuals receiving care in a nursing home, and, at state option, certain people receiving care in community-based settings who have transferred assets for less than fair-market value on or after a "look-back date." The "look-back date" is 36 months prior to application for Medicaid for income and most assets disposed of by the individual, and 60 months in the case of certain trusts.

Calculating the Length of the Penalty Period

The length of the delay in Medicaid eligibility is determined by dividing the total cumulative uncompensated value of all assets transferred by the individual (or individual's spouse) on or after the look-back date by the average monthly cost to a private patient of a nursing facility in the state (or, at the option of the state, in the community in which the individual is institutionalized) at the time of application. States use different methods for counting transfers and determining the length of a penalty period when more than one transfer is made during a limited time period. The Senate bill would impose certain requirements on how these calculations would be made in an attempt to ensure that such calculations result in longer, rather than shorter, penalty periods. Specifically, the provisions would (1) require states to count cumulative transfers (transfers made during *different* months) as one transfer, and (2) prohibit states from rounding down to shorten the penalty period.

Changing Non-Countable Assets to Countable Assets

Not all assets that an applicant may have are counted for the purposes of determining an applicant's eligibility for Medicaid long-term care services, or for determining if a transfer for less than fair-market value has been made — states generally follow rules established by the Supplemental Security Income (SSI) program for counting income and assets of applicants. Provisions in the Senate bill would change the status of certain types of assets from non-countable (or exempt) assets to countable assets to decrease the ways in which individuals might protect assets to meet Medicaid's means-testing requirements sooner than they otherwise would. Under this proposal, certain types of assets that are currently exempt, including certain types of annuities, promissory notes, loans, mortgages, and life estates, would be counted for the purposes of Medicaid eligibility determinations. The bill would also require that states treat the purchase of an annuity as the disposal of an asset for less than fair-market value unless the state is named as the remainder beneficiary in the first position (or in the second position after the community spouse) for at least the total amount of Medicaid expenditures paid on behalf of the annuitant.

Undue Hardship Waivers

To protect beneficiaries from unintended consequences of asset transfer penalties, current law requires states to establish procedures for waiving penalties for persons who, according to criteria established by the Secretary, show that a penalty would impose an undue hardship. The ways in which states implement this requirement vary significantly by state. Whereas a few states have formal application processes and specified eligibility criteria to apply to each application, most states have informal methods for evaluating each application and no formal method for notifying applicants of the availability of undue hardship waivers. The Senate bill would impose requirements on state practices to formalize and standardize the waiver application process. The bill would specify criteria that states would use to determine eligibility for a waiver and require states to provide notice to applicants about the availability of undue hardship waivers.

Medicaid Estate Recovery

Current law requires states to recover the private assets (e.g., countable and non-countable assets) of the estates of deceased beneficiaries who have received certain long-term care services. Recovery of Medicaid payments may be made only after the death of the individual's surviving spouse, and only when there is no surviving child under age 21 and no surviving child who is blind or has a disability. Estate recovery is limited to the amounts paid by Medicaid for services received by the individual and is limited only to certain assets that remain in the estate of the beneficiary upon his or her death. As a result, estate recovery is generally applied to a beneficiary's home, if available, and certain other assets within a beneficiary's estate. The Senate provision would make any remaining balance of an annuity subject to recovery by the state after a beneficiary's death.

Long-Term Care Insurance Partnership Program

Under Medicaid's long-term care (LTC) insurance partnership program, certain persons who have exhausted (or used at least some of) the benefits of a private long-term care insurance policy may access Medicaid without meeting the same means-testing requirements as other groups of Medicaid-eligible individuals. For these individuals, means-testing requirements are relaxed at (1) the time of application to Medicaid; and (2) the time of the beneficiary's death when Medicaid estate recovery is generally applied. Under current law, these provisions are limited to selected states.[2]

The Senate Committee's provision would allow additional states to implement long-term care partnership programs as long as the state long-term care insurance programs would provide for the disregard of assets in an amount equal to the amount of payments made to, or on behalf of, the LTC insurance policyholder. Long-term care partnership programs would be required to meet certain requirements. The Senate's bill would also require LTC insurance partnership programs already in existence to meet most of the specified requirements on or after two years after enactment.

LTC insurance policies sold under the LTC insurance partnership plan would be required to meet certain requirements specified in the National Association of Insurance Commissioners' (NAIC) Long-Term Care Insurance Model Regulations and Long-Term Care

Insurance Model Act. In addition, the Secretary, in consultation with specified entities, would be required to develop uniform standards for reciprocity, minimum reporting requirements, suitability, incontestability, nonforfeiture, independent certification for benefits assessment, rating requirements, and dispute resolution.

Fraud, Waste, and Abuse

Third Party Liability

With certain exceptions, Medicaid is a payer of last resort, meaning that states must ascertain the legal liability of third parties to pay for Medicaid care and services. They must also seek reimbursement for Medicaid costs from third parties when necessary. Examples of potentially liable third parties specified in current Medicaid law include health insurers, group health plans, service benefit plans, and health maintenance organizations. With respect to third-party liability, the Senate bill would clarify the right of states to obtain reimbursement from specific third parties — self-insured plans and pharmacy benefit managers — that are legally responsible for payment of claims for health care items or services provided to Medicaid beneficiaries. The bill would also require each state to have laws that in effect require third parties to provide eligibility and claims payment data for Medicaid-eligible individuals and to cooperate with payment and recovery efforts by Medicaid.

Medicaid Integrity Program

Under current law, states and the federal government — acting primarily through CMS and the Office of Inspector General within the Department of Health and Human Services (HHS) — share in the responsibility for safeguarding Medicaid program integrity. The Senate bill would establish a Medicaid Integrity Program, under which entities that meet certain contracting requirements (modeled after the Medicare Integrity Program) would review the actions of Medicaid providers, audit claims for payment, identify and recover overpayments, and provide education on payment integrity and benefit quality assurance issues. Appropriations for the Medicaid Integrity Program would total \$50 million in FY2006, \$49 million in each of FY2007 and FY2008, \$74 million in each of FY2009 and FY2010, and \$75 million in FY2011 and beyond. A Medicaid Chief Financial Officer and Medicaid Integrity Program Oversight Board would also be established, and an additional \$25 million would be appropriated in each of FY2006-FY2010 for Medicaid activities of the Office of Inspector General in HHS.

Other Provisions

Other fraud, waste, and abuse provisions in the Senate bill would require states to adhere to compensation standards for Medicaid consultants and other contractors issued by the Inspector General of HHS; encourage states to enact laws modeled after the federal False Claims Act by decreasing the percentage of Medicaid amounts recovered under such laws that must be repaid to the federal government; require that any entity receiving annual Medicaid payments of \$1 million or more educate its employees about state and federal false-claims laws, whistle-blower protections, and policies and procedures for detecting fraud, waste, and abuse; and prohibit states from billing Medicaid twice for the same drugs.

State Financing and Medicaid

Temporary FMAP Increases

Two provisions in the Senate bill would affect federal Medicaid reimbursement for states. First, for items and services furnished between August 28, 2005 and May 15, 2006, states would receive 100% reimbursement for Medicaid assistance provided to individuals who resided prior to Hurricane Katrina in one of the parishes in Louisiana or counties in Mississippi and Alabama specified in the bill. Costs directly attributable to related administrative activities would also be reimbursed at 100%. Second, the bill would provide that if Alaska's calculated federal medical assistance percentage (FMAP, which is based on a formula that provides higher reimbursement to states with lower per capita incomes relative to the national average and vice versa) for FY2006 or FY2007 is less than its FY2005 FMAP, the FY2005 FMAP shall apply.

Managed Care Organization Provider Tax Reform

States sometimes raise their share of Medicaid program costs by establishing provider taxes that federal law requires to be broad based. The statute defines broad based taxes as those that apply to all providers within a class of providers. Two examples of classes of providers are hospitals and physicians. One of the classes of providers that current law allows a state provider tax to apply to is Medicaid managed care organizations. The Senate bill would modify this class of providers (both Medicaid and non-Medicaid) to encompass all managed care organizations, so that, in the future, these taxes would be required to be more broad than are allowed under current law. States with existing provider specific taxes levied against Medicaid managed care organizations would be allowed to keep those taxes.

Disproportionate Share Hospital Allotment for the District of Columbia

Medicaid requires states to make payments to hospitals that treat disproportionate numbers of Medicaid beneficiaries and those who cannot pay for their care. The Senate bill would increase allotments for the District of Columbia for making such disproportionate share hospital (DSH) payments. The increased allotments would become available on October 1, 2005.

Changes to Medicaid Targeted Case Management Benefit

Targeted case management (TCM) is an optional benefit under the Medicaid state plan that is designed to help Medicaid beneficiaries access needed medical, social, educational, and other services. States that cover the TCM service do not have to offer the benefit statewide and can limit the service to specific groups of Medicaid beneficiaries (e.g., those with chronic mental illness). Several states extend the TCM services to individuals who may also be receiving certain case management services as part of another state and/or federal program (e.g., foster care, juvenile justice).

This proposal would clarify the activities that can be considered a TCM service, and those activities (primarily foster care-related activities) that may not be reimbursed as TCM services. The proposal also states that Medicaid funding would only be available for TCM services if there are no other third parties liable to pay for such services, including as reimbursement under a medical, social, educational, or other program. The proposal would take effect January 1, 2006.

Inclusion of Podiatrists as Physicians

Currently, states may provide Medicaid coverage for podiatrist services under an optional benefit category of "other practitioners." In contrast, physician services are a mandatory Medicaid benefit. The proposal would treat podiatrists as physicians, as is the case under Medicare, thereby making it mandatory for states to provide Medicaid coverage for the medical services of podiatrists.

Demonstration Project Providing Medicaid Coverage for Institutions for Mental Disease to Stabilize Emergency Medical Conditions

Current law prohibits Medicaid payments for residents of an Institution for Mental Disease (IMD) between the ages of 22 and 64. This proposal would require the Secretary of HHS to establish a three-year demonstration project in eligible states to provide Medicaid coverage for IMD services (not publicly-owned or operated) for Medicaid eligible individuals who are between the ages of 21 and 64, and who require IMD services to stabilize an emergency medical condition. Eligible states include Arizona, Arkansas, Louisiana, Maine, North Dakota, Wyoming, and four additional states to be selected by the Secretary. The proposal appropriates $30 million for FY2006 for the demonstration which would be available through December 31, 2008. The proposal also requires the Secretary to submit annual and final reports to Congress regarding the progress of the demonstration project.

Limitation on FMAP Reduction

The federal medical assistance percentage (FMAP), which has a statutory minimum of 50% and maximum of 83%, is the rate at which states are reimbursed for most Medicaid service expenditures. An enhanced FMAP is available for both services and administration under SCHIP, subject to the availability of funds from a state's SCHIP allotment. When state FMAPs are calculated by HHS for an upcoming fiscal year (usually in the preceding November), the state and U.S. per capita personal income amounts used in the formula are equal to the average of the three most recent calendar years of data on per capita personal income available from the Department of Commerce's Bureau of Economic Analysis (BEA). When BEA undertakes a comprehensive revision of its income data (reflecting methodological and other changes) every few years, there may be upward and downward revisions to each of the component parts of personal income (e.g., wages and salaries, supplements to wages and salaries such as employer contributions for employee pension and insurance funds, etc.). To calculate FMAPs for FY2006, HHS used per capita personal income data for 2001, 2002, and 2003 that reflected BEA's latest comprehensive revision. Under the Senate bill, FY2006 FMAPs would be re-computed so that no FY2006 FMAP would be less than the greater of (1) a state's FY2005 FMAP minus 0.5 percentage points (0.1 in the case of Delaware and Michigan, 0.3 in the case of Kentucky) or (2) the FY2006 FMAP that would have been determined for a state if per capita incomes for 2001 and 2002 that were used to calculate the state's FY2005 FMAP (i.e., pre-revision BEA data, which are not available for 2003) were used.

Authority to Continue Providing Certain Adult Day Health Care Services or Medical Adult Day Care Services

Adult day care services are generally community-based daytime programs for adults with disabilities or chronic conditions that provide health, social, and related support services in a setting outside the person's home. Most states currently offer these services to Medicaid beneficiaries through the rehabilitation or clinic benefits of the Medicaid state plan (in approximately 10 states) or, more commonly, through a home and community-based (HCBS) waiver under Section 1915(c) of the Social Security Act (in approximately 44 states through 102 HCBS separate waiver programs).[3] Because states define the state plan service criteria and tailor the HCBS waivers to specific groups of beneficiaries, states offer adult day care services under *both* the state plan and HCBS waiver(s) or under multiple HCBS waivers.

The way in which a state covers a Medicaid benefit makes a difference in terms of who can receive the benefit and what administrative steps may be necessary. The Medicaid state plan must be available statewide, and individuals who need the service are entitled to receive it. The HCBS waiver program, on the other hand, can be limited by the state, both in the number of people covered and its statewide availability. In addition, the HCBS waiver program is designed as an alternative to institutions (i.e., nursing home, hospital or intermediate care facility for those with mental retardation) and must meet a cost-neutrality provision (on average, the per-person cost of the HCBS waiver can not exceed the per-person cost of a comparable institution). This provision would prohibit the Secretary of HHS from denying federal Medicaid funding or withdrawing federal approval for adult day health care services or medical adult day care services under the Medicaid state plan, as defined by the state and approved by the Secretary on or before 1982.

Demonstration Project Regarding Medicaid Coverage of Low-Income HIV-Infected Individuals

Section 1115 of the Social Security Act gives the Secretary of HHS broad authority to modify virtually all aspects of the Medicaid program. Among other projects, the Secretary has used the Section 1115 waiver authority to approve benefit-specific demonstrations that provide targeted services to certain individuals so as to divert them from full Medicaid eligibility. For example, under existing HIV/AIDS demonstration waivers, the Secretary approved programs that provide a limited set of Medicaid benefits (e.g., case management, and pharmacy services) to individuals with HIV/AIDS who would not otherwise be eligible for Medicaid. Approved Section 1115 waivers are deemed to be part of a state's Medicaid (or SCHIP) state plan for purposes of federal reimbursement. Project costs associated with waiver programs are subject to that state's FMAP. Unlike regular Medicaid, CMS waiver guidance specifies that costs associated with waiver programs must be budget neutral to the federal government over the life of the waiver program. The federal and state government negotiate a budget neutrality spending cap beyond which the federal government has no fiscal responsibility.

This section of the bill would require the Secretary to allow states to seek approval for five-year Section 1115 demonstration projects that provide full Medicaid medical assistance coverage to specified HIV-infected individuals. For fiscal years 2006 through 2010 only, $450,000,000 in federal funds would be appropriated for such demonstrations. From these federal funds, the Secretary would allocate money to states and territories (without regard to existing federal Medicaid spending caps) with approved HIV Section 1115 demonstrations based on the availability of such funds. Allotment of funds among states and territories with approved demonstrations would be equal to the state's enhanced federal medical assistance percentage (enhanced-FMAP) for quarterly expenditures associated with medical assistance provided to individuals under the waiver up to the specified cap. Not later than December 31,

2010, the Secretary would be required to submit a report to Congress evaluating the cost-effectiveness and the impacts of the demonstrations on the Medicare, Medicaid, and Supplemental Security Income programs. This provision would be effective on January 1, 2006.

Improving the Medicaid and State Children's Health Insurance Programs

Family Opportunity Act

This provision would create a new optional Medicaid eligibility group for children with disabilities up to age 18 who meet the severity of disability required under the Supplemental Security Income (SSI) program, but whose family income is above the financial standards for SSI but below 300% of the federal poverty level (FPL). Under current law, children with disabilities have generally had to qualify for Medicaid using an income standard that is lower than 300% of FPL. Medicaid coverage for this optional group would be initially effective January 1, 2008 and would be fully phased in starting in FY2010. Within certain limits, states would be permitted to charge monthly premiums (based on income) and other cost-sharing fees under this new group. Finally, under this option, states must require the parents of Medicaid beneficiaries to enroll in any available employer-sponsored private insurance meeting certain criteria.

Demonstration Projects Regarding Home- and Community-Based Alternative to Psychiatric Residential Treatment Facilities for Children

This proposal would establish a five-year demonstration project in which up to 10 states could provide a broad range of home- and community-based services to children who would otherwise require services in a psychiatric residential treatment facility. Though these types of home- and community-based services are often allowed for other types of disability groups (e.g., children with developmental disabilities) under Section 1915(c) waivers of the Social Security Act, the waiver requirements prohibit states from developing home- and community-based services as an alternative to a psychiatric residential treatment facility. The demonstration would test the effectiveness of improving or maintaining the child's functional level, and the cost-effectiveness of providing these types of services as an alternative to psychiatric residential treatment services. These projects must also follow the existing requirements of the Section 1915(c) waiver. The demonstration project must be budget neutral and there must be an assurance that an interim and final evaluations will be conducted by an independent third party. The Secretary will also be required to complete evaluations of the project and report the findings to Congress. This proposal would authorize a total of $218 million for FY2007-FY2011 to carry out the demonstration.

Development and Support of Family-to-Family Health Information

This proposal would increase funding under the Special Projects of Regional and National Significance program (SPRANS) of the Maternal and Child Services Block Grant (Title V of the Social Security Act) for the development and support of new family-to-family health information centers. These family-to-family health information centers would assist families of children with disabilities to make informed decisions about health care options and available resources. The proposal would appropriate a total of $12 million for FY2007-

FY2009, and would authorize an additional $5 million, each year, for FY2010 and FY2011. The Secretary would be required to develop family-to-family health information centers in at least 25 states in FY2007, 40 states in FY2008, and all states in FY2009.

Restoration of Medicaid Eligibility for Certain SSI Beneficiaries

The provision would extend Medicaid eligibility to persons who are under age 21 and who are eligible for SSI, effective on the later of: (1) the date the application was filed, or (2) the date SSI eligibility was granted. Currently, SSI and Medicaid eligibility is effective on the first day of the month *following* the dates specified above. This provision would be effective one year after the date of enactment.

Grants to Promote Innovative Outreach and Enrollment under Medicaid and SCHIP

The provision would establish a new grant program under SCHIP to finance outreach and enrollment efforts to increase the participation of eligible children in both SCHIP and Medicaid. Currently, SCHIP administrative activities, which include outreach, cannot exceed 10% of total SCHIP expenditures. Various entities would be eligible to receive these grants, such as: state or local governments, Indian tribes, schools, non-profit organizations, and certain faith-based organizations. The proposal specifies several criteria the Secretary must use to prioritize grant awards, for example, entities that target geographic areas where there are a large number of eligible but not enrolled children. The provision would appropriate $25 million for FY2007 for these grants; 10% of the appropriation would be for grants to certain organizations that specifically provide health care services to Indian children.

Money Follows the Person Rebalancing Demonstration

The proposal would authorize the Secretary to award demonstration projects to states that provide 90% federal Medicaid reimbursement for home- and community-based long-term care services for 12 months for certain individuals relocating from an institution into the community. To participate in the demonstration, a person must be a Medicaid beneficiary who is residing in a hospital, nursing facility, intermediate care facility for a person with mental retardation, or an institution for mental disease (IMD) (to the extent that IMD services are covered in the state), and must have resided there for six months (up to a maximum of two years, as specified by the state).

State demonstrations must operate for at least two years in a five-year period starting in FY2007, and services for individuals must continue following the demonstration, so long as the person remains eligible for these services. States must also take steps to eliminate barriers to using Medicaid funding to provide long-term care services in the setting of a person's choosing, and meet maintenance of effort requirements. The Secretary would be required to provide technical assistance and oversight to state grantees and conduct and report the findings of a national evaluation. This proposal would appropriate $1.75 billion from January 1, 2009 through FY2013 (September 30, 2013) to carry out the demonstration.

State Children's Health Insurance Program (SCHIP)

Under current law, each state's federal SCHIP annual allotment is available for three years. At the end of the three-year period of availability, the unspent funds from the original allotment are reallocated based on methodologies that vary depending on the fiscal year. Unspent original allotments from FY2003 forward are to be redistributed according to the original Balanced Budget Act of 1997 (BBA97) methodology. That is, redistributed funds will go only to those states that spend all of their original allotments by the applicable three-year deadline, with the redistributed amounts determined by the Secretary of HHS and made available for one year only.

The provision would reduce the period of availability of the FY2004 and FY2005 original allotments from three years to two years, and would specify rules for the reallocation of unspent FY2003, FY2004, and FY2005 SCHIP original allotments. The reallocated FY2003 and FY2004 funds would be available in FY2006; the reallocated FY2005 funds would be available in FY2007. The proposal is projected to eliminate state shortfalls in FY2006. The proposal is projected to nearly eliminate state shortfalls in FY2007. Each of the 15 states expected to face a shortfall in FY2007 under the proposal would still be able to cover at least 97% of their federal SCHIP demand.

In addition, the provision would limit the types of payments that could be matched at the SCHIP enhanced matching rate for SCHIP expenditures drawn against the FY2003, FY2004, and FY2005 redistributed funds available to shortfall states. Specifically, the enhanced FMAP would be available for "targeted low-income children" but all other SCHIP expenses, such as, benefit expenditures for adults (other than pregnant women) would be matched at the regular FMAP. The provision would also limit the Secretary of HHS's Section 1115 waiver authority by prohibiting the approval of demonstration projects that allow federal SCHIP funds to be used to provide child health assistance or other health benefits coverage to nonpregnant childless adults. Finally, the proposal would permit the 11 qualifying states to use FY2004 and FY2005 funds under the 20% allowance, and would permit all states to use up to 10% of their FY2006 and FY2007 original allotments for expenditures on outreach activities incurred during FY2006 and FY2007 respectively.

MEDICARE

Physicians

Physicians are paid under the fee schedule which assigns relative values to services based on physician work, practice expense costs and malpractice costs. The relative values are then adjusted for geographic variations in costs. These adjusted relative values are converted into dollar payment amounts by a conversion factor. The conversion factor is updated annually according to a complex formula specified in the law. CMS has announced that the update for 2006 will be a *negative* 4.4%. The bill would override the formula by setting a minimum update for 2006 at a *positive* 1%.

Medicare Value-Based Purchasing Programs

The Medicare statute would be amended to establish value-based purchasing systems for each of the different Medicare providers. There would be separate value-based purchasing programs for hospitals, physicians and other practitioners, Medicare managed health care plans, ESRD providers and facilities, home health agencies, and skilled nursing facilities. Medicare payments to providers currently are not based on any measures of quality. The value-based purchasing programs, sometimes referred to as "pay-for-performance" programs, would introduce variations in provider payments reflecting differences in measured quality. Although the specifics of each program differ in the details, they all share some general principles:

- The value-based purchasing programs would begin collecting data on quality measures in the initial year of establishment, with incentive payments disbursed in subsequent years. Data from the initial year would be used to inform providers what their payments would have been for the year had the value-based purchasing program already been in place.
- Each value-based purchasing program would create an incentive pool funded by withholding up to 2% of total payments to that category of provider. The percentage of funds that goes towards the incentive pool would not decrease over time, and all funds collected for the incentive pool must be paid to providers as incentive payments.
- Participation in the value-based purchasing program would be voluntary, but providers would be required to report quality data in order to be eligible for incentive payments.
- Incentive payments would be paid to providers who meet certain thresholds for quality measurement. These thresholds would be based on either relative or absolute standards.
- The quality measures would be specific to each category of providers and would be revised over time, but the measures would be required to be evidence-based, easy to collect and report, address process, structure, outcomes, beneficiary experience, efficiency, over- and underuse of health care and to address disparities in health care provided and health outcomes between majority and minority groups. In the initial year, the measures would include at least one measure of health information technology infrastructure.

Because all the funds collected under the value-based purchasing programs would be paid out as incentive payments, the total payments over time would not change as a result of these provisions, but the timing of the incentive payments would be delayed a year compared to payments made in the absence of the value-based purchasing programs.

Medicare Advantage

Under Medicare Advantage (MA), Part C of the Medicare program, private health plans agree to provide Medicare covered benefits to beneficiaries who enroll in their plans. MA plans are paid a per capita monthly fee for providing all required Part A and Part B services to each plan enrollee, regardless of the amount of services used. An MA plan's per capita payment is adjusted to reflect the higher health care use of sicker enrollees. Though payments to plans are risk adjusted based on the demographics and health history of each enrollee, the risk adjustment method is imperfect and cannot account for all of the variation in health care use.

Phase-out of Risk Adjustment Budget Neutrality

Medicare payments to private plans under the Medicare Advantage program are risk adjusted to control for the variation in the cost of providing health care among beneficiaries. Congress urged the Secretary of HHS to implement risk adjustment without reducing overall payments to plans. The Secretary applied a budget neutrality adjustment to the risk adjusted rates to keep them from being reduced overall.

This provision directs the Secretary to (1) change the way the MA benchmarks are calculated to, in part, exclude budget neutrality, and (2) phase-out the budget-neutral implementation of risk adjustment. Overall, these changes will lower payments to plans. Budget neutrality is to be completely phased-out by 2011.

Elimination of Stabilization Fund

The Secretary is to establish an MA Regional Plan Stabilization Fund to provide incentives for plan entry in each region and plan retention in certain MA regions with below average MA penetration. Initially, $10 billion is to be available for expenditures from the fund beginning on January 1, 2007 and ending on December 31, 2013. Additional funds are to be available in an amount equal to 12.5% of average per capita monthly savings from regional plans that bid below the benchmark. The section which created this fund under the Medicare Modernization Act is repealed.

Other Medicare Provisions

The Senate provisions would make several other changes to the Medicare program, as described below.

Medicare Dependent Hospitals

Under current law, special reimbursement for facilities with Medicare dependent hospital (MDH) status will lapse in 2006. Certain rural hospitals with 100 beds or less that have at least 60% of their discharges or inpatient days attributable to Medicare patients in two of the last three years are classified as MDH hospitals. This provision would extend their status through discharges occurring before October 1, 2011. Also, MDHs could elect payment based on their adjusted FY2002 hospital-specific costs, beginning in FY2005, if that would result in higher Medicare payments.

Skilled Nursing Facility Bad Debt

Beginning October 1, 2005, the amount of bad debts otherwise treated as allowed costs, which are attributable to deductible and coinsurance amounts, would be reduced by 30% for services furnished in skilled nursing facilities (SNF).

Inpatient Rehabilitation Facilities

CMS requires that a facility treat a certain proportion of patients with specified medical conditions in order to qualify as an inpatient rehabilitation facility (IRF) and receive higher

Medicare payments. The "75% rule" established in regulation requires IRFs to meet a compliance threshold of 60% from July 1, 2005 and before July 1, 2006, 65% from July 1, 2006 and before July 1, 2007 and 75% thereafter. This legislation would reduce the current required proportion, or threshold to 50% from July 1, 2005 through June 30, 2007.

Physician Self Referrals

The prohibition on Medicare and Medicaid referrals to physician-owned limited service hospitals or specialty hospitals would be effective on or after December 8, 2003. Certain exceptions would be made to the definition of such hospitals, to include those hospitals where: (1) the percent investment by physician investors is no greater than the percent on June 8, 2005, (2) the percent investment by any physician investor is no greater than the percent on June 8, 2005, (3) the number of operating rooms is no greater than the number on June 8, 2005 and (4) the number of beds is no greater than the number on June 8, 2005.

Hold Harmless Provision for Small Rural and Sole Community Hospitals

Under current law, most services provided by hospital outpatient departments are paid under a prospective payment system, which began August 2000. Rural hospitals with no more than 100 beds and sole community hospitals located in rural areas, are to be held harmless through January 2006, that is they are to be paid no less under the prospective system than they would have been paid under prior law. This legislation would extend the hold harmless provisions through January 1, 2007.

Composite Rate for Dialysis Services

Medicare payments for dialysis services furnished either at a facility or in a patient's home are based on a basic case-mix adjusted prospective payment system. The system has two components: (1) the composite rate, which does not have to be updated annually; and (2) a drug add-on adjustment, which the Secretary of HHS is required to update annually beginning in 2006. The legislation would increase the composite rate by 1.6% for services beginning January 1, 2006.

Therapy Caps

The Balanced Budget Act of 1997 established annual per beneficiary payment limits on all outpatient therapy services provided by non-hospital providers beginning in 1999. Subsequent legislation suspended application of the limits beginning in 2000. A moratorium has been in place since then, except for a brief period in 2003. Under current law, the caps are again slated to go into effect in 2006. The bill would extend the moratorium for an additional year, through 2006.

Durable Medical Equipment Rentals

This provision would eliminate the semi-annual maintenance payment currently allowed for capped rental equipment and pay only for repairs when needed. The Secretary would determine the amount of payments for maintenance and service, which would only be made if deemed reasonable and necessary. With the exception of power-driven wheelchairs, the title to durable medical equipment in the capped rental category would be transferred by the supplier to the Medicare beneficiary after a 13-month rental period. The current option for beneficiaries to purchase power wheelchairs when initially furnished would be retained and the amount of any necessary maintenance and servicing payments would be established by the Secretary.

Rural Program of All-Inclusive Care for the Elderly (PACE) Provider Grant Program

The Program for All-Inclusive Care for the Elderly (PACE) makes available all services covered under Medicare and Medicaid without amount, duration or scope limitations, and without application of any deductibles, copayments or other cost sharing. Under the program, certain low-income individuals age 55 and older, who would otherwise require nursing home care, receive all health, medical, and social services they need. An interdisciplinary team of physicians, nurses, physical therapists, social workers, and other professionals develop and monitor care plans for enrollees. Monthly capitated payments are made to providers from both the Medicare and Medicaid programs. As specified in Medicare and Medicaid statutes, the amount of these payments from both programs must be less than what would have otherwise been paid for a comparable frail population not enrolled in PACE program. Payments are also adjusted to account for the comparative frailty of PACE enrollees. PACE providers assume the risk for expenditures that exceed the revenue from the capitation payments. The Balanced Budget Act of 1997 made PACE a permanent benefit category under Medicare and a state plan optional benefit under Medicaid.

The provision would create site development grants and provide technical assistance to establish PACE providers in rural areas. It would also create a fund for rural PACE providers to provide partial reimbursement for incurred expenditures above a ceratin level. The proposal would require the Secretary of HHS to establish a process and criteria for awarding up to $7.5 million in site development grants in up to 12 qualified PACE providers that have been approved to serve a geographic service area that is in whole or in part in a rural area, with each grant award not to exceed $750,000.

Waiver of Part B Late Enrollment Penalty

Generally, individuals who delay enrollment in Medicare Part B past their initial period of eligibility are subject to a penalty equal to 10% of the premium amount for each 12 months of delay. This provision would allow certain individuals to delay enrollment without a penalty, specifically those individuals who volunteered outside of the United States through a 12-month or longer program sponsored by a tax-exempt organization (defined by the Internal Revenue Code). Upon return to the United States, they would have a special enrollment period.

Federally Qualified Health Centers

This provision would allow federally qualified health centers (FQHC) to provide diabetes outpatient self management training services and medical nutrition therapy services provided by a registered dietician or nutritional professional. It would modify the definition of FQHC services so that only the primary preventative required services would be retained. Services would include those furnished to an outpatient of an FQHC that are provided by a health care professional under contract with the center, and payments would be made directly to the FQHC.

Delay of Medicare Payments

Medicare Parts A and B payments for services made by fiscal intermediaries and carriers would be delayed for seven business days at the end of FY2006. These payments would be made at the beginning of FY2007, thereby shifting payments from one fiscal year to the next.

Coverage of Ultrasound Screening for Abdominal Aortic Aneurysms

The provision would authorize Medicare coverage of ultrasound screening for abdominal aortic aneurysms for individuals who (1) received referrals for such screenings as a result of an initial preventive physical exam performed for new Medicare enrollees; (2) had not previously had such a test covered by Medicare; and (3) had a family history of abdominal aortic aneurysm or manifested risk factors included in a beneficiary category (not related to age) identified by the United States Preventive Services Task Force. The Part B deductible would not apply to these services.

Improving Patient Access to and Utilization of Colorectal Cancer Screening Services

The provision would establish national minimum payment amounts for specified facility and non-facility service codes that reflect a 5% increase above current amounts. The provision would also authorize Medicare coverage for an office visit or consultation prior to a screening colonoscopy or in connection with a beneficiary's decision to obtain such a screening. The Part B deductible would not apply for colorectal cancer screening tests.

Coverage of Marriage and Family Therapist Services and Mental Health Counselor Services under Medicare Part B

The provision would authorize coverage of marriage and family therapist services and mental health counselor services for the diagnosis and treatment of mental illness that the therapist or counselor is legally authorized to perform in the state.

HOUSE BILL

Under the budget resolution instructions, the House Energy and Commerce Committee was required to obtain $2 million in savings in FY2006 and $14.734 billion over the five-year budget period, FY2006-FY2010. The total House Energy and Commerce proposal, which includes changes in areas outside of health, is estimated to reduce federal outlays by $17.1 billion over the five-year budget window.[4] Proposed changes to the Medicaid program would result in an $11.9 billion reduction in spending over the five-year period. Katrina health care and energy relief would increase spending by $3.6 billion. Additional savings would result from Digital Television transition. This report summarizes provisions dealing only with Medicaid and SCHIP.[5] These provisions were incorporated into the larger bill reported by the House Budget Committee on November 3, 2005, the Deficit Reduction Act of 2005. Under a House rule, an amended Committee bill was introduced. The bill passed the House on November 18, 2005.

Subtitle A of Title III in the House bill reduces federal Medicaid spending by $11.9 billion over the FY2006-FY2010 five year budget period. Changes in outpatient prescription drug payments would result in $2.1 billion in savings over the period. Changes in Medicaid cost-sharing and benefits would result in $6.5 billion in savings over the period. Changes in asset transfer rules would reduce Medicaid spending by an additional $2.5 billion over the five year period. Changes in other provisions (e.g., changes in the treatment of state taxes on health care providers, and changes aimed at reducing Medicaid overpayment when a Medicaid recipient also has private insurance) would reduce Medicaid spending by an additional $1.8 billion over the five year period. Benefit expansions would add $1 billion in Medicaid spending. These expansions would include changes in benefits for individuals with long-term care needs in the community, and the establishment of health opportunity account demonstration programs (Medicaid-funded savings accounts that beneficiaries would use to pay for certain health care services). Under subtitle B, federal government spending for Medicaid and SCHIP would be temporarily increased for Medicaid-eligible individuals who lived or currently live in parts of Alabama, Louisiana, and Mississippi affected by Hurricane Katrina. The overall effect of this subtitle's changes would result in an increase in spending over the FY2006- FY2010 period of $2.5 billion. In total, the two health subtitles in the House Energy and Commerce proposal is estimated by CBO to result in net Medicaid and SCHIP savings of $9.3 billion over the five year budget period.

MEDICAID

Medicaid Outpatient Prescription Drugs

The Medicaid outpatient prescription drug provisions in the House bill would alter the federal upper limits that apply to Medicaid outpatient prescription drugs, provide for a minimum dispensing fee for multiple source drugs, and establish special reporting requirements for the prices of certain "authorized" generic drugs and certain outpatient drugs administered in physicians' offices. In addition, the bill would allow certain children's hospitals access to discounted drug prices and places an additional requirement on state prior authorization programs that seeks to limit access to atypical antipsychotic or antidepressant single source drugs.

Federal Upper Limits

The House bill would also replace the current FUL requirement so that state payments for single source drugs would qualify for federal reimbursement up to 106% of the RAMP, defined as the average price paid to a manufacturer by wholesalers as reported to CMS by the manufacturers. FULs for multiple source drugs would be equal to 120% of the volume weighted average RAMP for all drug products in the same multiple source drug billing and payment code. The provision would provide the Secretary with the authority to enter into contracts and engage the services of vendors to determine RAMP, and would allow the Secretary to implement an alternative FUL methodology based on survey prices. The implementation of the changes to the FUL would be delayed, however, if GAO were to find that the average prices paid by pharmacies are above the new reimbursable amounts.

In addition, this section of the bill would allow state Medicaid programs to have access to manufacturers' reported prices and would establish minimum dispensing fees of $8 for pharmacies dispensing multiple-source drugs.

Authorized Generics and Physician-Administered Drugs

The House bill would establish that when a manufacturer reports AMP and best price for their brand name product, they would include the prices of all drugs sold under the new drug application (which would include authorized generic versions). This provision is estimated to increase rebates resulting in savings to the Medicaid program, since authorized generic drugs are generally- less expensive than brand name versions of the same drug. In addition, the provision would require states to provide utilization and coding information to CMS for all single source physician-administered outpatient drugs and for the 20 most frequently provided physician administered multiple source drugs. This would improve the ability of CMS to ensure manufacturers pay rebates for those drugs.

Children's Hospitals and Access to Discounted Drug Products

The House bill includes a provision allowing Children's Hospitals access to the discounted outpatient prescription drugs prices negotiated under Section 340(B) of the Public Health Service Act. Section 340(B) allows certain health care providers, including many community health centers and disproportionate share hospitals, access to prescription drug prices that are similar to the prices paid by Medicaid agencies after being reduced by manufacturer rebates.

Prior Authorization for Mental Health Drugs

The bill would limit the ability of states to place atypical antipsychotic or antidepressant single source drugs on prior authorization lists imposing other restrictions unless a drug use review board has determined that doing so is not likely to harm patients or increase overall medical costs. It also would require states to pay for a 30 day supply of such drugs in cases where a request for authorization is not responded to within 24 hours after the prescription is transmitted.

Reform of Asset Transfer Rules

Lengthening Look-Back Period for All Disposals to Five Years

Current law requires states to impose penalties on individuals who transfer assets (all income and resources of the individual and of the individual's spouse) for less than fair market value (an estimate of the value of an asset if sold at the prevailing price at the time it was actually transferred). Specifically, the rules require states to delay Medicaid eligibility for certain Medicaid long-term care services for individuals applying for care in a nursing home, and, at state option, for certain people receiving care in community-based settings, who have transferred assets for less than fair market value on or after a "look-back date." The "look-back date" is 36 months prior to application for Medicaid for income and most assets disposed of by the individual, and 60 months in the case of certain trusts. The penalty, or period of ineligibility, begins with the first month during which the assets were transferred. The House bill would lengthen the look-back date to five years, or 60 months, for all income and assets disposed of by the individual. It would also change the start date of the ineligibility period for all transfers to the first day of a month during or before which assets have been transferred for less than fair market value, or the date on which the individual is eligible for medical assistance under the state plan and would be receiving certain long-term care services if it where not for the penalty, whichever is later.

Availability and Provisions Concerning Hardship Waivers

To protect beneficiaries from unintended consequences of the asset transfer penalties, current law requires states to establish procedures for not imposing penalties on persons who, according to criteria established by the Secretary of DHHS, can show that a penalty would impose an undue hardship. The House bill would add to existing law criteria for approving or disapproving applications for undue hardship waivers. It would also require states to provide applicants with notice about the availability of undue hardship waivers; to review applications under a timely process; and to establish an appeal process for beneficiaries who receive an adverse determination. The bill would also permit facilities to apply for waivers on behalf of, and with the consent of, institutionalized individuals. In addition, if the application for undue hardship of nursing facility residents meets criteria specified by the Secretary, the state would have the option of providing payments for nursing facility services to hold the bed for these individuals at a facility while an application is pending. Such payments could not be made for longer than 30 days.

Disclosure and Treatment of Annuities and of Large Transactions

Current law provides that the term "trust," for purposes of asset transfers and the look-back period, includes annuities only to the extent that the Secretary of DHHS defines them as such. CMS guidance (Transmittal Letter 64) asks states to determine the ultimate purpose of an annuity in order to distinguish those that are validly purchased as part of a retirement plan from those that abusively shelter assets. To be deemed valid in this respect, the life of the annuity must coincide with the average number of years of life expectancy for the individual (according to tables in the transmittal). If the individual is not reasonably expected to live longer than the guarantee period of the annuity, the individual will not receive fair market value for the annuity based on the projected return; in this case, the annuity is not "actuarially sound" and a transfer of assets for less than fair market value has taken place. The House bill would require applicants and their community spouses to report their ownership interest in annuities (or similar financial instruments). It would also require disclosure of all transfers greater than $100,000. Further it would also require that all transactions $5,000 or more within a single year would be treated as a single transaction.

Subject to certain requirements, the bill would also require the state to be made the remainder beneficiary under such annuities or similar financial instruments. The bill would also give the Secretary authority to provide guidance to states on categories of arms length transactions (such as the purchase of a commercial annuity) that could be generally treated as an asset transfer for fair market value.

Application of "Income-First" Rule in Applying Community Spouse's Income before Assets in Providing Support of Community Spouse

Current law includes provisions intended to prevent impoverishment of a spouse whose husband or wife seeks Medicaid coverage for long-term care services, allowing the community spouse to retain higher amounts of income and assets (on top of non-countable assets such as a house, car, etc.) than allowed under general Medicaid rules. The law allows community spouses with more limited income to retain at least a state specified amount set within federal guidelines. If the community spouse's monthly income amount is less than this amount, the institutionalized spouse *may* choose to transfer an amount of his or her income or assets to make up for the shortfall (i.e. the difference between the community spouse's monthly income and the state- specified minimum monthly maintenance needs allowance). The House bill would require that any transfer or allocation made from an institutionalized spouse to meet the need of a community spouse for a community spouse's monthly income allowance be first made from income of the institutionalized spouse. Only when sufficient income is not available, could resources of the institutionalized spouse be transferred or allocated.

Disqualification for Long-Term Care Assistance for Individuals with Substantial Home Equity

Under current law, states set asset standards, within federal parameters, that applicants must meet to qualify for coverage. These standards specify a limit on the amount of countable assets a person may have to qualify, as well as define which assets are not counted. In general, countable assets cannot exceed $2,000 for an individual. States generally follow SSI rules for computing both countable and non-countable assets. Current Medicaid and SSI asset counting practices exclude the entire value of an applicant's home. The House bill would exclude from Medicaid eligibility for nursing facility or other long-term care services, those individuals with an equity interest in their home of greater than $750,000. (The Secretary of DHHS would establish a process to waive application of this provision for demonstrated cases of hardship.) This amount would be increased, beginning in 2011, from year to year based on the percentage increase in the consumer price index for all urban consumers, rounded to the nearest $1,000. Individuals whose spouse, child under age 21, or child who is blind or disabled resides in the individual's home would *not* be excluded from eligibility.

Enforceability of Continuing Care Retirement Communities and Life Care Community Admission Contracts

The House bill would allow state-licensed, registered, certified, or equivalent continuing care retirement communities (CCRC) or a life care community to require in their admissions contracts that residents spend their resources (subject to Medicaid's rules concerning the resources and income allowances for community spouses), declared for the purposes of admission, on their care before they apply for Medicaid. It would also allow certain entrance fees for CCRCs or life care communities to be considered by states to be countable resources for purposes of the Medicaid eligibility determination.

Flexibility in Cost Sharing and Benefits

Many of the provisions in this chapter allow for changes to existing cost-sharing and benefit requirements through Medicaid state plan amendments, rather than the special waiver process that is required under current law.

State Option for Alternative Medicaid Premiums and Cost-Sharing

Under current law, premiums are generally prohibited under Medicaid except under specific circumstances. For example, for pregnant women and infants with family income that exceeds 150% of the federal poverty level (FPL), states are allowed to implement nominal premiums or enrollment fees (between $1 and $19 per month depending on family income) as defined in regulations. Other restrictions apply to service-related cost-sharing. For example, all service-related cost-sharing is prohibited for children under 18. Service-related cost-sharing is also prohibited for pregnant women for any pregnancy-related services or for services to treat other medical conditions that complicate pregnancy. Other groups and services are also exempt from service-related cost-sharing (e.g., emergency care, family planning services, services delivered to persons receiving Medicaid hospice care). For most other beneficiaries and services, nominal service-related cost-sharing (between $0.50 and $3 depending on the cost of the service provided) may be imposed.

The House bill would allow states to impose premiums and cost-sharing for any group of individuals for any type of service subject to several specific restrictions. Certain groups would be exempted from paying premiums (e.g., children under 18 in mandatory coverage groups, inpatients in certain medical institutions who must spend nearly all their income on medical care before Medicaid pays for services). Also, cost-sharing would be prohibited for specified services (e.g., preventive care for all children under 18, services provided to hospice patients, emergency care). The total amount of annual cost-sharing for all individuals in a family would be capped at 5% of family income for all families regardless of income. States would be allowed to impose higher cost-sharing amounts than is allowed under current law for individuals with family income over 100% of the FPL. States may exempt additional classes of individuals or services from premiums and service-related cost-sharing. Beginning in 2006, for individuals in families with incomes below 100% FPL, the Secretary of HHS would be required to increase nominal cost-sharing amounts over time based on the annual percentage increase in the medical care component of the consumer price index for all urban consumers.

The House bill would also allow states to condition the provision of medical assistance on the payment of premiums, and to terminate eligibility for Medicaid when the failure to pay a premium continues for at least 60 days. States may apply this provision to some or all groups, and may waive premium payments when they would be an undue hardship. In addition, states could permit Medicaid providers to require a Medicaid beneficiary to pay authorized cost-sharing as a condition of receiving services. Providers would also be allowed to reduce or waive cost-sharing amounts.

GAO would be required to conduct a study of the impact of premiums and cost-sharing under Medicaid on access to and utilization of services, with a report of findings due to Congress no later than January 1, 2008. All provisions would be effective for cost-sharing imposed on items and services furnished on or after January 1, 2006.

Special Rules for Cost-Sharing for Prescribed Drugs

Under current law, cost-sharing for outpatient prescription drugs follows the rules described above for all cost-sharing amounts. Many states require cost-sharing amounts that are slightly lower for generic drugs or for drugs listed on a preferred drug list.

The House bill would allow states to impose cost-sharing amounts that exceed the proposed state option limits described above for certain state-identified non-preferred drugs if specific conditions are met. Under this option, states may impose higher cost-sharing for non-preferred drugs within a class; waive or reduce cost-sharing otherwise applicable for preferred drugs within such class; and must not apply such cost-sharing for preferred drugs to persons exempt from service-related cost-sharing. Cost-sharing for non-preferred drugs would be based on multiples of the nominal amounts based on family income. For persons generally exempt from cost-sharing, the cost-sharing for non-preferred drugs may be applied. Such cost-sharing may not exceed nominal amounts, and aggregate caps on cost-sharing would still apply.

When a prescribing physician determines that the preferred drug would not be effective or would have adverse health effects or both, the state may impose the cost-sharing amount for preferred drugs on the prescribed non-preferred product.

States may exclude specified drugs or classes of drugs from these special cost-sharing rules. Finally, states would be prohibited from implementing these special cost-sharing rules for outpatient prescription drugs unless the state has instituted a system for prior authorization and related appeals processes. All provisions would be effective for cost-sharing imposed on items and services furnished on or after October 1, 2006.

Emergency Room Copayments for Non-Emergency Care

Under current law, waivers may be used to allow states to impose up to twice the otherwise applicable nominal cost-sharing amounts for non-emergency services provided in a hospital emergency room (ER). States may only impose these higher amounts if they have established that Medicaid beneficiaries have available and accessible alternative sources of non-emergency, outpatient services.

The House bill would allow states, through state plan amendments rather than waivers, to impose increased cost-sharing on state-specified groups for non-emergency services provided in an ER, when certain conditions are met. First, alternative non-emergency providers must be available and accessible to the person seeking care. Second, after initial screening but before the non-emergency care is provided at the ER, the beneficiary must be told: (1) the hospital can require a higher co-payments, (2) the name and location of an alternative non-emergency provider and that this provider uses a lower co-payments, and (3) the hospital can provide a referral. When these conditions are met, states could apply or waive cost-sharing for services delivered by the alternate provider.

For persons with income below 100% FPL, cost-sharing for non-emergency services in an ER could not exceed twice the nominal amounts. Individuals exempt from premiums or service-related cost-sharing may be subject to nominal copayments for non-emergency services in an ER, only when no cost-sharing is imposed for care in hospital outpatient departments or by other alternative providers in the area served by the hospital ER. Aggregate caps on cost-sharing would still apply.

Finally, the House bill would require the Secretary to provide for payments to states for the establishment of alternate non-emergency providers, or networks of such providers. It also authorizes and appropriates $100 million for paying such providers for the four-year period beginning with 2006. The Secretary would be required to give a preference to states that establish or provide for alternate non-emergency services providers (or networks) that serve rural or underserved areas where beneficiaries may have limited access to primary care providers, or in partnership with local community hospitals.

Use of Benchmark Benefit Packages

Medicaid benefits may differ for what are called categorically needy (CN) versus medically needy (MN) groups. In general, CN groups include families with children, the elderly, certain persons with disabilities, and certain other pregnant women and children who meet applicable financial standards. These financial criteria are tied to rules under two federal cash assistance programs — the former AFDC program for poor families with children or the SSI program for the poor elderly and persons with disabilities. Some groups of the elderly, pregnant women, and children must meet financial standards tied to specified percentages of the FPL instead. MN groups include the same types of individuals, but different, typically higher financial standards apply. Medical expenses (if any) may be subtracted from income in determining financial eligibility for the MN. For nearly all CN groups, medical expenses are not considered in determining Medicaid eligibility.

Examples of benefits that are mandatory for CN groups include inpatient and outpatient hospital services, services provided by federally qualified health centers (FQHC), physician services, and nursing facility care for persons age 21 and over. Examples of optional benefits for CN groups that are offered by many states include physician-directed clinic services, routine dental care, other licensed practitioner services (e.g., optometrists, podiatrists, psychologists), physical therapy, inpatient psychiatric care for the elderly and persons under age 21, and prescribed drugs (all states). In general, states may offer a more restrictive benefit package to the MN, but at a minimum, must offer (1) prenatal and delivery services, (2) ambulatory services for persons under 18 and those entitled to institutional services, and (3) home health services for those entitled to nursing facility care. Within a state, services available to all CN groups must be equal in amount, duration and scope. Likewise, services available to all MN groups must be equal in amount, duration and scope.

The House bill would give states the option to provide Medicaid to state-specified groups of beneficiaries through enrollment in benchmark and benchmark-equivalent coverage (described below). States could implement this option through a Medicaid state plan amendment rather than a waiver as would be required under current law. States could require "full-benefit eligible individuals" to enroll in such coverage. A full-benefit eligible would be a person eligible for all services covered for the CN, or under any other category of eligibility for full services as defined by the Secretary. Some individuals would be excluded from the definition of a full-benefit eligible (e.g., the MN, persons who spend-down their income for medical care to meet the financial requirements for Medicaid coverage). Several other specific groups would also be exempted from this option (e.g., mandatory pregnant women and children, dual eligibles, hospice patients, persons with special medical needs, individuals who qualify for Medicaid long-term care services). States could only apply this option to eligibility categories established before the date of enactment of this provision.

The benchmark and benchmark equivalent packages would be nearly identical to those offered under the State Children's Health Insurance Program (SCHIP), with some additions beyond the basic elements of SCHIP. Under this option, benchmark coverage would include (1) the standard Blue Cross/Blue Shield preferred provider option plan under the Federal Employees Health Benefits Program (FEHBP), (2) the health coverage offered and generally available to state employees, or (3) the health coverage offered by a health maintenance organization (HMO) with the largest commercial (non-Medicaid) enrollment. Benchmark-equivalent coverage would be defined as a package of benefits that has the same actuarial value as one of the benchmark benefit packages. Such coverage would include each of the benefits in the "basic benefits category," including (1) inpatient and outpatient hospital services, (2) physician's surgical and medical services, (3) lab and x-ray services, (4) well-baby and well-child care, including age-appropriate immunizations, and (5) other appropriate preventive services (designated by the Secretary). Such coverage must also include at least 75% of the actuarial value of coverage under the benchmark plan for each of the benefits in the "additional service category," including (1) prescription drugs, (2) mental health services, (3) vision services, and (4) hearing services.

Both benchmark and benchmark equivalent coverage would also include qualifying child benchmark dental coverage. A qualifying child would be a person under 18 with family income below 133% of the FPL. Benchmark dental coverage would be equivalent to or better than the dental plan that covers the greatest number of individuals in the state who are not eligible for Medicaid.

Finally, states could only enroll eligible beneficiaries in benchmark and benchmark-equivalent coverage if such persons have access to services provided by rural health clinics (RHC) and FQHCs, and the Medicaid prospective payment system for both types of providers remains in effect.

State Option to Establish Non-Emergency Medical Transportation Program

Federal regulations require states to ensure necessary transportation for recipients to and from providers and to describe the methods that they will use to meet this requirement in their Medicaid state plan. States may choose whether to provide transportation as an optional Medicaid service or claim it as an administrative expense.

If a state chooses to provide transportation as an optional Medicaid service, costs are reimbursed by the federal government using the federal medical assistance percentage (FMAP), which varies by state and has a statutory floor of 50% and ceiling of 83%. Under this option, states must meet a number of federal requirements that apply to all Medicaid services (e.g., enrollees must have freedom to choose among qualified providers) unless they have an approved waiver. Costs are only allowable for FMAP reimbursement if the transportation is furnished by a provider to whom a direct payment can be made. Other arrangements (e.g., payment to a broker who manages and pays transportation providers) must be claimed as an administrative expense. If a state chooses to claim transportation as an administrative expense, costs are reimbursed by the federal government at a rate of 50%, which is lower than the FMAP in many states, but there are fewer federal requirements that must be met.

Under the House bill, a state would have the option to establish a non-emergency medical transportation brokerage program in order to more cost-effectively provide transportation for Medicaid enrollees who need access to medical care or services and have no other means of transportation. Under the program, the state would not be required to provide comparable services for all Medicaid enrollees or freedom to choose among providers. The program could include wheelchair van, taxi, stretcher car, bus passes and tickets, and other transportation methods deemed appropriate by the Secretary, and could be conducted under contract with a broker who: (1) is selected through a competitive bidding process, (2) meets oversight requirements, (3) is subject to regular auditing by the state, and (4) complies with requirements related to prohibitions on referrals and conflict of interest established by the Secretary. Also, the HHS Inspector General would be required to submit a report to Congress examining this new program no later than January 1, 2007.

Exempting Women Covered under Breast or Cervical Cancer Program

Under current law, states may offer Medicaid to certain uninsured women who are under age 65, and are in need of treatment for breast or cervical cancer based on screening services provided under an early detection program run by the CDC. This group has access to the same Medicaid services offered to the CN in a given state, and are subject to Medicaid's nominal cost sharing rules.

Under the House bill, none of the proposed cost-sharing or benefit provisions described above would apply to women who qualify for Medicaid under the breast and cervical cancer eligibility group.

Benefit Expansions

Expanded Access to Home and Community-Based Services for the Elderly and Disabled

Under current law, states may provide a broad range of home and community-based services under a Medicaid waiver authorized by Section 1915(c) of the Social Security Act. These services, which may include, for example, respite, adult day care, and personal care, may be provided to Medicaid beneficiaries who would otherwise need the level of care provided in a nursing facility, intermediate care facility for persons with mental retardation (ICF-MR), or hospital. Approval of a Medicaid waiver is contingent on a state documenting the waiver's cost-neutrality (the average per person cost under the waiver cannot exceed the average per person cost of services in an institution.)

This proposal would allow states to cover these types of home and community-based services under the Medicaid state plan *without* requiring the state to seek a waiver or document the waiver's cost-neutrality. To cover this option, a state's existing waiver must have expired. Similar to rules governing the current waiver program, states would be able to: 1) define which services will be covered (room and board may not be paid for); 2) offer the waiver on a less-than-statewide basis; 3) limit the number of individuals who are eligible for services; and 4) establish a waiting list for services. This section would be effective for home and community-based services furnished on or after October 1, 2006.

Optional Choice of Self-Directed Personal Assistance Services (Cash and Counseling)

Traditionally, Medicaid personal care and other related benefits have been provided to beneficiaries through a local public or private agency. However, in the last decade, Medicaid programs have been increasing the discretion that Medicaid beneficiaries have over key elements of the service (e.g., what time a service provider comes to the home, who provides the service). This proposal would allow a state to establish and operate a program in which the Medicaid beneficiary could hire, supervise and manage the individuals providing his or her services (including personal care and related services or other home and community-based services). The beneficiary would have significant discretion within an approved service plan and budget. As part of this option, a state may limit the population eligible to receive these types of services and may limit the number of persons served.

Expansion of State Long-Term Care Partnership Program

Under Medicaid's long-term care (LTC) insurance partnership program, certain persons who have exhausted (or used at least some of) the benefits of a private long-term care insurance policy may access Medicaid without meeting the same means-testing requirements as other groups of Medicaid eligibles. For these individuals, means-testing requirements are relaxed at (1) the time of application to Medicaid (allowed with Secretary's approval, without changes to current law); and (2) the time of the beneficiary's death when Medicaid estate recovery is generally applied. Current law allows states with an approved state plan amendment *as of* May 14, 1993 to exempt individuals from Medicaid estate recovery who apply to Medicaid after exhausting their private long-term care insurance benefits. By that date, five states (California, Connecticut, Indiana, Iowa, and New York) had received CMS approval. Except for Iowa, all of these states have implemented partnership programs.

This provision would allow additional groups of individuals in states with state plan amendments approved *after* May 14, 1993 to be exempt from estate recovery requirements if the amendment provides for a qualified state long-term care insurance partnership program. New partnership programs would disregard any assets or resources of a Medicaid applicant and beneficiary in the amount equal to the amount of insurance benefit paid to or on behalf of an individual who is a beneficiary under a long-term care policy. Policies sold under new LTC partnership programs would be tax-qualified, cover an insured who was a resident of such state when coverage first became effective under the policy, require that policyholders be offered a policy with some level of inflation protection, and impose certain requirements on states concerning seller training. It would also require insurers to report information, as specified by the Secretary, concerning benefit payments, policy terminations, among others. Existing Partnership programs (programs in California, Connecticut, Indiana, Iowa, and New York) would not be subject to these requirements. The Secretary would also be subject to certain requirements concerning data reporting and the development of recommendations for certain uniform standards. Under the House bill, the Secretary would be permitted to develop portability standards for reciprocal recognition of partnership policies among certain states.

Health Opportunity Accounts

The bill would require the Secretary to establish demonstration programs within Medicaid for health opportunity accounts (HOA), effective January 1, 2006. No more than ten state programs could be established the first five years, though afterwards other programs would be allowed if the earlier ones were not unsuccessful. Among other things, state programs would have to make patients aware of the high cost of medical care, provide incentives for them to seek preventive care, and reduce inappropriate uses of health care. Eligibility for HOAs would be determined by the state, though individuals who are disabled, pregnant, or receiving terminal care or long-term care, would be among those who could not participate.

Participants would have both an HOA and coverage for medical items and services that, after an annual deductible is met, were available under the existing Medicaid state plan and waiver authorities. The deductible would have to be at least 100%, but no more than 110%, of the annual state contributions to the HOA. Both the deductible and the maximum for out-of-pocket cost-sharing could vary among families. The deductible need not apply to preventive care.

HOAs would be used to pay health care expenses specified by the state; payments could be restricted to licensed or otherwise authorized providers as well as to items and services that are medically appropriate or necessary. Withdrawals would be made by electronic transfer. Once account holders were no longer eligible for Medicaid they could continue to make withdrawals under these conditions, though accounts could then also be used to pay for health insurance or, at state option, for job training or education. Participants generally would be able to obtain services from Medicaid providers or managed care organizations at the same payment rates that would be applicable if the coverage deductible did not apply, or from any provider for payment rates not exceeding 125% of those rates.

HOA contributions could be made by the state or by other persons or entities, including charitable organizations. Including federal shares, state contributions generally could not exceed $2,500 for each adult and $1,000 for each child.

Other Medicaid Provisions

Managed Care Organization Provider Tax Reform

The House bill would, like the Senate bill, modify the class of providers that states can tax under the provider tax rules. The current law class of Medicaid managed care providers would be changed to encompass all managed care organizations, so that, in the future, these taxes would be required to be more broad than are allowed under current law. States with existing provider specific taxes levied against Medicaid managed care organizations would be allowed to keep those taxes in 2008, and would have to reduce the tax by half in 2009. After that, all states would be subject to the new rule.

Third Party Liability

With certain exceptions, Medicaid is a payer of last resort, meaning that states must ascertain the legally liability of third parties to pay for Medicaid care and services. They must also seek reimbursement for Medicaid costs from third parties when necessary. Examples of potentially liable third parties specified in current Medicaid law include health insurers, group health plans, service benefit plans, and health maintenance organizations. With respect to third party liability, the House proposal would clarify the right of states to obtain reimbursement from specific third parties — self-insured plans and pharmacy benefit managers —that are legally responsible for payment of claims for health care items or services provided to Medicaid beneficiaries. The proposal would also require each state to have laws in effect requiring third parties to provide eligibility and claims payment data for Medicaid-eligible individuals and to cooperate with payment and recovery efforts by Medicaid.

Reforms of Targeted Case Management Benefit

Targeted case management (TCM) is an optional benefit under the Medicaid state plan that is designed to help Medicaid beneficiaries access needed medical, social, educational, and other services. States that cover the TCM service do not have to offer the benefit statewide and can limit the service to specific groups of Medicaid beneficiaries (e.g., those with chronic mental illness). Several states extend the TCM services to individuals who may also be receiving certain case management services as part of another state and/or federal program (e.g., foster care, juvenile justice).

This proposal would clarify the activities that can be considered a TCM service, and those activities (primarily foster care-related activities) that may not be reimbursed as TCM services. The proposal also states that Medicaid funding would only be available for TCM services if there are no other third parties liable to pay for such services, including as reimbursement under a medical, social, educational, or other program. The proposal would take effect January 1, 2006.

Increase in Payments to Insular Areas

In the 50 states and the District of Columbia, Medicaid is an individual entitlement. There are no limits on the federal payments for Medicaid as long as the state is able to contribute its share of the matching funds. In contrast, Medicaid programs in the territories are subject to spending caps. These spending caps were set in FY1998 and adjusted for inflation in subsequent years. For each of fiscal years 2006 and 2007, the provision would increase the total annual cap on federal funding for the Medicaid programs in each of Puerto Rico, the Virgin Islands, Guam, the Northern Marianas, and American Samoa. For Puerto Rico the total annual Medicaid cap would be increased by $12 million; for the Virgin Islands and Guam, the FY2006 total annual Medicaid caps would be increased by $2.5 million and the FY2007 caps would be increased by $5.0 million. For the Northern Marianas, the FY2006 total annual Medicaid cap would be increased by $1.0 million and the FY2007 cap would be increased by $2.0 million. For American Samoa, the FY2006 total annual Medicaid cap would be increased by $2.0 million and the FY2007 cap would be increased by $4.0 million. For FY2008 and subsequent fiscal years, the total annual cap on federal funding for the Medicaid programs in each of Puerto Rico, the Virgin Islands, Guam, the Northern Marianas, and American Samoa would be calculated by increasing the FY2007 ceiling for inflation.

Medicaid Transformation Grants

Under the House proposal, in addition to the normal federal Medicaid reimbursement received by states, Secretary of DHHS would provide for payments to states for the adoption of innovative methods to improve the effectiveness and efficiency of Medicaid. Examples of innovative methods for which such funds may be used include (1) methods for reducing patient error rates through the implementation and use of electronic health records, electronic clinical decision support tools, or e-prescribing programs, (2) methods for improving rates of collection from estates owed to Medicaid, (3) methods for reducing waste, fraud, and abuse under Medicaid, (4) implementation of a medication risk management program as part of a drug use review program, and (5) methods for reducing expenditures for covered outpatient drugs by increasing generic utilization. Total payments under this provision would equal and not exceed $50 million in each of FY2007 and FY2008.

Citizenship Documentation

As a condition of an individual's eligibility for Medicaid benefits, Section 1137(d) of the Social Security Act requires a state to obtain a written declaration, under penalty of perjury, stating whether the individual is a citizen or national of the United States. Under current law, if an individual declares that he or she is not a citizen or national, the individual must declare that he or she is a qualified alien and must present additional documentary evidence. If an individual declares that he or she is a U.S. citizen or national, the state is not required to obtain additional evidence but may choose to do so. Under the House proposal, states would be required to obtain documentary evidence from individuals who declare that they are U.S. citizens or nationals.

Emergency Services Furnished by Non-Contract Providers for Medicaid Managed Care Enrollees

Medicaid law provides certain protections for beneficiaries enrolled in managed care, including assuring coverage of emergency services under each managed care contract awarded by the state.

Under the House bill, a Medicaid provider that does not have a contract with a Medicaid managed care entity (MCE) that furnishes emergency care to a beneficiary enrolled with that MCE must accept as payment in full the amount otherwise applicable outside of managed care (e.g., in the fee-for-service setting) — minus any payments for indirect costs of medical education and direct costs of graduate medical education. This provision would be effective on January 1, 2007.

FMAP Computation for Employer Pension Contributions

When state FMAPs are calculated by HHS for an upcoming fiscal year (usually in the preceding November), the state and U.S. per capita personal income amounts used in the formula are equal to the average of the three most recent calendar years of data on per capita personal income available from the Department of Commerce's Bureau of Economic Analysis (BEA). The definition of personal income used by BEA is comprised of many parts, including supplements to wages and salaries such as employer contributions for employee pension and insurance funds. When BEA undertakes a comprehensive revision of its income data every few years, there may be upward and downward revisions to each of these parts, the sum of which has a net effect on overall personal income. For example, in describing its most recent comprehensive revision, BEA reported that upward revisions to employer contributions for pensions beginning with 1989 were the result of methodological improvements and more complete source data. However, BEA reported upward and downward revisions to other parts of personal income as well (e.g., wages and salaries). Under the House proposal, for purposes of computing states FMAPs beginning with FY2006, employer contributions toward pensions that exceed a specified threshold would be excluded from the per capita income of a state.

Katrina Health Care Relief

Targeted Medicaid Relief

The federal medical assistance percentage (FMAP), which has a statutory minimum of 50% and maximum of 83%, is the rate at which states are reimbursed for most Medicaid service expenditures. Medicaid administrative costs are generally reimbursed at a flat rate of 50%. An enhanced FMAP is available for both services and administration under SCHIP, subject to the availability of funds from a state's SCHIP allotment. Under the House proposal, for items and services furnished during the period August 28, 2005 through May 15, 2006, states would receive 100% FMAP reimbursement for Medicaid and SCHIP assistance provided to: (1) any individual residing in a parish of Louisiana, a county of Mississippi, or a major disaster county of Alabama and (2) individuals who resided during the week preceding Hurricane Katrina in a parish or county for which a major disaster has been declared as a result of the hurricane and for which the President has determined, as of September 14, 2005, warrants individual assistance under the Robert T. Stafford Disaster Relief and Emergency Assistance Act. Costs directly attributable to related administrative activities would also be reimbursed at 100%.

FMAP Hold Harmless

When state FMAPs are calculated by HHS for an upcoming fiscal year (usually in the preceding November), the state and U.S. per capita personal income amounts used in the formula are equal to the average of the three most recent calendar years of data on per capita personal income available from the Department of Commerce's Bureau of Economic Analysis (BEA). For example, to calculate FY2006 FMAPs, HHS used per capita personal income data for 2001, 2002, and 2003 that became available from BEA in October 2004. Under the House bill, in computing Medicaid and SCHIP FMAPs for any year after 2006 for a state that the Secretary of HHS determines has a significant number of individuals who were evacuated to and live in the state as a result of Hurricane Katrina as of October 1, 2005, the Secretary would disregard such evacuees and their income.

Conference Agreement, as Passed by the Senate

On December 19, 2005, the House agreed to a conference report on S. 1932. However, the Senate amended the report, removing a few provisions as the result of a point of order raised associated with the "Byrd Rule."[6] The amended agreement passed the Senate on December 21, 2006, and was returned to the House for further action. It is expected that the agreement will be taken up in the early part of the session.

Title V and Title VI of the Deficit Reduction Act of 2005 contain provisions dealing with Medicare (Title V) and Medicaid, SCHIP and Hurricane Katrina relief (Title VI). Preliminary estimates from the Congressional Budget Office indicate $3.4 billion in Medicare savings in direct spending for FY2006, and $8.3 billion in Medicare savings in direct spending from FY2006-FY2010. Preliminary Medicaid savings estimates show a $1 billion increase in Medicaid spending for FY2006, and over the five-year period, FY2006-FY2010, savings of $6.9 billion. The SCHIP provisions are estimated to cost $170 million in FY2006 and $20 million over the FY2006-FY2010 period. Finally, the conference agreement provides for $2.0 billion in funding for Katrina-related health care costs in FY2006. Over the five-year period, estimated costs of the Katrina provisions would equal $2.1 billion.

MEDICARE

Medicare's Update Factor to Increase Operating Payments to Acute-Care Hospitals

Medicare's annual increase in its operating payments to hospitals is determined in part by the projected annual change in the hospital market basket (MB), a measure that estimates price inflation affecting hospitals. Congress establishes this update for Medicare's inpatient prospective payment system (IPPS), often several years in advance. Currently, through FY2007, the IPPS operating update has been established as the MB for hospitals that submit specific quality information and as the MB minus 0.4 percentage points for hospitals that do not provide such information.

Under the conference agreement, hospitals that do not submit the required data in FY2007 and each subsequent year will have the applicable MB percentage increase reduced by two percentage points. Any reduction applies only to the fiscal year in question and does not affect subsequent fiscal years. The conference agreement establishes that the Secretary will expand the number of quality indicators required from acute care hospitals.

Value-Based Purchasing for Acute-Care Hospitals

Under the conference agreement, the DHHS Secretary is required to develop a plan to implement a value-based purchasing program for inpatient payments to acute care hospitals beginning with FY2009. The plan is required to consider specified factors such as (1) the development, selection, and modification process for quality measures; (2) data reporting, collection, and validation; (3) the structure of value-based payment adjustments and sources of its funding; and (4) the disclosure of information on hospital performance.

DRG Adjustment for Certain Hospital Acquired Infections

Medicare discharges are classified into diagnosis-related groups (DRGs) primarily on the basis of the diagnosis and procedure code information included on the beneficiary's claim. The information includes the principal diagnosis (or main problem requiring inpatient care), up to eight secondary diagnoses codes as well as up to six procedures performed during the stay. Certain secondary diagnoses are considered to be complications or comorbidities (CC). When present as a secondary condition (with a specific principal diagnosis), these diagnosis codes are considered to increase the length of stay by least one day in at least 75% of the patients. Paired DRGs are split into higher- and lower-paid DRGs on the presence or the absence of a CC. CMS has added and deleted codes from the standard list of CCs, but has never conducted a comprehensive review of the list. It is planning to systematic review of the CC list for FY2007 Medicare payments.

Under the conference agreement, starting for discharges on October 1, 2007, hospitals are required to report any secondary diagnosis codes applicable to patients at their admission in order to be paid. By October 1, 2007, the Secretary is required to identify at least two high-cost or high-volume (or both high-cost and high-volume) diagnosis codes with a DRG assignment that has a higher payment weight when present as a secondary diagnosis. These codes represent conditions, including certain hospital-acquired infections, that could reasonably have been prevented through the use of evidence-based guidelines. Starting for discharges on October 1, 2008, the DRG assigned to a discharge with the identified diagnosis codes will be the lower-paid DRG.

Clarification of Inclusion of Medicaid Patient Days in Medicare's Computation of Its Disproportionate Share Hospital (DSH) Adjustment

Hospitals that serve a certain number of low-income Medicare and Medicaid beneficiaries will receive a DSH adjustment that increases their Medicare IPPS payments. Most hospitals receive the additional payments based on their DSH patient percentage, which is calculated using proportion of the hospital's total days provided to Medicaid recipients added to the proportion of the hospital's Medicare inpatient days provided to poor Medicare beneficiaries. The policy of whether inpatient days provided to a patient covered under demonstration projects established by Section 1115 waivers could be included in the Medicare DSH calculation has changed over time. Policies on these issues were established through regulation.

Under the conference agreement, the Secretary can include inpatient hospital days of patients eligible for medical assistance under a Section 1115 demonstration waiver in the Medicare DSH calculation. These days will be counted as if they were provided to patients who were eligible for medical assistance under an approved Medicaid state plan. The provision ratifies existing regulations.

Improvements to the Medicare-Dependent Hospital (MDH) Program

Under current law, special reimbursement for facilities with Medicare dependent hospital (MDH) status will lapse in 2006. Certain rural hospitals with 100 beds or less that have at least 60% of their discharges or inpatient days attributable to Medicare patients in two of the last three years are classified as MDH hospitals. Under the conference agreement, their MDH status would be extended for discharges occurring before October 1, 2011. Starting for discharges on October 1, 2006, an MDH would be able to elect payments based on 50% of its FY2002 hospital-specific costs if that would result in higher Medicare payments. MDH's payments would be based on 75% of their adjusted hospital-specific costs starting for discharges on October 1, 2006. MDH's that qualify for a disproportionate share hospital (DSH) adjustment would not have the adjustment capped at 12%.

Reduction in Payments to Skilled Nursing Facilities (SNFs) for Bad Debt

Medicare pays the costs of certain items on a reasonable cost basis (outside of the applicable prospective payment system), including the unpaid debt for beneficiaries' coinsurance and deductible amounts. Historically, CMS has reimbursed certain providers (e.g., SNFs) for 100% of the debt. Effective for cost reports starting in FY2001, Medicare began reimbursing acute care hospitals for 70% of the reasonable costs associated with beneficiaries' allowable bad debt. Under the conference agreement, Medicare payments to SNFS for allowable bad debts would be reduced to 70% for beneficiaries who are not eligible for both Medicare and Medicare. Medicare's payments for allowable bad debts attributed to dual eligible beneficiaries would remain at 100%.

Extend Phase-in of the Inpatient Rehabilitation Facility (IRF) Compliance Thresholds

CMS requires that a facility treat a certain proportion of patients with specified medical conditions in order to qualify as an inpatient rehabilitation facility (IRF) and receive higher Medicare payments. The "75% rule" established in regulation requires IRFs to meet a compliance threshold of 60% from July 1, 2005 and before July 1, 2006, 65% from July 1, 2006 and before July 1, 2007 and 75% thereafter. Under the conference agreement, the compliance threshold for IRFs is established at 60% during the 12-month period beginning on July 1, 2006; at 65% during the 12-month period beginning on July 1, 2007; and at 75% beginning on July 1, 2008 and subsequently.

Development of a Strategic Plan Regarding Physician Investment in Specialty Hospitals

Physicians are generally prohibited from referring Medicare and Medicaid patients to facilities in which they (or their immediate family member) have financial interests. This prohibition does not extend to patient referrals to hospitals where physicians have ownership or investment interest in the whole hospital itself (and not merely in a subdivision of the hospital). Section 507 of MMA established that the exception for physician investment and self-referral would not extend to specialty hospitals for a period of 18 months from enactment (or until June 8, 2004). This moratorium has been extended administratively by CMS, which has not issued provider numbers to new specialty hospitals while it examines the criteria used to award such numbers. Under the conference agreement, the Secretary is required to develop a strategic and implementing plan regarding physician investment in specialty hospitals. An interim report is due within three months, and the final report is due no later than six months after the date of enactment. The Secretary will continue to suspend enrollment of new specialty hospitals until the earlier date of either the submission of the report or six months after the date of enactment. If the Secretary does not submit the final report within the six-month time period, then the enrollment suspension will be extended an additional two months. The Secretary will also provide an appropriate certification of the failure to Congressional committees of jurisdiction.

Gainsharing Demonstration Project

In 2004, a federal district court stopped CMS from implementing an eight-hospital gainsharing demonstration project because of civil monetary penalty concerns. Under the conference agreement, the Secretary will establish a gainsharing demonstration project to evaluate arrangements between IPPS hospitals and physicians and practitioners. Up to six projects (with at least two in rural areas) will be approved by November 1, 2006, and operational no later than January 1, 2007. The sum of $6 million will be appropriated from the Treasury in FY2006 to carry out the projects and will remain available for expenditure through FY2010.

Post-Acute Care Payment Reform Demonstration Program

Under the conference agreement, the DHHS Secretary is required to establish a three-year demonstration program to assess the costs and outcomes across different post-acute care sites by January 1, 2008. Six million dollars will be transferred from Medicare's Hospital Insurance Trust Fund for the costs of carrying out the demonstration program.

Beneficiary Ownership of Certain DME and Oxygen Equipment

Medicare Part B pays for certain items of durable medical equipment such as hospital beds, nebulizers and power-driven wheelchairs under the capped rental category. Most items in this category are provided on a rental basis for a period that can not exceed 15 months. After using the equipment for 10 months, beneficiaries must be given the option of purchasing it effective 13 months after the start of the rental period. If they choose the purchase option, the title to the equipment is transferred to beneficiaries. If the purchase option is not chosen, the supplier retains ownership of the equipment. Medicare payments to suppliers for maintenance and servicing differ based on whether the beneficiary has purchased the equipment or whether the supplier continues to own it. Oxygen equipment rentals continue for the entire period of medical need and are not subject to a maximum number of months.

The conference agreement would require the supplier to transfer the title of durable medical equipment in the capped rental category to the beneficiary after a 13-month rental period. The option for a 15-month rental period with the supplier retaining ownership of the item would be eliminated. Automatic payment for maintenance and servicing would be eliminated. Such payments (for parts and labor not covered by the supplier's or manufacturer's warranty) would only be made if the Secretary determined them to be reasonable and necessary. Rental payments for oxygen equipment (including portable oxygen equipment) are converted to ownership at 36 months. The supplier is required to transfer the title of the equipment to the beneficiary after a 36-month rental period. After transfer of the title, monthly payments for oxygen contents will continue to be made. Payments for maintenance and servicing (for parts and labor not covered by the supplier's or manufacturer's warranty) will be made if the Secretary determines them to be reasonable and necessary.

Adjustments in Payments for Imaging Services

Medicare has a longstanding policy of reducing payment for multiple surgical procedures performed by the same physician on the same patient on the same day. Full payment is made for the highest priced procedure, with any subsequent procedure paid at 50%. In 1995, the policy was extended to certain nuclear medicine diagnostic procedures. On November 21, 2005, CMS issued its final physician fee schedule regulation for 2006. This regulation provided for a reduction in the a component of payments (the technical component) for the subsequent imaging procedure performed on contiguous body parts. The conference agreement specifies that, effective for fee schedules established beginning with 2007, the reduced expenditures attributable to the multiple procedure payment reduction for imaging (under the final rule published November 21, 2005) will not be taken into account for purposes of the budget neutrality calculation for fee schedules for 2006 and 2007. The agreement further provides that for specified imaging services furnished on or after January 1, 2007, the technical component for a service will be reduced if it exceeds (without regard to the geographic wage adjustment factor) the outpatient department (OPD) fee schedule amount for the service established under the prospective payment system for hospital outpatient departments.

Limitation on Medicare Payments for Procedures in Ambulatory Care Surgical Centers (ASCs)

Medicare uses a fee schedule to pay for the facility services related to a surgery provided in an ASC. The associated physician services (surgery and anesthesia) are reimbursed under the physician fee schedule. The Secretary is required to implement a new ASC payment system no later than January 2008. Medicare reimbursement for hospital outpatient department (OPD) services is based on a fee schedule established by a separate prospective payment system (OPPS). Under OPPS, the unit of payment is the individual service or procedure as assigned to an ambulatory payment classification (APC). The payment rate for each service is determined by multiplying the relative weight for the service's APC by the conversion factor. Under the conference agreement, starting for surgical procedures on January 1, 2007, when the ASC facility payment (without application of any geographic price differences) is greater than the Medicare OPD fee schedule amount established under OPPS (without application of any geographic adjustment) for the same service, the ASC will be paid the OPD fee schedule amount. This adjustment applies to ASC payments until the revised ASC payment system is implemented. Total payments to ASCs under the revised payment system can be no more than those under the existing ASC payment system, including the reduced expenditures that result from the application of this provision.

Update for Physicians' Services for 2006

Medicare payments for services of physicians and certain nonphysician practitioners are made on the basis of a fee schedule. The fee schedule assigns relative values to services that reflect physician work (i.e., the time, skill, and intensity it takes to provide the service), practice expenses, and malpractice costs. The relative values are adjusted for geographic variations in costs. The adjusted relative values are then converted into a dollar payment amount by a conversion factor. The conversion factor is the same for all services. It is updated each year according to a formula specified in law. Under the formula, a negative 4.4% update goes into effect in 2006. The conference agreement overrides application of the formula for 2006 by setting the update at zero. In effect, this means that the 2006 conversion factor is the same as the 2005 conversion factor. The agreement also requires the Medicare Payment Advisory Commission (MedPAC) to submit a report to Congress by March 1, 2007 on mechanisms that could be used to replace the sustainable growth rate system (SGR). The sustainable growth rate (SGR) which is essentially a cumulative target for Medicare spending growth over time (with 1996 serving as the base period).

Three Year Hold Harmless Transition for Small Rural Hospitals into the Outpatient Prospective Payment System (OPPS)

Rural hospitals with no more than 100 beds and sole community hospitals (SCH) located in rural areas are paid no less under OPPS than they would have received under the prior reimbursement system for covered outpatient department services provided until January 1, 2006. Under its administrative authority, starting for services on January 1, 2006, CMS has increased OPPS payments to rural SCHs by 7.1%. Under the conference agreement, certain small rural hospitals (with no more than 100 beds that are not SCHs) can receive additional Medicare payments if their outpatient payments under OPPS are less than under the old payment system. For calendar year (CY) 2006, these hospitals will receive 95% of any difference. The hospitals will receive 90% of the difference in CY2007 and 85% of the difference in CY2008.

Update to the Composite Rate Component of the Basic Case-Mix Adjusted Prospective Payment System for Dialysis Services

The basic case-mix adjusted reimbursement system for dialysis has two components: (1) the composite rate, which covers services, including dialysis; and (2) a drug add-on adjustment for the difference between the payment amounts for separately billable drugs and biologicals and their acquisition costs. The basic case-mix adjusted payment amounts are to be updated annually beginning with 2006, but only for that portion of the case-mix adjusted system that is represented by the add-on adjustment and not for the portion represented by the composite rate. The conference agreement increases the composite rate component of the basic case-miz adjusted system by 1.6% for services beginning January 1, 2006.

Revisions to Payments for Therapy Services

The Balanced Budget Act of 1997 established annual per beneficiary payment limits on all outpatient therapy services provided by non-hospital providers beginning in 1999. Subsequent legislation suspended application of the limits beginning in 2000. A moratorium has been in place since then, except for a brief period in 2003. Under current law, the caps are again slated to go into effect in 2006. The conference agreement does not extend the moratorium. However, the Secretary is required to implement an exceptions process for expenses incurred in 2006. The agreement also requires the Secretary, by July 1, 2006, to implement clinically appropriate code edits for physical therapy services, occupational therapy services, and speech language pathology services. The edits are to identify and eliminate improper payments.

Accelerated Implementation of Income-Related Reduction in Part B Premium Subsidy

Since the inception of Medicare, all Part B enrollees have paid the same Part B premium, regardless of their income level. MMA increased the Part B premiums for higher income enrollees beginning in 2007. The increase is to be phased-in over five years. The agreement accelerates the phase-in period from five years to three years, with the provision fully effective in 2009.

Medicare Coverage of Ultrasound Screening for Abdominal Aortic Aneurysms

The conference agreement would authorize Medicare coverage of ultrasound screening for abdominal aortic aneurysms for individuals who (1) received referrals for such screenings as a result of an initial preventive physical exam performed for new Medicare enrollees; (2) had not previously had such a test covered by Medicare; and (3) had a family history of abdominal aortic aneurysm or manifested risk factors included in a beneficiary category (not related to age) identified by the United States Preventive Services Task Force. The Part B deductible would not apply to these services.

Improving Patient Access to, and Utilization of, Colorectal Cancer Screening under Medicare

The conference agreement provides that the Part B deductible does not apply to colorectal cancer screening tests, effective January 1, 2007.

Expansion and Payment for Services Provided by Federally Qualified Health Centers (FQHC)

Medicare pays FQHCs to provide primary and other preventative services. MMA specified that a SNF Part A resident who receives FQHC services from a physician or appropriate practitioner would be excluded from SNF consolidated billing and receive separate Medicare payments. Under the conference agreement, FQHCs may provide diabetes self-management training and nutrition therapy benefits, as covered under Medicare, and be paid under the all-inclusive per visit payment. FQHCs would receive direct payment for any FQHC service provided by a health care professional under contract to the center.

Waiver of Part B Late Enrollment Penalty for Certain International Volunteers

The conference agreement permits certain individuals to delay enrollment in Part B without a delayed enrollment penalty. Those individuals permitted to delay enrollment would be those who volunteered outside of the United States for at least 12 months through a program sponsored by a tax-exempt organization defined under Section 501(c)(3) of the Internal Revenue Code. The individuals must demonstrate they had health insurance coverage while serving in the international program. Individuals permitted to delay enrollment will have a special Part B enrollment period.

Home Health Payments

The Medicare home health prospective payment system, which was implemented on October 1, 2000, provides a standardized payment for a 60-day episode of care furnished to a Medicare beneficiary. Medicare's payment is adjusted to reflect the type and intensity of care furnished and area wages as measured by the hospital wage index. Each year Medicare's payment to home health agencies is updated by the projected annual change in the home health market basket (HHMB), with specified reductions in some years. The Medicare Prescription Drug Improvement and Modernization Act of 2003 provided for a one-year 5% additional payment for home health services furnished in rural areas. The temporary payment began for episodes and visits ending on or after April 1, 2004 and before April 1, 2005.

The conference agreement eliminates the update for home health payments in 2006. It also extends the 5% additional payment for rural home health episodes or visits beginning on or after January 1, 2006 and before January 1, 2007. Starting in 2007, the conference agreement directs home health agencies to submit to the Secretary health care quality data in a form, manner, and time period specified by the Secretary. In 2007 and subsequent years, a home health agency that does not submit the required quality data will receive an update of the market basket minus two percentage points. The conference agreement directs the Medicare Payment Advisory Commission to submit a report to Congress no later than June 1, 2007 on a value-based purchasing program for home health services.

Delay of Medicare Payments

The conference agreement delays Medicare Part A and B payments by nine days at the end of the FY2006. Claims that would otherwise be paid on September 22, 2006 through September 30, 2006 would be paid on the first business day of October 2006. No interest or late penalty would be paid for any delay in a payment during the period.

Increase in Medicare Integrity Program (MIP) Funding

Certain Hospital Insurance Trust Fund amounts were appropriated for specific activities, including the Medicare Integrity Program (MIP) that focuses on anti-fraud activities. Under the conference agreement, MIP funding is increased by $100 million for FY2006.

Phase-out of Risk Adjustment Budget Neutrality in Determining the Amount of Payments to Medicare Advantage Organizations

Beginning in 2007, this section (1) would change the way MA area-specific non-drug monthly benchmarks (or MA benchmarks) are calculated, and (2) would specify an adjustment to the benchmarks to phase-out overall increases in MA rates that are the result of the budget neutral implementation of risk adjustment.

Establishment of PACE Provider Grant Program

The Program for All-Inclusive Care for the Elderly (PACE) makes available all services covered under Medicare and Medicaid without amount, duration or scope limitations, and without application to any deductibles, copayments or other cost-sharing. Under the program, certain low-income individuals age 55 and older, who would otherwise require nursing home care, receive all health, medical, and social services in a community setting through a capitated managed care program. The conference agreement establishes a grant program for no more than 15 pilot PACE providers in rural areas. For FY2006, $7.5 million is appropriated to the Secretary for a grant distribution in amounts of no greater than $750,000 per pilot site (for specified purposes) to remain available through FY2008. Technical assistance programs are also created to help establish and support rural PACE pilot sites. The conference agreement also establishes an outlier reimbursement fund for recognized outlier costs (as defined in the provision). Under this fund, the Secretary makes payments equal to 80% of costs greater than $50,000 for an eligible outlier participant, with total outlier payments per eligible individual not exceeding $100,000 for a 12-month period. Total payments, for all outlier eligibles at a particular site, may not exceed $500,000 in a 12-month period. For this purpose, $10 million is appropriated to remain available through FY2010. The Secretary conducts an evaluation of rural PACE pilot sites no later than 60 months after enactment.

MEDICAID

Outpatient Prescription Drugs

Modification of Federal Upper Payment Limit (FUL) for Multiple Source Drugs; Definition of Multiple Source Drugs

The conference agreement applies FULs to multiple source drugs for which the FDA has rated two or more products to be therapeutically and pharmaceutically equivalent. For those drugs, starting in CY2007, the FUL would be equal to 250% of the average manufacturer price. In addition, the definition of AMP is altered to exclude customary prompt pay discounts extended to wholesalers from those amounts. The price reporting requirements are also modified such that manufacturers would be required to submit, not later than 30 days after the last day of each rebate period, the customary prompt pay discounts extended to wholesalers in addition to the AMP and best price reporting required under current law. The agreement contains additional provisions on reporting including provisions on sales of Medicaid covered drugs that are made at a nominal prices; and that AMP would be reported and calculated on a monthly basis. In addition, the agreement allows states to have access to reported AMP data for multiple source drugs for the purpose of carrying out the Medicaid programs and would require the Secretary to disclose such information through a website accessible to the public. Additionally, the conference agreement allows the Secretary to contract for services for the determination of retail survey prices for covered outpatient drugs that represent a nationwide average of consumer purchase prices for such drugs, net of all discounts and rebates. Funds are made available beginning in 2006 for this purpose.

Collection and Submission of Utilization Data for Certain Physician Administered Drugs

Certain drugs administered by physicians in their offices or in another outpatient setting, such as chemotherapy, have often been excluded from the drug rebate program although there is no specific statutory exclusion. This is because providers use Healthcare Common Procedure Coding System (HCPCS) J-codes to bill the Medicaid program for injectible prescription drugs, including cancer drugs. The HCPCS J-codes do not, however, provide states with the specific manufacturer information necessary to enable them to seek rebates. The conference agreement requires that states provide for the collection and submission of utilization and coding information for each Medicaid single source drug that is physician administered.

Improved Regulation of Drugs Sold under a New Drug Application Approved under Section 505(c) of the Federal Food, Drug, and Cosmetic Act

The conference agreement modifies the existing drug price reporting requirements to include, for single source drugs, innovator multiple source drugs, and any other drugs sold under a new drug application approved (under Section 505c of the Federal Food, Drug and Cosmetic Act, FFDCA) by FDA, both the average manufacturer's price and the manufacturer's best price for such drugs.

The definition of AMP would be modified to include, in the case of a manufacturer that approves, allows, or otherwise permits an authorized generic or any other drug of the manufacturer to be sold under an NDA to be inclusive of the average price paid for such drugs.

In addition, the definition of best price would be modified so that it is inclusive, in the case of a manufacturer that approves, allows, or otherwise permits any other drug of the manufacturer to be sold under a new drug application approved under Section 505(c) of the FFDCA, of the lowest price for an authorized drug available from the manufacturer during the rebate period to any manufacturer, wholesaler, retailer, provider, health maintenance organization, nonprofit entity, or governmental entity within the U.S.

Children's Hospital Participation in Drug Discount Program

Section 340(B) of the Public Health Service Act allows certain health care providers, including community health centers and disproportionate share hospitals, access to prescription drug prices that are similar to the prices paid by Medicaid agencies after being reduced by manufacturer rebates. The conference agreement includes a provision adding Children's Hospitals to the list of providers that may have access to 340(B) discounted prices.

Asset Transfers

Lengthening Look-Back Period

Current law requires states to impose penalties on individuals who transfer assets (all income and resources of the individual and of the individual's spouse) for less than fair market value. the rules require states to delay Medicaid eligibility for certain Medicaid long-term care services for individuals applying for care in a nursing home, and, at state option, for certain people receiving care in community-based settings, who have transferred assets for less than fair market value on or after a "look-back date." The "look-back date" is 36 months prior to application for Medicaid for income and most assets disposed of by the individual, and 60 months in the case of certain trusts. The conference agreement would lengthen the look-back period to five years, for all income and assets disposed of by the individual after enactment.

Change in Beginning Date for Period of Ineligibility

The period of ineligibility, or penalty period, begins on the first day of the first month during or after which assets have been improperly transferred. The conference agreement would change the start date of the ineligibility period for all transfers made on or after the date of enactment, to begin on the first day of a month during or after which assets have been transferred for less than fair market value, or the date on which the individual is eligible for Medicaid and would otherwise be receiving institutional level care.

Availability of Hardship Waivers; Additional Provisions on Hardship Waivers

The conference agreement adds requirements that states approve undue hardship requests when the asset transfer penalty would deprive the individual of (a) medical care such that the individual's health or life would be endangered; or (b) food, clothing, shelter, or other necessities of life. States are required to provide notice to recipients about the hardship waivers; a timely processing of the waivers; and, an appeals process. Institutions may file hardship applications on behalf of residents. States may pay nursing facilities to hold beds of residents while applications are pending.

Disclosure and Treatment of Annuities

The conference agreement requires individuals applying for Medicaid-covered LTC services, upon Medicaid application and recertification of eligibility, to disclose to the state a description of any interest the individual or community spouse has in an annuity (or similar financial instrument, as specified by the Secretary), regardless of whether the annuity is irrevocable or is treated as an asset. The purchase of an annuity is treated as an improper transfer unless the state would be named as a remainder beneficiary to the asset for amounts up to certain Medicaid expenditures. The conference agreement also makes certain annuities subject to estate recovery.

Application of "Income-First" Rule in Applying Community Spouse's Income before Assets in Providing Support of Community Spouse

Current law includes provisions intended to prevent impoverishment of a spouse whose husband or wife seeks Medicaid coverage for long-term care services, allowing the community spouse to retain higher amounts of income and assets (on top of non-countable assets such as a house, car, etc.) than allowed under general Medicaid rules. The law allows community spouses with more limited income to retain at least a state specified amount set within federal guidelines. If the community spouse's monthly income amount is less than this amount, the institutionalized spouse may choose to transfer an amount of his or her income or assets to make up for the shortfall (i.e., the difference between the community spouse's monthly income and the state-specified minimum monthly maintenance needs allowance). The conference agreement requires states to consider that all income of the institutionalized spouse that could be made available to the community spouse, in accordance with the calculation of the post-eligibility allocation of income or additional income allowance allocated at a fair hearing, has been made before states allocate to the community spouse resources from the institutionalized spouse to provide the difference between the minimum monthly maintenance needs allowance and all income available to the community spouse.

Disqualification for Long-Term Care Assistance for Individuals with Substantial Home Equity

The conference agreement would exclude from Medicaid eligibility for nursing facility or other long-term care services, certain individuals with an equity interest in their home of greater than $500,000. A state may elect to substitute an amount that exceeds $500,000 but does not exceed $750,000. Beginning in 2011, these dollar amounts are increased,, from year to year based on the percentage increase in the consumer price index for all urban consumers (all items, United States city average) rounded to the nearest $1,000. Individuals whose spouse, child under age 21, or child who is blind or disabled who lawfully resides in the home would not be excluded from eligibility. This provision would not prevent an individual from using a reverse mortgage or home equity loan to reduce the individual's total equity interest in the home.

Enforceability of Continuing Care Retirement Communities (CCRC) and Life Care Community Admission Contracts

The conference agreement would allow state-licensed, registered, certified, or equivalent continuing care retirement communities (CCRC) or a life care community to require in their admissions contracts that residents spend their resources (subject to Medicaid's rules concerning the resources and income allowances for community spouses), declared for the purposes of admission, on their care before they apply for Medicaid. It would also allow certain entrance fees for CCRCs or life care communities to be considered by states to be countable resources for purposes of the Medicaid eligibility determination.

Requirement to Impose Partial Months of Ineligibility

The conference agreement requires that a state shall not round down, or otherwise disregard any fractional period of ineligibility when determining the penatly period (or ineligibility period) with respect to the disposal of assets.

Authority for States to Accumulate Multiple Transfers into One Penalty Period

Under the conference agreement, for an individual or an individual's spouse who disposes of multiple fractional assets in more than one month for less than fair market value on or after the applicable look-back date, states may determine the penalty period by treating the total, cumulative uncompensated value of all assets transferred by the individual (or individual's spouse) during all months as one transfer. States would be allowed to begin such penalty periods on the earliest date which would apply to such transfers.

Inclusion of Transfer of Certain Notes and Loans Assets

The conference agreement would make additional assets subject to the look-back period, and thus a penalty, if established or transferred for less than fair market value. Such assets would include funds used to purchase a promissory note, loan or mortgage, unless the repayment terms are actuarially sound, provide for payments to be made in equal amounts during the term of the loan and with no deferral nor balloon payments, and prohibit the cancellation of the balance upon the death of the lender.

Inclusion of Transfers to Purchase Life Estates

The conference agreement would redefine the term 'assets,' with respect to the Medicaid asset transfer rules, to make the purchase of a life estate interest in another individual's home subject to asset transfer penalties unless the purchaser resides in the home for at least one year after the date of purchase.

Expanded Access to Certain Benefits

Expansion of State Long-Term Care Partnership Program

Under Medicaid's long-term care (LTC) insurance partnership program, certain persons who have exhausted (or used at least some of) the benefits of a private long-term care insurance policy may access Medicaid without meeting the same means-testing requirements as other groups of Medicaid-eligible individuals. For these individuals, means-testing requirements are relaxed at (1) the time of application to Medicaid; and (2) the time of the beneficiary's death when Medicaid estate recovery is generally applied. Under current law, these provisions are limited to selected states.

The conference agreement: (1) requires that existing partnership programs not allow consumer protection standards to be less stringent than those applying under the state plan amendment as of December 31, 2005; and (2) allows certain individuals in states with state plan amendments approved after May 14, 1993 to be exempt from estate recovery requirements if the amendment provides for the disregard of any assets or resources in the amount equal to the amount of insurance benefits made to or on behalf of an individual who is a beneficiary under a LTC policy, if the program meets NAIC LTC model regulations and other requirements. In addition, the DHHS Secretary is to develop recommendations for Congress to fund a minimum electronic data set of the LTC insurance partnerships and reciprocal recognition of the policies among states.

Fraud, Waste and Abuse

Encouraging the Enactment of State False Claims Acts

States may have a variety of laws in place to facilitate prosecution of Medicaid fraud, and some have established their own versions of a false claims act. With limited exceptions, a state must repay the federal share (generally determined by the federal medical assistance percentage, or FMAP) of any provider overpayment within 60 days of discovering the overpayment, regardless of whether or not the state has recovered the overpayment to the provider. Under the conference agreement, if a state has in effect a law relating to false or fraudulent claims that meets requirements specified in the bill, the FMAP, with respect to any amounts recovered under a state action brought under such a law, is decreased by 10 percentage points.

Employee Education About False Claims Recovery

Under the conference agreement, a state is required to provide that any entity that receives annual Medicaid payments of at least $5 million, as a condition of receiving such payments, must: (1) establish written policies for all employees (and any contractor or agent) of the entity that provide detailed information on state and federal false claims laws and whistle-blower protections under such laws, (2) include in such written polices detailed provisions regarding the entity's policies and procedures for detecting and preventing fraud, waste, and abuse, and (3) include in any employee handbook for the entity a specific discussion of such laws, the rights of employees to be protected as whistleblowers, and the entity's policies and procedures for detecting and preventing fraud, waste, and abuse.

Prohibition on Restocking and Double Billing of Prescription Drugs

The conference agreement would prohibit federal matching payments for the ingredient cost of a covered outpatient drug for which the pharmacy has already received payment (other than a reasonable re-stocking fee).

Medicaid Integrity Program

The conference agreement establishes a Medicaid Integrity Program, under which the Secretary of HHS shall enter into contracts with eligible entities to carry out its activities, including review of the actions of individuals or entities, audit of claims for payment, identification of overpayments, and education with respect to payment integrity and quality of care. Appropriations for the program total $5 million in FY2006, $50 million in FY2007-FY2008, and $75 million each year thereafter. In each year of FY2006-FY2010, $25 million is appropriated for Medicaid actitivities of the HHS Office of Inspector General. The conference agreement also establishes a national expansion of the Medicare-Medicaid data match project (referred to as the Medi-Medi Program) as a required activity of the Medicare Integrity Program.

Enhancing Third Party Identification and Payment

With certain exceptions, Medicaid is a payer of last resort in cases where another party is legally liable to pay for a beneficiary's care. The conference agreement amends the list of third parties for which states must take all reasonable measures to ascertain legal liability to include self-insured plans, pharmacy benefit managers, and other parties that are legally responsible (by statute, contract, or agreement) for payment of a claim for a health care item or service. It also amends that section to include these entities in the list of health insurers that states must prohibit from taking an individual's Medicaid status into account when enrolling the individual or making payments for benefits to or on behalf of the individual. In addition, it requires a state to provide assurances satisfactory to the Secretary of HHS that it has laws in effect requiring third parties to provide, upon request of the state, information to determine health insurance coverage and to cooperate with payment and recovery efforts by Medicaid.

Improved Enforcement of Documentation Requirements

Under the conference agreement, states are prohibited from receiving federal Medicaid reimbursement for an individual who has not provided satisfactory documentary evidence of citizenship or nationality. The agreement provides a listing of acceptable documentation. The requirements do not apply to aliens who are entitled to or enrolled for Medicare benefits, receiving Supplemental Security Income (SSI) benefits, or eligible for Medicaid on such other basis as the Secretary may specify that satisfactory evidence had been previously presented.

Flexibility in Cost Sharing and Benefits

State Option for Alternative Premiums and Cost Sharing

The conference agreement allows states to impose premiums and cost-sharing for any group of individuals for any type of service (except prescribed drugs which are treated separately; see below), through Medicaid state plan amendments (rather than waivers), subject to specific restrictions. Premiums and cost-sharing provisions in current law for workers with disabilities are not affected.

In general, for individuals in families with income between 100 and 150% FPL: (1) no premiums may be imposed, (2) cost sharing for any item or service cannot exceed 10% of the cost of the item or service, and (3) the total aggregate amount of all cost-sharing (including cost sharing for prescribed drugs and emergency room copayments for non-emergency care; see below) cannot exceed 5% of family income as applied on a quarterly or monthly basis as specified by the state. For individuals in families with income above 150% FPL: (1) the total aggregate amount of all cost sharing (including cost sharing for prescribed drugs and emergency room copayments for non-emergency care) cannot exceed 5% of family income as applied on a quarterly or monthly basis as specified by the state, and (2) cost-sharing for any item or service cannot exceed 20% of the cost of the item or service.

Certain groups are exempt from paying premiums under this option. There are additional limitations on service-related cost sharing and certain groups and services are exempt from these provisions. Such cost-sharing provisions would be indexed over time.

The agreement allows states to condition the provision of medical assistance on the payment of premiums, and to terminate Medicaid eligibility on the basis of failure to pay a premium if that failure continues for at least 60 days. Providers can also deny care for failure to pay service-related co-payments.

Special Rules for Cost Sharing for Prescription Drugs

Under the conference agreement, states may impose higher cost-sharing amounts for state-identified non-preferred drugs within a class; waive or reduce the cost-sharing otherwise applicable for preferred drugs within such class; and must not apply such cost-sharing for preferred drugs to persons exempt from cost-sharing. Cost-sharing limits for non-preferred drugs are associated with income classes. In cases in which a prescribing physician determines that the preferred drug would not be effective or would have adverse health effects or both, the state may impose the cost-sharing amount for preferred drugs on the prescribed non-preferred product.

Emergency Room Co-Payments for Non-Emergency Care

The conference agreement would allow states, through a state plan amendment, to impose increased cost-sharing on state-specified groups for non-emergency services provided in an ER, when certain conditions are met. The agreement also provides for limitations on the cost-sharing. The Secretary is required to provide for payments to states for the establishment of alternate non-emergency providers, or networks of such providers.

Use of Benchmark Benefit Packages

The conference agreement gives states the option to provide Medicaid to state-specified groups through enrollment in benchmark and benchmark-equivalent coverage. States can only exercise this option for eligibility groups that were established under the state plan on or before the date of enactment of this option. States may choose to provide other wrap-around and additional benefits. Specific groups are exempted from mandatory enrollment in the benefit package option. Benchmark and benchmark-equivalent packages would be nearly identical to those offered under SCHIP, with some additions. For any child under age 19 in one of the major mandatory and optional eligibility groups, wrap-around benefits to the benchmark or benchmark-equivalent coverage includes ESPDT.

State Financing under Medicaid

Managed Care Organization (MCO) Provider Tax

States' ability to use provider-specific taxes to fund Medicaid expenditures is limited. If a state establishes provider-specific taxes to fund the state's share of program costs, reimbursement of the federal share will not be available unless the tax program meets specific rules. One of these rules stipulates that the tax must be broad-based. To meet the broad base requirement under current law an MCO tax must apply to all Medicaid MCOs. The conference agreement would expand the Medicaid MCO provider class to include all MCOs. To qualify for federal reimbursement, a state's provider tax would need to apply to both Medicaid and non-Medicaid MCOs.

Reforms of Case Management and Targeted Case Management (TCM)

The conference agreement clarifies the activities that can be considered case management or targeted case management, and those activities (primarily foster care-related activities) that may not be reimbursed as case management services or TCM.

Additional FMAP Adjustments

Under the conference agreement, if Alaska's FY2006 or FY2007 FMAP for Medicaid or SCHIP is less than its FY2005 FMAP, the FY2005 FMAP shall apply. In addition, in computing Medicaid and SCHIP FMAPs for any year after 2006 for a state that the Secretary of HHS determines has a significant number of individuals who were evacuated to and live in the state as a result of Hurricane Katrina as of October 1, 2005, the Secretary shall disregard such evacuees and their incomes.

DSH Allotment for the District of Columbia

States and the District of Columbia are required to recognize, in establishing hospital payment rates, the situation of hospitals that serve a disproportionate number of Medicaid beneficiaries and other low-income patients with special needs. DSH payments are made to each qualifying hospital. Total federal reimbursement for each state's DSH payments, however, are capped at a statewide ceiling, referred to as the state's DSH allotment. The conference agreement would raise the allotments for the District of Columbia for FY2000, 2001, and 2002 from \$ 32 million to \$ 49 million. The higher allotments would be used to calculate DSH allotments beginning with FY2005 amounts.

Increase in Medicaid Payments to the Insular Areas

For each of FYs 2006 and 2007, the conference Agreement increases the federal Medicaid funding caps in the insular areas. For Puerto Rico, the federal Medicaid cap is increased by \$12 million in each of FY2006 and FY2007. For the Virgin Islands and Guam, the federal Medicaid caps is increased by \$2.5 million in FY2006, and by \$5.0 million in FY2007. For the Northern Marianas, the federal Medicaid cap is increased by \$1.0 million in FY2006, and by \$2.0 million in FY2007. For American Samoa, the federal Medicaid cap is increased by \$2.0 million in FY2006, and by \$4.0 million in FY2007. Caps in subsequent years will be indexed.

OTHER PROVISIONS

Family Opportunity Act

Opportunity for Families of Disabled Children to Purchase Medicaid Coverage for Such Children

This provision would create a new optional Medicaid eligibility group for children with disabilities up to age 18 who meet the severity of disability required under the Supplemental Security Income (SSI) program, but whose family income is above the financial standards for SSI but below 300% of the federal poverty level (FPL). Under current law, children with disabilities have generally had to qualify for Medicaid using an income standard that is lower than 300% of FPL. Medicaid coverage for this optional group would be initially effective January 1, 2008 and would be fully phased in starting in FY2010. Within certain limits, states would be permitted to charge monthly premiums (based on income) for Medicaid coverage provided to this new group. Finally, under this option, states must require the parents of Medicaid beneficiaries to enroll in any available employer-sponsored private insurance meeting certain criteria.

Demonstration Projects Regarding Home and Community-Based Alternatives to Psychiatric Residential Treatment Facilities for Children

The conference agreement establishes a five-year demonstration project in which up to 10 states could provide a broad range of home- and community-based services to children who would otherwise require services in a psychiatric residential treatment facility.

Development and Support of Family-to-Family Health Information Centers

The conference agreement increases funding for the development and support of new family-to-family health information centers. The purpose of the family-to-family health information centers is to: (1) assist families of children with disabilities or special health care needs to make informed choices about health care so as to promote good treatment decisions, cost-effectiveness, and improved health outcomes for such children; (2) provide information regarding the health care needs of, and resources available for children with disabilities or special health care needs; (3) identify successful health delivery models; (4) develop a model for collaboration between families of such children and health professionals; (5) provide training and guidance with regard to the care of such children; and (6) conduct outreach activities to the families of such children, health professionals, schools, and other appropriate entities and individuals.

Restoration of Medicaid Eligibility for Certain SSI Beneficiaries

The agreement extends Medicaid eligibility to persons who are under age 21 and who are eligible for SSI, effective on the later of: (1) the date the application is filed, or (2) the date SSI eligibility is granted.

Money Follows the Person Rebalancing Demonstration

Money Follows the Person Rebalancing Demonstration

The conference agreement authorizes the Secretary to conduct a demonstration project in states to (1) increase the use of home and community-based care instead of institutions by relocating individuals from institutions into the community, (2) expand the state's capacity to provide home and community-based long-term care services for individuals who choose to transition into the community; and (3) to ensure that procedures are in place to provide quality assurance and continuous quality improvement, that is at least comparable to other Medicaid home and community-based services.

State demonstrations would receive additional federal funding for 12 months for home and community based services following an individual's relocation from institutions to the community. The amount of additional funding would be based on a Money Follows the Person enhanced federal matching percentage. State demonstrations must operate for at least two years in a five-year period starting in FY2007, and services for individuals must continue following the demonstration, so long as the person remains eligible for these services. States must also take steps to eliminate barriers to using Medicaid funding to provide long-term care services in the setting of a person's choosing, and meet maintenance of effort requirements. The Secretary would be required to provide technical assistance and oversight to state grantees and conduct and report the findings of a national evaluation. The conference agreement appropriates $250 million for the portion of FY2007 which begins on January 1, 2007, and ends on September 30, 2007; $300 million in FY2008; $350 million in FY2009; $400 million in FY2010; and $450 million in FY2011 to carry out the demonstration project.

Miscellaneous

Medicaid Transformation Grants

The conference agreement requires that the Secretary of HHS shall provide for payments to states for the adoption of innovative methods to improve the effectiveness and efficiency in Medicaid.

Examples of innovative methods for which funds may be used include (1) methods for reducing patient error rates through the implementation and use of electronic systems, (2) methods for improving rates of Medicaid collection from estates, (3) methods for reducing waste, fraud, and abuse, (4) implementation of a medication risk management program, (5) methods for reducing outpatient drug expenditures by increasing the utilization of generics, and (6) methods for improving access to primary and specialty physician care for the uninsured using integrated university-based hospital and clinic systems. Total payments will equal and not exceed $75 million in each of FY2007 and FY2008.

Health Opportunity Accounts

The conference agreement requires the Secretary to establish demonstration programs within Medicaid for health opportunity accounts (HOA), effective January 1, 2006. No more than 10 state programs could be established the first five years, though afterwards other programs would be allowed if the earlier ones were not unsuccessful. Among other things, state programs would have to make patients aware of the high cost of medical care, provide incentives for them to seek preventive care, and reduce inappropriate uses of health care. Eligibility for HOAs would be determined by the state, though individuals who are disabled, pregnant, or receiving terminal care or long-term care, would be among those who could not participate.

Participants would have both an HOA and coverage for medical items and services that, after an annual deductible is met, were available under the existing Medicaid state plan and waiver authorities. The deductible would have to be at least 100%, but no more than 110%, of the annual state contributions to the HOA. Both the deductible and the maximum for out-of-pocket cost-sharing could vary among families. The deductible need not apply to preventive care.

HOAs would be used to pay health care expenses specified by the state; payments could be restricted to licensed or otherwise authorized providers as well as to items and services that are medically appropriate or necessary. Withdrawals would be made by electronic transfer. Once account holders were no longer eligible for Medicaid they could continue to make withdrawals under these conditions, though accounts could then also be used to pay for health insurance or, at state option, for job training or education. Participants generally would be able to obtain services from Medicaid providers or managed care organizations at the same payment rates that would be applicable if the coverage deductible did not apply, or from any provider for payment rates not exceeding 125% of those rates.

HOA contributions could be made by the state or by other persons or entities, including charitable organizations. Including federal shares, state contributions generally could not exceed $2,500 for each adult and $1,000 for each child.

State Option to Establish Non-Emergency Medical Transportation Program

The agreement allows states to establish a non-emergency medical transportation brokerage program for beneficiaries who need access to medical care but have no other means of transportation. States are not required to provide such services on a statewide basis, comparable services for all Medicaid enrollees, nor freedom of choice among providers.

Extension of Transitional Medical Assistance (TMA) and Abstinence Education Program

States are required to continue Medicaid benefits for certain low-income families who would otherwise lose coverage because of changes in their income. This continuation of benefits is known as transitional medical assistance (TMA). The conference agreement extends a provision of law that requires states to provide up to 12 months of TMA coverage through December 31, 2006.

Emergency Services Furnished by Non-Contract Providers for Medicaid Managed Care Enrollees

Medicaid law provides certain protections for beneficiaries enrolled in managed care, including assuring coverage of emergency services under each managed care contract awarded by the state. A Medicaid provider that does not have a contract with a Medicaid managed care entity (MCE) that furnishes emergency care to a beneficiary enrolled with that MCO must accept as payment in full no more than the amount otherwise applicable outside of managed care (e.g., in the fee-for-service setting) minus any payments for indirect costs of medical education and direct costs of graduate medical education. In a state where rates paid to hospitals under the state Medicaid plan are negotiated by contract and not publicly released, the payment amount applicable under this provision must be the average contract rate that would apply under the state plan for general acute care hospitals or the average contract rate that would apply under the plan for tertiary hospitals.

Expansion of Home and Community-Based Services

Medicaid home and community-based service (HCBS) waivers authorized by Section 1915(c) of the Social Security Act allow states to provide home and community-based services to Medicaid beneficiaries who would otherwise need institutional care. The conference agreement establishes home and community-based services as an optional Medicaid benefit that would not require a waiver and that meets certain other requirements for individuals whose income does not exceed 150% of the federal poverty level. States that offer this new benefit must establish needs-based criteria to determine an individual's eligibility for HCBS services, and the specific HCBS the individual will receive. The individual does not have to meet an institutional level of care to qualify for services. A state may limit the number of individuals who can participate in this benefit and establish waiting lists. A state is required to use an independent evaluation for determining an individual's eligibility for the HCBS option. The state must establish a written individualized care plan for all individual participating in the HCBS option. For this new benefit, a state may also allow an individual or the individual's representative to receive self-directed home and community-based services.

Optional Choice of Self-Directed Personal Assistance Services (Cash and Counseling)

Medicaid beneficiaries with disabilities or chronic conditions and federal and state policymakers have been increasing the discretion that beneficiaries have over key elements of the service (e.g., what time a personal care worker comes to the home to help the beneficiary, who provides the service, etc.) These types of programs are broadly known as 'self-directed' or 'consumer-directed' programs. The conference agreement would allow a state to cover, under the Medicaid program, payment for part or all of the cost of self-directed personal assistance services (other than room and board) based on a written plan of care.

State Children's Health Insurance Program (SCHIP)

Additional Allotments to Eliminate Fiscal Year 2006 Funding Shortfalls

The conference agreement authorizes and appropriates $283, million for the purpose of providing additional SCHIP allotments to shortfall states and territories in FY2006. From the additional FY2006 SCHIP appropriation, after a 1.05% set aside for distribution among the territories, each FY2006 shortfall state would receive an allotment to cover its projected shortfall. Such additional SCHIP allotments are available for one year only. The conference agreement limits the types of payments that may be matched at the SCHIP enhanced matching rate for SCHIP expenditures drawn against the additional FY2006 appropriation available to shortfall states to include child health assistance payments made on behalf of targeted low-income children.

Prohibition Against Covering Nonpregnant Adults with Schip Funds

The conference agreement limits the Secretary of Health and Human Services' Section 1115 waiver authority by prohibiting the approval of new waiver, experimental, pilot, or demonstration projects (approved on or after October 1, 2005) that allow federal SCHIP funds to be used to provide child health assistance or other health benefits coverage to nonpregnant childless adults. The Secretary can continue to approve projects that expand the SCHIP program to caretaker relatives of Medicaid or SCHIP-eligible children and to pregnant adults. It also allows the continuation of existing Medicaid or SCHIP waiver projects (and/or extensions, amendments, or renewals to such projects) approved under the Section 1115 waiver authority before the date of enactment of this act.

Continued Authority for Qualifying States to Use Certain Funds for Medicaid Expenditures

Current law permits qualifying states to receive the SCHIP enhanced federal matching rate for the coverage of certain children enrolled in regular Medicaid. The maximum amount that qualifying states may claim under this allowance is the lesser of the following two amounts: (1) 20% of the state's available FY1998-FY2001 original SCHIP allotments; and (2) the state's balance (calculated quarterly) of any available FY1998-FY2001 federal SCHIP funds (original allotments or reallocated funds). If there is no balance, states may not claim 20% spending. Under current law, no 20% spending will be permitted in FY2006 or any fiscal year thereafter. The conference agreement continues the authority for states to apply federal SCHIP matching funds toward the coverage of certain children enrolled in regular Medicaid. Tthe conference agreement allows qualifying states to use any available FY2004 and FY2005 SCHIP funds (i.e., FY2005 original allotments, and/or FY2004 and FY2005 retained allotments or redistributed funds, as the case may be) for such Medicaid services made on or after October 1, 2005 under the 20% allowance.

Katrina Relief

Additional Federal Payments under Hurricane-Related Multi-State Section 1115 Demonstrations

The conference agreement appropriates $2 billion (in addition to any funds made available for the National Disaster Medical System under the Department of Homeland Security for health care costs related to Hurricane Katrina) for use by the Secretary of HHS to pay eligible states (those who have provided care to affected individuals or evacuees under a Section 1115 project) for: (1) the non-federal (i.e., state) share of expenditures for health care provided to affected individuals (those who resided in a county or parish designated for individual assistance pursuant to the Stafford Act as a result of Hurricane Katrina and continue to reside in the same state) and evacuees (affected individuals displaced to another state) under approved multi-state Section 1115 demonstration projects; (2) reasonable administrative costs related to such projects; (3) only with respect to affected counties and parishes, the non-federal share of expenditures for medical assistance provided to individuals under existing Medicaid and SCHIP state plans; and (4) other purposes, if approved by the Secretary, to restore access to health care in impacted communities

REFERENCES

[1] Congressional Budget Office Cost Estimate, Reconciliation, *Recommendations of the Senate Committee on Finance,* as approved by the Senate Committee on Finance on Oct. 25, 2005.

[2] Section 1917 of the Social Security Act (amended by the Omnibus Budget Reconciliation Act of 1993, P.L. 103-66) allows states with an approved state plan amendment as of May 14, 1993 to exempt individuals from Medicaid estate recovery who apply to Medicaid after exhausting their private long-term care insurance benefits. By that date, five states (California, Connecticut, Indiana, Iowa, and New York) had received CMS approval for such exemptions. All of these states, except Iowa, have implemented partnership programs.

[3] CRS analysis of Medicaid state chart as published by CCH: Internet Research Network and the Home- and Community-based waiver database from the Centers for Medicare and Medicaid Services, July 2003.

[4] Congressional Budget Office. Cost Estimate. Reconciliation Recommendations of the House Committee on Energy and Commerce, as approved by the House Committee on Energy and Commerce on October 28, 2005.

[5] Specifically, this report does not discuss provisions that alter the Public Health Services Act (PHSA). These provisions are in sections 3202, 3203, and 3204. In addition, the report does not discuss subtitle C, Katrina and Rita Energy Relief, and subtitle D, Digital Television Transition of Title III.

[6] See CRS Report RL33132, Budget Reconciliation Legislation in 2005, by Robert Keith.

In: State Children's Health Insurance Program (SCHIP) ISBN: 978-1-60456-333-7
Editor: Mary T. Ewing, pp. 57-98

Chapter 2

MEDICAID, SCHIP, AND HEALTH INSURANCE: FY2008 BUDGET ISSUES*

April Grady, Evelyne P. Baumrucker, Bernadette Fernandez, Jean Hearne, Elicia J. Herz, Bob Lyke, Chris L. Peterson, Julie Stone and Julie M. Whittaker

ABSTRACT

Each year, the President is required to submit a comprehensive federal budget proposal to Congress no later than the first Monday in February. The House and Senate Budget Committees then develop their respective budget resolutions. Differences between the houses are supposed to be resolved by April 15, but this deadline is rarely met. Although it is not binding, the resolution provides a framework for subsequent legislative action.

The President's FY2008 budget contains a number of proposals that would affect Medicaid and the State Children's Health Insurance Program (SCHIP). While certain proposals would require legislative action, others would be implemented administratively (e.g., via regulatory changes, issuance of program guidance, or other possible methods). The President's budget also contains a number of proposals that would affect health insurance.

On May 17, the House and Senate adopted a conference agreement on the budget resolution (H.Rept. 110-153 accompanying S.Con.Res. 21). The FY2008 budget resolution provides a reserve fund of up to $50 billion for SCHIP legislation that is deficit-neutral in the Senate and deficit/surplus-neutral in the House, a variety of other deficit-neutral reserve funds, up to $383 million for health care fraud and abuse control, and two "sense of the Congress" provisions regarding health care cost growth and affordable health coverage.

To date, a number of Medicaid and SCHIP issues have seen legislative action in the 110th Congress. A war supplemental appropriations bill enacted on May 25 (H.R. 2206, P.L. 110-28) contains SCHIP funding, delays implementation of certain Medicaid administrative proposals, requires the use of tamper-resistant pads for Medicaid

* Excerpted from CRS Report RL33866, dated October 15, 2007.

prescriptions, and provides a Medicaid Pharmacy Plus waiver extension. Legislation was also enacted to temporarily extend Medicaid transitional medical assistance (TMA) through September 30, 2007 (S. 1701, P.L. 110-48). Another bill to extend TMA and the QI-1 program through December 31, 2007, apply an asset verification pilot to Medicaid for five years, and delay implementation of the new Medicaid tamper-resistant prescription pad requirement for six months (H.R. 3668, P.L. 110-90) was enacted at the end of September.

On the issue of SCHIP reauthorization, numerous bills have been introduced, including the Senate-passed Children's Health Insurance Program Reauthorization Act of 2007 (S. 1893/H.R. 976) and the House-passed Children's Health and Medicare Protection Act of 2007 (H.R. 3162). A bicameral agreement on SCHIP reauthorization passed the House on September 25 and the Senate on September 27 as an amendment to H.R. 976. President Bush vetoed the legislation on October 3. A continuing resolution that contains short-term funding for SCHIP (H.J.Res. 52, P.L. 110-92) was enacted at the end of September.

INTRODUCTION

Each year, the President is required to submit a comprehensive federal budget proposal to Congress no later than the first Monday in February. Once it is submitted, the Congressional Budget Office (CBO) analyzes the proposal using its own economic assumptions and estimation techniques. The House and Senate Budget Committees then develop their respective budget resolutions after reviewing the President's budget, the views of other committees, and information from CBO. Differences between the houses are supposed to be resolved by April 15, but this deadline is rarely met. Although it is not binding, the resolution provides a framework for subsequent legislative action.

This report provides information on Medicaid, the State Children's Health Insurance Program (SCHIP), and health insurance issues. It will be updated as the FY2008 budget process unfolds. Congressional Research Service (CRS) staff contact information by topic area is provided in tables 3 and 4 at the end of the report.

MEDICAID AND SCHIP IN THE PRESIDENT'S FY2008 BUDGET

The President's FY2008 budget contains a number of proposals that would affect Medicaid and SCHIP. Some are program expansions, and others are designed to reduce federal spending. For each of the proposals, this report provides:

- background;
- a description of the proposal based on available information;[1]
- a description of recent action (if any); and
- a list of relevant CRS reports.

The proposals generally are presented in the order in which they appear in the Department of Health and Human Services' (HHS) *Fiscal Year 2008 Budget in Brief*. The description of each proposal includes HHS and CBO estimates of its cost or savings in FY2008 and over the FY2008-FY2012 period. These estimates are summarized in table 1.

As described below, proposals that have seen recent legislative or administrative action include:

- Medicaid: Require Tamper-Resistant Prescription Pads;
- Medicaid: Expand Asset Verification System;
- Medicaid: Transitional Medical Assistance;
- Medicaid: Extend Qualified Individual Program;
- Medicaid: Revise Payments for Government Providers;
- Medicaid: School-Based Services;
- Medicaid: Eliminate Medicaid Graduate Medical Education;
- Medicaid: Clarify Rehabilitation Services;
- Medicaid: Clarify Provider Tax Policy; and
- SCHIP: Reauthorization.

Legislative Versus Administrative Proposals

As shown in table 1, some of the President's proposals would require legislative action, while others would be implemented administratively (e.g., via regulatory changes, issuance of program guidance, etc.).

In their analyses of the President's budget, both CBO and executive branch agencies such as HHS and the Office of Management and Budget (OMB) provide baseline (current law) estimates of Medicaid and SCHIP spending along with estimated costs and savings of proposed changes. However, CBO and the executive branch differ in their treatment of legislative and administrative proposals.

In executive branch documents describing the President's budget, implementation of proposed administrative changes is assumed in estimates of baseline Medicaid and SCHIP spending,[2] and estimates for legislative proposals are presented separately. In general, CBO assesses the likelihood that a particular administrative action will take place before adjusting its baseline,[3] and only provides separate estimates for legislative proposals. For this reason and others, CBO and executive branch estimates of Medicaid and SCHIP spending will differ.

Table 1. Cost (Savings) of Medicaid and SCHIP Proposals in the President's FY2008 Budget

Proposal	Outlays in millions			
	HHS estimate		CBO estimate	
	FY2008	FY2008-FY2012	FY2008	FY2008-FY2012
Medicaid				
Legislative proposals	($1,942)	($13,016)	($2,273)	($19,600)
Streamline administrative match rates	(945)	(5,315)	(1,160)	(8,380)
Implement cost allocation	(280)	(1,770)	(280)	(1,770)
Require state reporting and link performance to reimbursement	0	(330)	0	(350)
Reimburse targeted case management at 50%	(200)	(1,160)	(225)	(1,370)

Table 1. Cost (Savings) of Medicaid and SCHIP Proposals in the President's FY2008 Budget

Proposal	Outlays in millions			
	HHS estimate		CBO estimate	
	FY2008	FY2008-FY2012	FY2008	FY2008-FY2012
Rationalize pharmacy reimbursement	(160)	(1,200)	(325)	(2,225)
Allow optional managed formulary	(160)	(870)	(10)	(175)
Require tamper-resistant prescription pads	(35)	(210)	(15)	(150)
Replace best price with budget-neutral rebate	0	0	0	0
Expand asset verification demonstration	(65)	(640)	(50)	(460)
Enhance third party liability	(10)	(85)	(40)	(235)
Define home equity limit at $500,000	(70)	(430)	(70)	(415)
Extend Section 1915(b) waiver period	0	0	—	—
Modify HIPAA	0	0	—	—
Extend TMA (Medicaid impact)	460	665	470	965
Extend Qualified Individual program (net Medicaid impact)	0	0	76	0
Other legislative proposals with an impact on Medicaid				
Refugee extension exemption	33	99	5	12
Funding for disability reviews	—	—	(48)	(1,502)
SCHIP reauthorization (Medicaid impact)	(510)	(1,770)	(601)	(3,545)
Administrative proposals	(1,515)	(12,715)	—	—
Revise payments for government providers	(530)	(5,000)	—	—
School-based services — eliminate administration and transportation	(615)	(3,645)	—	—
Eliminate graduate medical education	(140)	(1,780)	—	—
Clarify rehabilitation services	(230)	(2,290)	—	—
Issue guidance defining 1915(b)(3) services	0	0	—	—
Third party liability — eliminate pay and chase for pharmacy	0	0	—	—
Clarify provider tax policy	0	0	—	—
Codify disproportionate share hospital provisions in regulation	0	0	—	—
SCHIP				
Legislative proposals	1,220	5,930	933	5,457
SCHIP reauthorization (SCHIP impact)	1,220	5,930	939	5,463
Other legislative proposals with an impact on SCHIP				
Extend TMA (SCHIP impact)	—	—	(6)	(6)
Total Medicaid and SCHIP	(2,237)	(19,801)	(1,340)	(14,143)
Health Care Fraud and Abuse Control account (Medicaid and SCHIP financial management)	10.1	10.1	—	—

Source: Department of Health and Human Services, *Fiscal Year 2008 Budget in Brief*, available at [http://www.hhs.gov/budget/docbudget.htm], and Congressional Budget Office, *CBO Estimates of Medicaid and SCHIP Proposals in the President's Budget for Fiscal Year 2008*, available at [http://cbo.gov/budget/factsheets/2007b/medicaid_schip_pres.pdf].

Note: Numbers in parentheses represent savings. Estimates for proposals that do not show a dollar figure were not provided in the documents cited above. In executive branch documents describing the President's budget, implementation of proposed administrative changes is assumed in estimates of baseline Medicaid and SCHIP spending, and estimates for legislative proposals are presented separately. In general, CBO only adjusts its baseline estimates to account for administrative changes as they are implemented — rather than as they are proposed — and only provides separate estimates for legislative proposals.

Medicaid: Streamline Administrative Match Rates

Background

The federal government pays a share of every state's spending on Medicaid services and program administration. For Medicaid services, this share is called the federal medical assistance percentage (FMAP). The FMAP is based on a formula that provides higher reimbursement to states with lower per capita incomes (and vice versa); it has a statutory minimum of 50% and maximum of 83%. The federal match for administrative expenditures does not vary by state and is generally 50%, but certain administrative functions have a higher federal match. Functions with a 75% federal match include:

- compensation or training of skilled professional medical personnel (and their direct support staff) of the state Medicaid or other public agency;
- preadmission screening and resident review for individuals with mental illness or mental retardation who are admitted to a nursing facility;
- survey and certification of nursing facilities;
- operation of an approved Medicaid Management Information System (MMIS) for claims and information processing;
- performance of medical and utilization review activities or external independent review of managed care activities; and
- operation of a state Medicaid fraud control unit (MFCU).

In the case of MMISs and MFCUs, the federal match is 90% for startup expenses. There is a 100% match for the implementation and operation of immigration status verification systems. Section 1903(a)(7) of the Social Security Act specifies that a 50% match will be provided for remaining expenditures that are found necessary by the Secretary of HHS for the proper and efficient administration of the state Medicaid program.

Proposal

The President's budget seeks legislation to align all administrative reimbursement rates in Medicaid at 50%. HHS estimates that the proposal would save $945 million in FY2008, and $5.315 billion over the FY2008-FY2012 period. CBO estimates that the proposal would save $1.160 billion in FY2008, and $8.380 billion over the FY2008-FY2012 period.

Reports

See CRS Report RS22101, State Medicaid Program Administration: A Brief Overview, by April Grady.

Medicaid: Implement Cost Allocation

Background

Because of the overlap in eligible populations, states often undertake administrative activities that benefit more than one program. Under the former Aid to Families with Dependent Children (AFDC) cash welfare program, AFDC and Medicaid program eligibility were linked, and many AFDC families also qualified for food stamps. As a result, states often collected necessary information for all three programs during a single eligibility interview or performed other shared administrative tasks and charged the full amount of the cost to AFDC as a matter of convenience. Since the federal government reimbursed states for 50% of administrative expenditures for all three programs, total federal spending was not affected by the way in which states allocated the programs' common administrative costs.

When Congress replaced AFDC with the Temporary Assistance for Needy Families (TANF) block grant program in 1996, the 50% federal match for expenditures related to cash welfare assistance ended and the automatic link between cash welfare and Medicaid eligibility was severed. Later, HHS clarified that states are required to allocate common administrative costs for TANF, Medicaid, and food stamps based on the relative benefits derived by each program. A remaining issue of controversy stems from the fact that TANF block grants are calculated in part on the basis of pre-1996 federal welfare spending, including any amounts received by states as reimbursement for common administrative costs. As a result, TANF block grants are higher in many states than they would be if common administrative costs attributable to Medicaid and food stamps were excluded from block grant calculations. To compensate, Congress has permanently reduced federal reimbursement for food stamp administrative costs in most states by a flat dollar amount that reflects the administrative costs attributable to food stamps that are included in each state's TANF block grant (the annual reductions total nearly $200 million). Congress has not reduced federal reimbursement for Medicaid administrative costs in a similar manner.

Proposal

The President's budget seeks legislation to recoup Medicaid administrative costs assumed in states' TANF block grants. HHS and CBO both estimate that the proposal would save $280 million in FY2008, and $1.770 billion over the FY2008-FY2012 period.

Reports

See CRS Report RS22101, State Medicaid Program Administration: A Brief Overview, by April Grady.

Medicaid: Require State Reporting and Link Performance to Reimbursement

Background

The Budget Act of 1997 mandated performance monitoring as a tool for ensuring the delivery of quality services in Medicaid and SCHIP. Among several initiatives, the Centers for Medicare and Medicaid Services (CMS) formed the Performance Measurement Partnership Project (PMPP) to select a common set of measures that can be used by Medicaid and SCHIP programs on a voluntary basis to assess the quality of care.

Proposal

The President's budget proposal would seek legislation to require states to monitor and report on Medicaid performance measures aimed at improving quality of care, program integrity, and efficiency, and would link performance to federal Medicaid grant awards. Reporting would begin in FY2008 with a three-year phase-in for each of the measures.

Beginning in 2011, states that fail to meet targeted thresholds for each performance measure would be subject to an FMAP or Medicaid grant award reduction, depending on the performance measure. These reductions would remain in effect until the state meets the designated thresholds for specific performance measures. Budget documents further indicate that performance measures currently being considered include increasing estate recovery collection rates and reducing the prevalence of daily physical restraints in nursing homes. For this proposal, HHS estimates no cost impact in FY2008, and a savings of $330 million over the FY2008-FY2012 period. CBO estimates no cost impact in FY2008, and a savings of $350 million over the FY2008-FY2012 period.

Medicaid: Reimburse Targeted Case Management at 50 Percent Rate

Background

Under current law, case management is an optional benefit under the Medicaid state plan that assists Medicaid beneficiaries in gaining access to needed medical, social, educational and other services. The term "targeted case management" refers to situations in which these services are not provided statewide to all Medicaid beneficiaries but rather are provided only to specific classes of individuals (e.g., those with AIDS, tuberculosis, chronic physical or mental illness, developmental disabilities, or children in foster care) or to persons who reside in a specific area. The federal government matches payments for such services using the federal medical assistance percentage (FMAP), which is the rate applicable to Medicaid benefits. FMAPs can range from 50% to 83% (statutory upper boundary) depending on the state. In FY2008, 13 states will have an FMAP equal to 50%.

Case management can also be claimed as an administrative activity rather than as a Medicaid benefit. When claimed as an administrative service, the federal government matches case management at the 50% rate applicable to most administrative services.

Proposal

The President's budget seeks legislation that would set the federal reimbursement rate for all case management activities at 50% to ensure that such services are reimbursed in a cost effective and efficient manner. The Administration maintains that case management activities are inherently the same, regardless of how federal matching funds are claimed, and that the availability of different matching rates has resulted in states choosing to submit claims for case management that will yield the highest reimbursement rate. For example, states may claim case management services as a benefit rather than as an administrative activity when the FMAP for the state is higher than the standard 50% match rate for administrative activities. HHS estimates that the proposal would save $200 million in FY2008, and $1.160 billion over the FY2008-FY2012 period. CBO estimates that the proposal would save $225 million in FY2008 and $1.370 billion over the FY2008-FY2012 period.

Reports

For general information on Medicaid administrative costs, see CRS Report RS22101, *State Medicaid Program Administration: A Brief Overview*, by April Grady.

Medicaid: Rationalize Pharmacy Reimbursement

Background

Under current law, state Medicaid programs set the prices paid to pharmacies for Medicaid outpatient drugs. Federal reimbursements for those drugs, however, are limited to a federal upper limit (FUL). The FUL that applies to drugs available from multiple sources (generic drugs, for the most part) is calculated by CMS to be equal to 250% of the average manufacturer's price (AMP, the average price paid by wholesalers to manufacturers) as reported to CMS by the manufacturers.

Proposal

The President's budget seeks legislation that would build on changes made by the Deficit Reduction Act of 2005 (DRA) to achieve additional savings in the Medicaid program. The proposal would reduce the FULs on multiple source drugs from 250% of the AMP to 150% of the AMP of the lowest priced drug in the group. HHS estimates that the proposal would save $160 million in FY2008, and $1.200 billion over the FY2008-FY2012 period. CBO estimates that the proposal would save $325 million in FY2008 and $2.225 billion over the FY2008-FY2012 period.

Reports

For more information on the Medicaid provisions of DRA 2005, see CRS Report RL33131, *Budget Reconciliation FY2006: Medicaid, Medicare, and State Children's Health Insurance Program (SCHIP) Provisions*, by Evelyne P. Baumrucker, et al. and CRS Report RL33251, *Side-by-Side Comparison of Medicare, Medicaid, and SCHIP Provisions in the Deficit Reduction Act of 2005*, by Karen Tritz et al. Additional background information on Medicaid prescription drugs can be found in CRS Report RL30726, *Prescription Drug Coverage Under Medicaid*, by Jean Hearne.

Medicaid: Allow Optional Managed Formulary

Background

Federal statute allows state Medicaid programs to establish formularies, or lists of preferred pharmaceuticals to be made available to Medicaid beneficiaries. When health care insurers or providers cover only those drugs on the list and deny payment for others, the list is referred to as a "closed formulary." Medicaid formularies are seldom as restrictive as the closed formularies found in the private market for insurance because of two requirements: (1) states are required to provide any non-formulary drug (with the exception of drugs in specific categories, described below) that is specifically requested and approved through a prior authorization process, and (2) states are required to cover all drugs offered by manufacturers entering into rebate agreements with the Secretary of HHS.

States, on the other hand, are permitted to exclude certain categories of drug products from Medicaid coverage. These include drugs used: (a) to treat anorexia, weight loss or weight gain; (b) to promote fertility; (c) for cosmetic purposes or hair growth; (d) for the relief of coughs and colds; (e) for smoking cessation; and (f) prescription vitamins and mineral products (except prenatal vitamins and fluoride preparations); (g) non-prescription drugs; (h) barbiturates; (i) benzodiazepines; and (j) drugs requiring tests or monitoring that can only be provided by the drug manufacturer. Formularies may also exclude a drug for which there is no significant therapeutic advantage over other drugs that are included in the formularies as long as there is a written explanation of the reason for its exclusion and the explanation is available to the public. As of January 1, 2006, federal law also prohibits federal Medicaid funds from being used to pay for drugs for the treatment of sexual or erectile dysfunction.

Proposal

The President's budget seeks legislation to allow states to use private sector management techniques to leverage greater discounts through negotiations with drug manufacturers. The "managed formulary" is described as a list of prescription drug products that are not covered under the program. HHS estimates that the proposal would save $160 million in FY2008, and $870 million over the FY2008-FY2012 period. CBO estimates that the proposal would save $10 million in FY2008 and $175 million over the FY2008-FY2012 period.

Reports

For a general background on Medicaid prescription drug benefits, formularies, and other cost control mechanisms used in administering those benefits, see CRS Report RL30726, *Prescription Drug Coverage Under Medicaid*, by Jean Hearne.

Medicaid: Require Tamper-Resistant Prescription Pads

Background

There are currently no federal Medicaid laws or rules regarding the use of prescription pads. Thirteen states, however, utilize tamper-resistant pads.

Proposal

The President's budget proposed to require all states where providers use hand-written prescription pads to use "tamper-resistant" pads. HHS estimates that the proposal would save $35 million in FY2008, and $210 million over the FY2008-FY2012 period. CBO estimates that the proposal would save $15 million in FY2008, and $150 million over the FY2008-FY2012 period.

Recent Action

A war supplemental appropriations bill that was vetoed on May 1, 2007 (H.R. 1591), included a provision that would have required the use of tamper-resistant pads for Medicaid prescriptions. A subsequent war supplemental enacted on May 25 (H.R. 2206, P.L. 110-28) includes the same provision, which will apply to prescriptions executed after September 30, 2007. Legislation to delay implementation of the new requirement for six months (H.R. 3668, P.L. 110-90) was enacted at the end of September.

Reports

For a general background on Medicaid prescription drug benefits, formularies, and other cost control mechanisms used in administering those benefits, see CRS Report RL30726, *Prescription Drug Coverage Under Medicaid*, by Jean Hearne.

Medicaid: Replace Best Price with Budget Neutral Rebate

Background

Under Medicaid, drug manufacturers that wish to have their drugs available for Medicaid enrollees are required to enter into rebate agreements with the Secretary of HHS, on behalf of the states. Under the agreements, pharmaceutical manufacturers must provide state Medicaid programs with rebates on drugs paid on behalf of Medicaid beneficiaries. The formulas used to compute the rebates are intended to ensure that Medicaid pays the lowest price that the manufacturers offer for the drugs. Rebate calculations depend on the type of drug. For single source and innovator multiple source drugs, basic rebate amounts are determined by comparing the average manufacturer price (AMP) for a drug (the average price paid by wholesalers) to the "best price," which is the lowest price offered by the manufacturer in the same period to any wholesaler, retailer, nonprofit, or public entity. The basic rebate is the greater of 15.1% of the AMP or the difference between the AMP and the best price. Additional rebates are required if the weighted average prices for all of a given manufacturer's single source and innovator multiple source drugs rise faster than inflation. For non-innovator multiple source drugs, basic rebates are equal to 11% of the AMP.

Proposal

The President's budget seeks legislation to eliminate the "best price" from the rebate formula for single source and innovator multiple source drugs, changing the best price-based formula to a flat rebate. This change is intended to be made in a budget neutral manner. HHS explanatory materials describe the proposal as a way to simplify drug rebate calculations and as a way to allow private purchasers to negotiate lower prices without affecting Medicaid drug costs. HHS and CBO both estimate that the proposal would have no cost impact in FY2008 or over the FY2008-FY2012 period.

Reports

For a general background on Medicaid prescription drug coverage and pricing including a description of drug rebates, see CRS Report RL30726, *Prescription Drug Coverage Under Medicaid*, by Jean Hearne.

Medicaid: Expand Asset Verification System

Background

The Social Security Administration is piloting a financial account verification system (in field offices located in New York and New Jersey) that uses an electronic asset verification system to help confirm that individuals who apply for Supplemental Security Income (SSI) benefits are eligible. The process permits automated paperless transmission of asset verification requests between SSA field offices and financial institutions. Part of this pilot involved a comprehensive study to measure the value of such a system for SSI applicants as well as recipients already on the payment rolls. This study identified a small percentage (about 5 percent) of applicants and recipients who were overpaid based on this financial account verification system.

Proposal

The President's budget seeks legislation to expand the SSA pilot to CMS programs whose eligibility criteria include limitations on financial resources. CMS would work with states to establish Medicaid pilots in the same locations as SSA. HHS estimates that the proposal would save $65 million in FY2008, and $640 million over the FY2008-FY2012 period. CBO estimates that the proposal would save $50 million in FY2008 and $460 million over the FY2008-FY2012 period.

Recent Action

H.R. 3162, the SCHIP reauthorization bill passed by the House on August 1, would implement a similar proposal. Legislation (H.R. 3668, P.L. 110-90) to apply the SSA pilot to Medicaid beginning on October 1, 2007, and ending on September 30, 2012, was enacted at the end of September. A bicameral agreement on SCHIP reauthorization, which passed the House and Senate as an amendment to H.R. 976 but was vetoed on October 3, would apply the pilot beginning on October 1, 2012.

Reports

For information on the provisions in SCHIP reauthorization legislation, see CRS Report RL34129, *Medicaid and SCHIP Provisions in H.R. 3162 and S. 1893/H.R. 976*, by Evelyne Baumrucker et al.

Medicaid: Enhance Third Party Liability

Background

Third party liability (TPL) refers to the legal obligation of third parties — individuals, entities, or programs — to pay all or part of the expenditures for medical assistance furnished under Medicaid. In general, federal law requires Medicaid to be the payer of last resort, meaning that all other available third parties must meet their legal obligation to pay claims before the Medicaid program pays for the care of an individual.

States are required to take all reasonable measures to ascertain the legal liability of third parties to pay for care and services available under the state Medicaid plan. If a state has determined that probable liability exists at the time a claim for reimbursement is filed, it generally must reject the claim and return it to the provider for a determination of the amount of third-party liability (referred to as "cost avoidance"). If probable liability has not been established or the third party is not available to pay the individual's medical expenses, the state must pay the claim and then attempt to recover the amount paid (referred to as "pay and chase").

States are generally required to cost avoid claims unless they have an approved waiver that allows them to use the pay-and-chase method. However, there are two statutory exceptions to this rule. In the case of prenatal and preventive pediatric care, states are required to use pay and chase. In the case of a Medicaid beneficiary whose parent provides medical support (e.g., health insurance coverage via an employer) as part of a child support order being enforced by the state, the state must use pay and chase if a provider has not been paid under the medical support arrangement within 30 days.

In some cases, a Medicaid beneficiary may be required to reimburse the state for Medicaid expenses paid on his or her behalf. To facilitate such reimbursement, the state may place a lien on the Medicaid beneficiary's property. With certain exceptions, federal law generally prohibits states from imposing Medicaid liens on the property of living beneficiaries. In contrast, federal law permits Medicaid liens on the estates of deceased beneficiaries in a wider variety of situations.

Proposal

The President's budget seeks legislation to allow states to avoid costs for prenatal and preventive pediatric claims where a third party is responsible; collect for medical child support where a health insurance is derived from a non-custodial parent's obligation to provide coverage; and recover Medicaid expenditures from beneficiary liability settlements. HHS estimates that the proposal would save $10 million in FY2008 and $85 million over the FY2008-FY2012 period. CBO estimates that the proposal would save $40 million in FY2008 and $235 million over the FY2008-FY2012 period.

Medicaid: Define Home Equity Limit at $500,000

Background

The Deficit Reduction Act of 2005 amended the Social Security Act to exclude from Medicaid eligibility for nursing facility or other long-term care services, certain individuals with an equity interest in their home of greater than $500,000. Under the law, the state may elect without regard to Medicaid's requirements concerning statewideness and comparability, to substitute an amount that exceeds $500,000 but does not exceed $750,000. These dollar amounts are increased, beginning in 2011, from year to year based on the percentage increase in the consumer price index for all urban consumers (all items, United States city average), rounded to the nearest $1,000. The Secretary establishes a process for waiving this provision in the case of a demonstrated hardship. Individuals whose spouse, child under age 21, or child who is blind or disabled (as defined by the Section 1614 of the Social Security Act) lawfully resides in the individual's home would not be excluded from eligibility.

Proposal

The President's budget seeks legislation that would limit the allowable home equity amount to $500,000 for all states by eliminating the state option to increase the equity limit to a number between $500,000 and $750,000. HHS estimates that the proposal would save $70 million in FY2008, and $430 million over the FY2008-FY2012 period. CBO estimates that the proposal would save $70 million in FY2008, and $415 million over the FY2008-FY2012 period.

Reports

For more information about home equity and Medicaid eligibility, see CRS Report RL33593, *Medicaid Coverage for Long-Term Care: Eligibility, Asset Transfers, and Estate Recovery*, by Julie Stone.

Medicaid: Extend Section 1915(b) Waiver Period

Background

Section 1915(b) of the Social Security Act gives the Secretary of HHS the authority to waive certain Medicaid program requirements (including statewideness, comparability of services, and freedom of choice of provider)[4] to allow states to establish mandatory managed care programs that restrict the providers from whom a beneficiary may obtain covered services, or that create a "carve out" delivery system for specialty care as long as such programs do not negatively impact beneficiary access and quality of care of services. Prior to passage of the Balanced Budget Act of 1997 (BBA 97), a state had to obtain a Section 1115 or a Section 1915(b) ("freedom-of-choice") waiver from the Secretary of HHS if it wanted to require Medicaid recipients to enroll in a managed care program.[5]

Section 1915(b) waiver programs are generally approved for a two-year period and must be cost effective (cannot cost more than what the Medicaid program would have cost without the waiver). They may not be used to expand eligibility to individuals not otherwise eligible under the approved Medicaid state plan, but cost savings achieved under the waivers may used to provide additional services (i.e., those not typically provided under the state plan) to Medicaid beneficiaries.

Proposal

The President's budget seeks legislation to extend the renewal period for 1915(b) "freedom of choice" waivers from two years to three years. HHS estimates that the proposal would have no cost impact in FY2008 or over the FY2008-FY2012 period. CBO did not provide an estimate for the proposal.

Reports

For more information on Medicaid managed care, see CRS Report RL33711, *Medicaid Managed Care: An Overview and Key Issues for Congress* by Elicia J. Herz.

Medicaid: Modify the Health Insurance Portability and Accountability Act (HIPAA)

Background

The Health Insurance Portability and Accountability Act of 1996 (HIPAA, P.L. 104-191) established a number of rules for employer-based health insurance plans to improve access to and portability of plans for people enrolled or enrolling into those plans. One of those provisions requires employer-based health plans to allow for new enrollment into the plan during periods outside of the typical annual open enrollment period for certain special reasons. Examples of those reasons include when an eligible employee (or their dependent) exhausts COBRA continuation coverage, or when an employee gains a new dependent through birth or adoption. Another HIPAA provision limits the ability of private health insurance plans to exclude coverage for pre-existing conditions during what are known as "preexisting condition exclusion periods." The allowable length of such pre-existing condition exclusion periods depends on the amount of time the new enrollee had been covered by prior "creditable" health insurance coverage.[6] A beneficiary can prove they have had prior creditable coverage by providing certificates issued by insurers at the end of each year. Because HIPAA was created in law before SCHIP was established, SCHIP was not included on the list of types of health insurance that can be considered as prior creditable coverage.

Proposal

The President's budget seeks several legislative changes relating to HIPAA. The first would define a determination of Medicaid or SCHIP eligibility as a qualifying event allowing for a special enrollment period into employer-based health insurance plans. This provision is intended to improve Medicaid and SCHIP programs' ability to coordinate coverage with private employer-offered coverage. The second proposal would require SCHIP programs to issue certificates of creditable coverage. This provision is intended to improve the reach of HIPAA's portability provisions by recognizing SCHIP coverage as prior creditable coverage. Both of these interpretations have previously been promulgated in a final regulation implementing HIPAA's portability for group health plan provisions.[7] HHS estimates that the proposal would have no cost impact in FY2008 or over the FY2008-FY2012 period. CBO did not provide an estimate for the proposal.

Reports

For general information on HIPAA, see CRS Report RL31634, *The Health Insurance Portability and Accountability Act (HIPAA) of 1996: Overview and Guidance on Frequently Asked Questions*, by Hinda Chaikind, Jean Hearne, Bob Lyke, and C. Stephen Redhead.

Medicaid: Transitional Medical Assistance

Background

States are required to continue Medicaid benefits for certain low-income families who would otherwise lose coverage because of changes in their income. This continuation of benefits is known as transitional medical assistance (TMA). Federal law permanently requires four months of TMA for families who lose Medicaid eligibility due to increased child or spousal support collections. It also permanently requires four months of TMA for families who lose Medicaid eligibility due to an increase in earned income or hours of employment.

However, Congress expanded work-related TMA benefits in 1988, requiring states to provide at least six, and up to 12, months of TMA coverage to families losing Medicaid eligibility due to increased hours of work or income from employment, as well as to families who lose eligibility due to the loss of a time-limited earned income disregard (such disregards allow families to qualify for Medicaid at higher income levels for a set period of time). Congress has acted on numerous occasions to extend these expanded TMA requirements (which are outlined in Section 1925 of the Social Security Act) beyond their original sunset date of September 30, 1998. They are currently set to expire on June 30, 2007.

Proposal

The President's budget seeks legislation to extend expanded TMA requirements through September 30, 2008. HHS estimates that the President's proposal would cost Medicaid $35 million in FY2007, $460 million in FY2008, and $665 million over the FY2008-FY2012 period (the budgetary effects extend beyond FY2008 because families are still entitled to up to 12 months of TMA if they qualify on or before the expiration date). CBO estimates that the proposal would have no cost impact on Medicaid in FY2007 and that it would cost Medicaid $470 million in FY2008 and $965 million over the FY2008-FY2012 period; it also estimates that the proposal would have no cost impact on SCHIP in FY2007, and that it would cost SCHIP $6 million in FY2008 and $6 million over the FY2008-FY2012 period.

Recent Action

Legislation to temporarily extend TMA through September 30, 2007 (S. 1701, P.L. 110-48), was enacted on July 18. An extension through December 31, 2007 (H.R. 3668, P.L. 110-90), was enacted at the end of September. H.R. 3162, the SCHIP reauthorization bill passed by the House on August 1, would modify and extend TMA through September 30, 2011. The FY2008 budget resolution also includes a deficit-neutral reserve fund for extending TMA.

Reports

See CRS Report RL31698, *Transitional Medical Assistance (TMA) Under Medicaid*, by April Grady. For information on the provision in SCHIP reauthorization legislation, see CRS Report RL34129, *Medicaid and SCHIP Provisions in H.R. 3162 and S. 1893/H.R. 976*, by Evelyne Baumrucker et al.

Medicaid: Extend Qualified Individual Program

Background

Congress requires state Medicaid programs to cover the Medicare Part B premiums for a certain group of low-income Medicare beneficiaries. The Qualifying Individual (QI-1) program includes individuals who would otherwise be Qualified Medicare Beneficiaries (QMBs) but whose income is between 120% and 135% of the federal poverty level. The Balanced Budget Act of 1997 established this group of eligibles for a temporary period between January 1998 and December 2002. Congress has extended eligibility for this group several times since its expiration. The most recent extension was authorized under the QI, TMA, and Abstinence Programs Extension and Hurricane Katrina Unemployment Relief Act of 2005 (P.L. 109-91), which extended the QI-1 program from September 2005 through September 2007. Without changes to current law, eligibility for this group would expire in September 2007.

Proposal

The President's budget seeks legislation to extend premium assistance for QI-1s through September 30, 2008. HHS estimates that the net cost to Medicaid would be zero in FY2008 and over the FY2008-FY2012 period (amounts paid by Medicaid for the Medicare Part B premium costs of QI-1s are offset by a reimbursement from Medicare Part B). CBO estimates that the proposal would cost Medicaid $76 million in FY2008, and that the net cost to Medicaid would be zero over the FY2008-FY2012 period.

Recent Action

An extension of the QI-1 program through December 31, 2007 (H.R. 3668, P.L. 110-90), was enacted at the end of September.

Reports

For more information about the QI-1 program, see CRS Report RL32977, *Dual Eligibles: A Review of Medicaid's Role in Providing Services and Assistance*, by Karen Tritz.

Medicaid: Refugee Exemption Extension

Background

Under current law, most legal immigrants who entered the country on or after August 22, 1996, and some who entered prior to that date, are not eligible for Supplemental Security Income (SSI) benefits — and thus, SSI-related Medicaid — until they have resided in the country for five years or have obtained citizenship. Refugees and asylees are currently exempted from this ban for the first seven years they reside in the United States.

Proposal

The President's budget seeks legislation to extend the exemption for refugees and asylees from seven years to eight years, allowing additional time for individuals to complete the citizenship process without penalty. HHS estimates that the proposal would cost $33 million in FY2008, and $99 million over the FY2008-FY2012 period. CBO estimates that the proposal would cost $5 million in FY2008, and $12 million over the FY2008-FY2012 period.

Reports

For general background information, see CRS Report RL31269, *Refugee Admissions and Resettlement Policy*, by Andorra Bruno; CRS Report RL31630, *Federal Funding for Unauthorized Aliens' Emergency Medical Expenses*, by Alison M. Siskin; and CRS Report RL33809, *Noncitizen Eligibility for Federal Public Assistance: Policy Overview and Trends*, Ruth Ellen Wasem.

Medicaid: Revise Payments for Government Providers

Background

Aggregate Medicaid payments to specific groups of institutional providers (e.g., hospitals and nursing facilities) cannot exceed a reasonable estimate of what would have been paid under Medicare payment principles. This is called the Medicaid upper payment limit (UPL) rule. In many states, Medicare payment rates for hospital and nursing home care are higher than corresponding Medicaid payment rates. The UPL based on Medicare payment principles has enabled some states to draw down additional federal dollars that exceed what they would have received based on Medicaid payment rates. These additional funds are paid to government providers which are sometimes required by states to transfer all or a portion of the extra payments received (i.e., some or all of the difference between the Medicare and Medicaid payment rates) back to the state through an intergovernmental transfer (IGT). Instead of financing more or improved Medicaid services, in some cases states have used the additional federal dollars for non-health services, or to make up part of the state share of Medicaid costs to draw down another round of federal dollars.

During 2000-2002, Congress and the Clinton and Bush Administrations revised UPL rules by changing permissible accounting methods used to claim federal matching payments. These changes significantly reduced the excess federal dollars states received under approved UPL plans that involved IGTs. However, these reforms did not eliminate all such excess payments because no changes were made to the Medicaid UPL standard which remains tied to the Medicare payment rate, nor to federal statute or regulations governing IGTs. Administration officials have taken additional steps to curb what they have identified as improper state financing mechanisms, especially certain intergovernmental transfers. In late 2003, CMS began requesting detailed information regarding the sources of the state share of Medicaid costs from states applying for Medicaid waivers and submitting Medicaid state plan amendments. In some cases, these proposals were modified to minimize the use of improper IGTs (i.e., IGTs that use "recycling mechanisms" under which payments to providers are returned to the state, artificially inflating the federal matching rate).

Proposal

The President's budget would, through administrative action: (1) clarify that only units of government are able to contribute to the financing of the non-federal share of Medicaid costs, (2) establish minimum requirements for documenting cost when using a certified public expenditure as part of the non-federal share, (3) cap payments to government providers to no more than the cost of providing services to Medicaid beneficiaries, rather than to Medicare payment principles, (4) establish a new regulatory provision requiring that providers receive and retain the total computable amount of their Medicaid payments, and (5) make corresponding and conforming changes to SCHIP. On January 18, 2007, the Administration published a proposed rule detailing these actions.

HHS estimates that the President's proposal would save \$530 million in FY2008, and \$5.000 billion over the FY2008-FY2012 period. CBO did not provide an estimate for the proposal (see earlier discussion under "Legislative Versus Administrative Proposals").

Recent Action

On May 29, 2007, CMS published a final rule on payments for government providers that addresses IGTs and other issues (a related proposed rule on outpatient hospital services was published on September 28). A war supplemental appropriations bill that was vetoed on May 1, 2007 (H.R. 1591), included a provision that would have delayed implementation for one year. A subsequent war supplemental enacted on May 25 (H.R. 2206, P.L. 110-28) includes the same provision. The FY2008 budget resolution also includes a deficit-neutral reserve fund for delayed implementation.

Reports

See CRS Report RL31021, Medicaid Upper Payment Limits and Intergovernmental Transfers: Current Issues and Recent Regulatory and Legislative Action, by Elicia J. Herz, and CRS Congressional Distribution Memorandum, Proposed Medicaid Regulation to Establish a Cost Limit for Providers Operated by Units of Government and Provisions to Ensure the Integrity of Federal-State Financial Partnership, by Jean Hearne (available upon request).

Medicaid: School-Based Services — Eliminate Administration and Transportation

Background

Medicaid pays for covered medical services provided to Medicaid-eligible children with Individualized Family Service Plans (IFSP) and Individualized Education Plans (IEP), pursuant to the Individuals with Disabilities Education Act (IDEA). In the President's FY2007 budget proposal, the Administration noted that Medicaid claims for services in the school setting were prone to abuse and overpayment, especially with respect to administrative and transportation services. Over the past few years, several GAO and HHS OIG studies have reached similar conclusions.[8]

For transportation services, examples of inappropriate Medicaid billing include (1) no verification that transportation was in fact provided, (2) a Medicaid-covered school health service other than transportation was not provided on the day that transportation was billed, and (3) child/family plans did not include a recommendation for transportation services, or there was no IEP or IFSP.

School districts may perform administrative functions for Medicaid purposes, including for example, outreach, eligibility intake, information and referrals, health service coordination and monitoring, and interagency coordination. Examples of inappropriate Medicaid billing include (1) payments based on inaccurate time studies used to allocate the cost of these administrative activities across funding sources including Medicaid, (2) expenditures for school employees who do not perform Medicaid administrative activities, (3) expenditures for operating costs such as nursing supplies, non-Medicaid outreach supplies, and education-related expenditures, (4) expenditures for personnel funded by other federal programs, and (5) payments for personnel who render only direct medical services.

Proposal

The President's FY2008 budget would, through administrative action, phase out Medicaid reimbursement for certain school-based IDEA-related transportation and school administrative claiming. The Administration says that appropriate medical services and transportation to and from these services under IDEA would continue to be reimbursed as under current law.

HHS estimates that the President's proposal would save $615 million in FY2008 ($167 million attributable to transportation cost savings and $448 million attributable to state and local administration savings), and $3.645 billion over the FY2008-FY2012 period. CBO did not provide an estimate for the proposal (see earlier discussion under "Legislative Versus Administrative Proposals").

Recent Action

On September 7, 2007, CMS published a proposed rule regarding Medicaid payments for school-based administration and transportation. H.R. 3162, the SCHIP reauthorization bill passed by the House on August 1, 2007, would prohibit the Secretary of HHS from taking any action to restrict Medicaid coverage or payments for school-based administration, transportation, or medical services for one year. A bicameral agreement on SCHIP reauthorization, which passed the House and Senate as an amendment to H.R. 976 but was vetoed on October 3, would prohibit the Secretary from taking any action on this issue prior to May 28, 2008. The FY2008 budget resolution also includes a deficit-neutral reserve fund for delayed implementation.

Reports

See CRS Report RS22397, The Link Between Medicaid and the Individuals with Disabilities Education Act (IDEA): Recent History and Current Issues, by Elicia J. Herz and CRS Report RL31722, Individuals with Disabilities Education Act (IDEA) and Medicaid, by Richard N. Apling and Elicia J. Herz. For information on the provisions in SCHIP reauthorization legislation, see CRS Report RL34129, Medicaid and SCHIP Provisions in H.R. 3162 and S. 1893/H.R. 976, by Evelyne Baumrucker et al.

Medicaid: Eliminate Medicaid Graduate Medical Education

Background

Medicare reimburses teaching hospitals for graduate medical education (GME) training through an indirect medical education (IME) adjustment within its hospital prospective payment system (PPS) and with direct graduate medical education (DGME) payments made outside of PPS. IME payments are designed to cover the higher patient costs associated with the training function (such as additional laboratory tests ordered by residents). DGME payments cover the costs of salaries and fringe benefits paid to medical residents, interns and teaching faculty. While Medicare has a statutory requirement to support GME, Medicaid does not. Nonetheless, most states make GME payments, primarily designed to cover DGME costs, through the Medicaid fee-for-service delivery system. Many states also make IME payments to teaching hospitals as well. On average, GME payments comprise about 8 to 9 percent of total Medicaid inpatient hospital expenditures.

Proposal

The Administration maintains that paying for GME is outside Medicaid's primary purpose, which is to provide medical care to low-income populations, and that current law does not explicitly authorize such payments. Through administrative action, the Administration proposes to eliminate funding for GME under Medicaid.

HHS estimates that the President's proposal would save $140 million in FY2008, and $1.780 billion over the FY2008-FY2012 period. CBO did not provide an estimate for the proposal (see earlier discussion under "Legislative Versus Administrative Proposals").

Recent Action

On May 23, 2007, CMS published a proposed rule to clarify that GME is not federally reimbursable under Medicaid. A war supplemental appropriations bill that was vetoed on

May 1, 2007 (H.R. 1591), included a provision that would have delayed implementation of this proposal for one year. A subsequent war supplemental enacted on May 25 (H.R. 2206, P.L. 110-28) includes the same provision. The FY2008 budget resolution also includes a deficit-neutral reserve fund for delayed implementation.

Medicaid: Clarify Rehabilitation Services

Background

Since the inception of Medicaid in 1965, states have been authorized to cover "other diagnostic, screening, preventive, or *rehabilitative* services" as an optional Medicaid service. In subsequent legislation (OBRA 90, P.L. 101-508), Congress clarified the benefit as "including any medical or remedial service (provided in a facility, a home, or other setting) recommended by a physician or other licensed practitioner of the healing arts within the scope of their practice under state law, for the maximum reduction of physical or mental disability and restoration of an individual to the best possible functional level." The rehabilitation benefit allows states to cover a broad range of services to individuals with various types of conditions and disabilities. Under the rehabilitation benefit, states often cover ongoing mental health and/or substance abuse services, early intervention services for children with disabilities, rehabilitation for individuals with physical disabilities, school-based rehabilitation, and services for children in foster care and juvenile justice programs.

Both the Government Accountability Office (GAO) and the HHS Office of the Inspector General (OIG) have reported that the Medicaid rehabilitation benefit has been used by some states to bill Medicaid for activities that are not allowable as rehabilitation services, and/or to pay rehabilitation providers using methods that did not meet the statutory requirement for being "efficient and economical."[9,10] Further, CMS financial management officials reported to GAO that they believed that states "were inappropriately filing claims for services that were the responsibility of other state programs."[11]

Proposal

The President's budget seeks to clarify, through regulation, which services may be claimed as Medicaid rehabilitation services. HHS estimates the President's proposal would save $230 million in FY2008, and $2.290 billion over the FY2008-FY2012 period. CBO did not provide an estimate for the proposal (see earlier discussion under "Legislative Versus Administrative Proposals").

Recent Action

On August 13, 2007, CMS published a proposed rule on rehabilitation services under Medicaid. H.R. 3162, the SCHIP reauthorization bill passed by the House on August 1, would prohibit the Secretary of HHS from taking any action to restrict Medicaid coverage or payments for rehabilitation services for one year. A bicameral agreement on SCHIP reauthorization, which passed the House and Senate as an amendment to H.R. 976 but was vetoed on October 3, would prohibit the Secretary from taking any action on this issue prior to May 28, 2008. The FY2008 budget resolution includes a deficit-neutral reserve fund for delayed implementation.

Reports

For information on the provisions in SCHIP reauthorization legislation, see CRS Report RL34129, *Medicaid and SCHIP Provisions in H.R. 3162 and S. 1893/H.R. 976*, by Evelyne Baumrucker et al.

Medicaid: Issue Guidance Defining 1915(b)(3) Services

Background

See the "Extend Section 1915(b) Waiver Period" proposal described earlier.

Proposal

The President's budget would, through administrative action, clarify which additional services may be provided under Section 1915(b)(3) out of cost savings achieved under Section 1915(b) waiver programs. HHS estimates that the proposal would have no cost impact in FY2008 or over the FY2008-FY2012 period. CBO did not provide an estimate for the proposal (see earlier discussion under "Legislative Versus Administrative Proposals").

Reports

For more information on Medicaid managed care, see CRS Report RL33711, *Medicaid Managed Care: An Overview and Key Issues for Congress* by Elicia J. Herz.

Medicaid: Third Party Liability — Eliminate Pay and Chase for Pharmacy

Background

As described earlier (under the "enhance third party liability" proposal), if a state has determined that probable third party liability exists at the time a claim for reimbursement is filed, it generally must reject the claim and return it to the provider for a determination of the amount of third party liability (referred to as "cost avoidance"). If probable liability has not been established or the third party is not available to pay the individual's medical expenses, the state must pay the claim and then attempt to recover the amount paid (referred to as "pay and chase"). States are generally required to cost avoid claims unless they have an approved waiver that allows them to use the pay and chase method.

Proposal

The President's budget would, through administrative action, require states to use cost avoidance and eliminate the pay and chase waiver option for pharmacy claims. HHS estimates that the proposal would have no cost impact in FY2008 or over the FY2008-FY2012 period. CBO did not provide an estimate for the proposal (see earlier discussion under "Legislative Versus Administrative Proposals").

Medicaid: Clarify Provider Tax Policy

Background

Under federal law and regulations, a state's ability to use provider-specific taxes to fund its state share of Medicaid expenditures is limited. If states establish provider-specific taxes, the taxes must be broad based in that they apply to all providers within a class, they cannot exceed 25% of the state (or non-federal) share of Medicaid expenditures and the state cannot provide a guarantee to the providers that the taxes will be returned to them. However, if the taxes returned to a provider are less than 6% of the provider's revenues (a ceiling created in regulation by HHS), the prohibition on guaranteeing the return of tax funds is not violated. As a result, a state could impose a provider tax of 6% of revenues, return those revenues to the provider in the form of a Medicaid "payment," and receive a federal match for those amounts. In effect, the state has temporarily borrowed funds from the provider for the purpose of inflating federal matching funds. In 2006, Congress included a provision in the Tax Relief and Health Care Act of 2006 (TRHCA, P.L. 109-432) preventing the Secretary of HHS from taking action to reduce this percentage. The law fixed the provider tax ceiling in statute at 6%, except for the period January 1, 2008-September 31, 2011, during which the rate is fixed at 5.5%.

Proposal

The President's budget seeks to revise existing rules to more explicitly state the policies and procedures CMS uses when evaluating states' provider taxes. HHS estimates that the proposal would have no cost impact in FY2008 or over the FY2008-FY2012 period. CBO did not provide an estimate for the proposal (see earlier discussion under "Legislative Versus Administrative Proposals").

Recent Action

On March 23, 2007, CMS published a proposed rule on health-care-related taxes to reflect the TRHCA change and clarify existing provisions.

Reports

For background information on provider taxes, see CRS Report 97-483, *Medicaid Disproportionate Share Payments*, by Jean Hearne.

Medicaid: Clarify DSH Provisions in Regulation

Background

States and the District of Columbia are required to recognize, in establishing hospital payment rates, the situation of hospitals that serve a disproportionate number of Medicaid beneficiaries and other low-income patients with special needs. Under broad federal guidelines, each state determines which hospitals receive disproportionate share hospital (DSH) payments and the payment amounts to be made to each qualifying hospital. The federal government shares in the cost of state DSH payments at the same federal matching percentage as for most other Medicaid services. Total federal reimbursement for each state's DSH payments are capped at a statewide ceiling, referred to as the state's DSH allotment, and DSH payments to each hospital are capped at a hospital-specific ceiling.

Proposal

The President's budget seeks to clarify, through regulation, provisions related to the allowable uses of DSH funds. HHS estimates that the proposal would have no cost impact in FY2008 or over the FY2008-FY2012 period.

CBO did not provide an estimate for the proposal (see earlier discussion under "Legislative Versus Administrative Proposals").

Reports

For background information on Medicaid DSH payments, see CRS Report 97-483, *Medicaid Disproportionate Share Payments*, by Jean Hearne.

SCHIP: Reauthorization

Background

The Balanced Budget Act of 1997 established SCHIP. In general, this program allows states to cover targeted low-income children with no health insurance in families with income that is above Medicaid eligibility levels. States may choose among three benefit options when designing their SCHIP programs. They may enroll targeted low-income children in Medicaid, create a separate state program, or devise a combination of both approaches. All states, the District of Columbia, and five territories have SCHIP programs. Nearly $40 billion has been appropriated for SCHIP for FY1998-FY2007. The authorized appropriation for FY2007 is $5.04 billion. Annual allotments among the states are determined by a formula that is based on a combination of the number of low-income children, and low-income uninsured children in the state, and includes a cost factor that represents the average health service industry wages in the state compared to the national average.

States that set up an SCHIP program are entitled to federal reimbursement, up to a cap, for a percentage of the incurred costs of covering enrolled individuals. This percentage, which varies by state, is called the enhanced federal medical assistance percentage (FMAP). It is based on the FMAP used for the Medicaid program but is higher in SCHIP than in Medicaid. In other words, the federal government contributes more toward the coverage of individuals in SCHIP (65% to 83% in FY2008) than it does for those covered under Medicaid (50% to 76% in FY2008).[12]

States have three years to spend each annual allotment (e.g., states have until the end of FY2007 to spend their FY2005 allotments). At the end of the applicable three-year period, unspent funds are reallocated among states based on year-specific rules. In the early years of the SCHIP, both states that did and did not fully exhaust their original allotments received unspent funds. For more recent years, only those states that fully exhaust their original allotments receive unspent funds. Some states have experienced shortfalls in SCHIP funds, meaning at the end of a given fiscal year, they have spent all federal SCHIP funds available to them at that point in time, including original allotments and reallocations of unspent funds from other states.

Although no SCHIP appropriations are currently slated for FY2008 forward, both OMB and CBO assume that the program continues at the FY2007 appropriation level of $5.04 billion.

Proposal

Federal SCHIP funds would pay the enhanced FMAP only for enrolled children or pregnant adults with family income at or below 200% of poverty. States would receive the regular FMAP for all other enrollees (that is, non-pregnant adults and children with family income above 200% of poverty). The President's budget also proposes prohibiting any further expansion of coverage to parents or, in states already covering them, childless adults. SCHIP eligibility could not be expanded to new groups of non-pregnant adults.[13]

For FY2008, the President's budget calls for no more additional SCHIP appropriations above the $5.04 billion assumed in the baseline. However, the President's budget would reduce the period of availability of original allotments from three years to a single year. This means that as of the end of FY2007, any remaining balances of states' FY2006 and FY2007 federal SCHIP funds would be available for redistribution (in addition to the redistribution of unspent FY2005 funds slated under current law). CRS currently projects that reducing the period of availability of these original allotments would make nearly $4 billion of federal SCHIP funds available for potential redistribution in FY2008. Depending on how the funds are targeted, this could be enough to cover the FY2008 projected shortfalls (less any applicable reduction in shortfalls from the reduction in the FMAP discussed above).

Although no additional SCHIP appropriations are called for in FY2008 (because of the availability of redistribution funds, as described above), $4.813 billion in additional allotment funds would be appropriated over the FY2009-FY2012 period.

HHS estimates that the proposal would have no impact on SCHIP outlays in FY2007 and that it would increase SCHIP outlays by $1.220 billion in FY2008 and by $5.930 billion over the FY2008-FY2012 period; it also estimates that the proposal would have no impact on Medicaid outlays in FY2007 and that it would reduce Medicaid outlays by $510 million in FY2008 and by $1.770 billion over the FY2008-FY2012 period. CBO estimates that the proposal would increase SCHIP outlays by $735 million in FY2007, by $939 million in FY2008, and by $5.463 billion over the FY2008-FY2012 period; it also estimates that the proposal would reduce Medicaid outlays by $287 million in FY2007, by $601 million in FY2008, and by $3.545 billion over the FY2008-FY2012 period.

Recent Action

A war supplemental appropriations bill that was vetoed on May 1, 2007 (H.R. 1591), included funding to cover projected FY2007 shortfalls. A subsequent war supplemental enacted on May 25 (H.R. 2206, P.L. 110-28) includes the same shortfall funding. In addition, a number of SCHIP reauthorization bills have been introduced in the 110th Congress.

Reports

See CRS Report RL34129, Medicaid and SCHIP Provisions in H.R. 3162 and S. 1893/H.R. 976, by Evelyne Baumrucker et al.; CRS Report RS22712, What Happens if SCHIP Is Not "Reauthorized"? by Chris L. Peterson; CRS Report RL30473, State Children's Health Insurance Program (SCHIP): A Brief Overview, by Elicia J. Herz and Chris L. Peterson; SCHIP Provisions of H.R. 6164 (NIH Reform Act of 2006), by Chris L. Peterson; CRS Report RL32807, SCHIP Financing: Funding Projections and State Redistribution Issues, by Chris L. Peterson; CRS Report RL33366, SCHIP Original Allotments: Description and Analysis, by Chris L. Peterson; and CRS Report RL33251, Side-by-Side Comparison of

Medicare, Medicaid, and SCHIP Provisions in the Deficit Reduction Act of 2005, by Karen Tritz et al.

Health Care Fraud and Abuse Control Account

Background

The Health Insurance Portability and Accountability Act of 1996 (HIPAA) established a national Health Care Fraud and Abuse Control (HCFAC) account within the federal Hospital Insurance (HI, also known as Medicare Part A) trust fund. The HCFAC account funds the Medicare Integrity Program within CMS, certain health care fraud and abuse activities within the Federal Bureau of Investigation, and HCFAC program activities carried out by HHS agencies and the Department of Justice. Annual mandatory minimum and maximum HCFAC appropriations are specified in statute.

Proposal

The President's budget seeks legislation to increase HCFAC funding with a discretionary appropriation. While the proposal would not directly affect Medicaid or SCHIP spending, it would fund Medicaid and SCHIP financial management activities and supplement HCFAC funding overall. HHS estimates that the Medicaid and SCHIP financial management portion of the proposal (which provides funding in FY2008 only) would cost $10.1 million in FY2008 and over the FY2008-FY2012 period. CBO did not provide an estimate for the proposal.

Reports

For information on discretionary HHS funding levels, see CRS Report RL34076, *Labor, Health and Human Services, and Education: FY2008 Appropriations*, by Pamela W. Smith.

HEALTH INSURANCE IN THE PRESIDENT'S FY2008 BUDGET

The President's FY2008 budget contains a number of proposals that would affect health insurance. For each of the proposals, this report provides:

- background information;
- a description of the proposal based on available information;[14] and
- a list of relevant CRS reports.

The description of each proposal includes Administration and JCT estimates of its cost or savings in FY2008 and over the FY2008-FY2017 period. These estimates are summarized in table 2.

Table 2. Revenue and Outlay Effects of Health Insurance Proposals in the President's FY2008 Budget

Proposal	Millions of dollars			
	Administration estimate		JCT estimate	
	FY2008-FY2012	FY2008-FY2017	FY2008-FY2012	FY2008-FY2017
Net revenue effect — provide a flat $15,000 deduction for family coverage ($7,500 for individual coverage)	—	—	($22,757)	$333,635
Revenue effect	($121,201)	$5,150	—	—
Outlay effect	$14,280	$37,886	$30,800	$77,000
Net revenue effect — expand and make HSAs more flexible	—	—	($389)	($1,451)
Revenue effect	($3,669)	($10,366)	—	—
Outlay effect	—	—	—	—
Net revenue effect — improve the Health Coverage Tax Credit	—	—	($116)	($265)
Revenue effect	($18)	($51)	—	—
Outlay effect	$55	$139	—	—
Establishing association health plans	—	—	—	—
Creating a competitive marketplace across state lines	—	—	—	—
Reforming medical liability law	—	—	—	—
Fostering affordable choices	—	—	—	—

Source: OMB, Budget of the United States Government, Fiscal Year 2008, available at [http://www.whitehouse.gov/omb/budget/fy2008/]; JCT, Estimating The Revenue Effects of the Administration's Fiscal Year 2008 Proposal Providing a Standard Deduction for Health Insurance: Modeling and Assumptions, Mar. 20, 2007, available at [http://www.house.gov/jct/x-17-07.pdf]; and JCT, Description of Revenue Provisions Contained in the President's Fiscal Year 2008 Budget Proposal, March 2007, available at [http://www.house.gov/jct/s-2-07.pdf].

Note: Numbers in parentheses are negative. Estimates for proposals that do not show a dollar figure were not provided in the documents cited above.

Although bills that would implement proposals similar to those in the President's budget have not been acted on in the 110th Congress to date, the FY2008 budget resolution and the SCHIP reauthorization bill passed by the Senate on August 2 (see CRS Report RL34107, *S. 1893/H.R. 976: The Children's Health Insurance Program Reauthorization Act of 2007*, by Evelyne Baumrucker et al.) do contain some provisions related to private health insurance and affordable coverage.

Health Insurance: Tax Deduction and Other Tax Changes

The President's budget proposes repealing the income and FICA exclusions for employer-paid health coverage, the self-employed health deduction, and itemized medical expenses for individuals not enrolled in Medicare. Instead, a new standard deduction for health insurance would be available. Other provisions would expand the availability and attractiveness of Health Savings Accounts. Background on these proposals is provided below.

Background on Tax Deduction

Health insurance paid by employers generally is excluded from employees' gross income in determining their income tax liability; it also is not considered for either the employee's or the employer's share of employment taxes (i.e., Social Security, Medicare, and unemployment taxes). The income and employment tax exclusions apply to both single and family coverage, which includes the employee's spouse and dependents. The employee's share of the premium may be paid with after-tax dollars (in which case they can be taken in consideration for the medical expenses itemized deduction) or subject to a premium conversion arrangement.

Insurance benefits paid from employment-based plans are generally excluded from gross income if they are reimbursements for medical expenses or payments for permanent physical injuries. Benefits not meeting these tests are taxable in proportion to the share of the insurance costs paid by the employer that were previously excluded from gross income. Benefits received by highly compensated employees under discriminatory self-insured plans may be partly taxable. A self-insured plan is one in which the employer assumes the risk for a health care plan and does not shift it to a third party.

Employers may deduct their insurance and other health care payments as a business expense. The deduction is not a tax benefit but a calculation necessary for the proper measurement of the net income that is subject to taxation. Revenue loss attributable to this deduction is not considered a tax expenditure.

Background on Premium Conversions

Under a cafeteria plan option known as premium conversion, employees may elect to reduce their taxable wages in exchange for having their share of health insurance premiums paid on a pretax basis.[15] The arrangement saves both income and employment taxes. Premium conversion is not available to retirees. However, employer payments for retiree health insurance is excluded from taxes, just as they are for active workers. For many retirees, the employer pays much of the premium.

Background on Flexible Spending Accounts

Flexible spending accounts (FSAs) are employer-established benefit plans that reimburse employees for specified expenses as they are incurred. FSA reimbursements funded through salary reduction agreements (the most common arrangement) are exempt from income and employment taxes under cafeteria plan provisions because employees have a choice between cash (their regular salary) and a nontaxable benefit. In contrast, FSA reimbursements funded by nonelective employer contributions are exempt from taxation directly under provisions applying to employer-paid dependent care or health insurance.

Background on Unreimbursed Medical Expenses Itemized Deduction

Taxpayers who itemize their deductions may deduct unreimbursed medical expenses that exceed 7.5% of adjusted gross income (AGI). Medical expenses include health insurance premiums paid by the taxpayer, principally premiums for individual market policies and the employee's share of premiums for employment based coverage (aside from those subject to a premium conversion arrangement). More generally, medical expenses include amounts paid for the "diagnosis, cure, mitigation, treatment, or prevention of disease, or for the purpose of affecting any structure or function of the body." They also include certain transportation and lodging expenditures, qualified long-term care costs, and long-term care insurance premiums that do not exceed certain amounts.

The JCT estimated that the FY2007 tax expenditure attributable to the medical expense deduction (including long-term care expenses) will be about $8.2 billion.

Proposal

The President's budget proposes a new health insurance tax deduction of $7,500 for self-only coverage or $15,000 for family coverage. The deduction would apply to both income and payroll taxes and would be the same regardless of the cost of the insurance or whether it was obtained in the individual and small group markets or through one's employer.

The proposal would terminate:

- the exclusion for employer provided health insurance;
- the self-employed premium deduction;
- the exclusion or deduction of health care spending for insurance premiums and out-of-pocket expenses (except for expenses covered under HSAs);
- the exclusion of FSAs from income and employment taxes; and
- the itemized deduction for medical expenses for those not enrolled in Medicare.

Employers would be required to report the value of health insurance coverage to their employees on their annual Form W-2 and such amounts would be subject to withholding and employment taxes. Businesses would continue to deduct employer-provided health insurance as a business expense.

The exclusion and deduction for Health Savings Account contributions would not be affected.

Effective for tax years beginning after 2008, OMB estimates that the proposal would increase outlays by $231 million and reduce revenue by $31.433 billion in 2009; increase outlays by $14.280 billion and reduce revenue by $121.201 billion over the 2008-2012 period; and increase outlays by $37.886 billion and increase revenue by $5.150 billion over the 2008-2017 period.

JCT estimates that repealing the provisions of existing law and providing the new standard health insurance deduction would reduce *net* revenue (including outlay effects) by $13.790 billion in 2009; reduce net revenue by $22.757 billion over the 2008-2012 period; and increase net revenue by $333.6 billion over the 2008-2017 period.

Reports

See CRS Report RL33505, *Tax Benefits for Health Insurance and Expenses: Overview of Current Law and Legislation*, by Bob Lyke and Julie M. Whitaker; CRS Report RL32656, *Health Care Flexible Spending Accounts*, by Bob Lyke and Chris L. Peterson; and CRS Report RS21573, *Tax-Advantaged Accounts for Health Care Expenses: Side-by-Side Comparison*, by Bob Lyke and Chris L. Peterson.

Health Insurance: Health Savings Accounts

Background

Health Savings Accounts (HSAs) are one way people can pay for unreimbursed medical expenses (deductibles, copayments, and services not covered by insurance) on a tax-advantaged basis. HSAs can be established and funded by eligible individuals when they have a qualifying high deductible health plan (HDHP, i.e., high deductible insurance) with a deductible in 2007 of at least $1,100 for self-only coverage and $2,200 for family coverage. Qualifying HDHPs must also limit out-of-pocket expenses for covered benefits to certain amounts. With some exceptions, eligible individuals cannot have other health insurance coverage.

HSA tax advantages can be significant for some people: contributions are deductible (or excluded from income that is taxable if made by employers), withdrawals are not taxed if used for medical expenses, and account earnings are tax exempt. HSAs are included in what some call "consumer-driven health plans." One objective of these plans is to encourage individuals and families to set money aside for their health care expenses. Another is to give them a financial incentive for spending health care dollars prudently. Still another goal is to give them the means to pay for health care services of their own choosing, without constraint by insurers or employers.

Proposal

The President's FY2008 budget proposes to allow health plans to be considered HSA-eligible if they meet all the existing requirements of an HDHP except that, in lieu of satisfying the minimum deductible requirement, they have at least a 50% coinsurance requirement and a minimum out-of-pocket risk that, under guidelines established by the Secretary, would result in the same (or lower) premium as a HDHP would under current law.

The proposal includes additional changes be made to HSAs, including (1) allowing family coverage to include coverage where each individual in the family can receive benefits once they have reached the minimum deductible for an individual HDHP; (2) allowing both spouses to contribute the catch-up contribution to a single HSA owned by one spouse if both spouses are eligible individuals; (3) allowing an individual to be covered by a flexible spending arrangement (FSA) or health reimbursement arrangement (HRA) with first dollar coverage and still contribute to an HSA, but offset the maximum allowable HSA contribution by the level of FSA or HRA coverage; (4) allowing qualified medical expenses to include any medical expense incurred on or after the first day of HDHP coverage if individuals have established an HSA by their return filing date for that year; and (5) excluding from the comparability rules extra employer contributions to HSAs on behalf of employees who are chronically ill or employees who have spouses or dependents who are chronically ill. All of the HSA-related proposals would be effective for years beginning after December 31, 2007.

While the President's proposal would replace the current law tax exclusion of employer-provided health insurance with a flat deduction, the current exclusion or deduction for HSA contributions would not be affected.

OMB estimates that the proposal would reduce revenue by $318 million in 2008, by $3.669 billion for 2008 through 2012, and by $10.366 billion for 2008 through 2017. JCT estimates that the proposal would reduce net revenue by $19 million in 2008, by $389 million for 2008 through 2012, and by $1.451 billion for 2008 through 2017.

Reports

For more information on HSAs, see CRS Report RL33257, *Health Savings Accounts: Overview of Rules for 2007*, by Bob Lyke and CRS Report RS21573, *Tax-Advantaged Accounts for Health Care Expenses: Side-by-Side Comparison*, by Bob Lyke and Chris L. Peterson.

Health Insurance: Health Coverage Tax Credit

Background

The Trade Act of 2002 (P.L. 107-210) authorized a federal income tax credit of 65% of what eligible taxpayers pay for qualified health insurance for themselves and their family members. The credit is refundable, so taxpayers may claim the full credit even if they have little or no federal income tax liability. The credit can also be advanced, so taxpayers need not wait until they file their tax returns in order to benefit from it.

Eligibility for the HCTC is limited to three groups of taxpayers. The first two consist of individuals who are eligible for Trade Adjustment Assistance allowances because they have lost manufacturing jobs due to increased foreign imports or shifts in production outside the United States. The third consists of individuals whose defined benefit pension plans were taken over by the Pension Benefit Guaranty Corporation (PBGC) due to financial difficulties. Eligible individuals cannot be enrolled in certain other health insurance (e.g., Medicaid) or entitled to certain other coverage (e.g., Medicare Part A).

Eligible individuals can claim the HCTC only if they make payments for qualified insurance. The statute limits qualified insurance to ten different categories of coverage. Three of the coverage categories are known as automatically qualified health plans. The other seven categories of coverage are known as state qualified plans; individuals may choose these options only if their state has chosen or established these plans to be included as qualified coverage.

Coverage under state qualified plans must provide consumer protections to all qualifying individuals. Plans must guarantee issue (offer coverage to all qualifying applicants) and not deny coverage based on preexisting conditions. Premiums (without regard to subsidies) must not be greater for qualifying individuals than for other similarly situated individuals, and benefits for qualifying individuals must be the same as or substantially similar to those for others. In short, the statute attempts to ensure that state qualified plans are open to all qualifying applicants and do not charge more or provide fewer benefits to people who are receiving the credit. The consumer protections do not preclude use of medical underwriting to set premiums.

Proposal

The President's FY2008 budget includes a proposal that would allow state qualified plans to impose a pre-existing condition exclusion for a period of up to 12 months, provided the plan reduces the restriction period by the length of the eligible individual's creditable coverage as of the date of application for the state qualified plan.

The FY2008 budget also proposes allowing the spouse of an HCTC-eligible individual to claim the credit when the HCTC-eligible individual becomes entitled to Medicare. The spouse would have to be at least 55 years of age.

OMB estimates that the proposal would increase outlays by $4 million and reduce revenue by $1 million in 2008, increase outlays by $55 million and reduce revenue by $18 million for 2008 through 2012, and increase outlays by $139 million and reduce revenue by $51 million for 2008 through 2017.

JCT estimates that the proposal would reduce *net* revenue by $15 million in 2008, by $116 million for 2008 through 2012, and by $265 million for 2008 through 2017.

Reports

For information on the Health Care Tax Credit, see CRS Report RL32620, Health Coverage Tax Credit Authorized by the Trade Act, by Bob Lyke and Julie Stone and CRS Report RL33505, Tax Benefits for Health Insurance and Expenses: Overview of Current Law and Legislation, by Bob Lyke and Julie M. Whitaker.

Health Insurance: Establishing Association Health Plans

Background

Most individuals obtain their health insurance at work, with both employers and workers contributing to the cost, or monthly premiums, of the health insurance plans. Sometimes employers will sponsor health insurance coverage offered through trade or professional associations. For smaller employers, insurance purchased through such an association can be easier to obtain compared with having to negotiate through the confusing offerings of the private insurance market on their own. Associations with members that cross state lines, however, have argued that their plans could be more affordable if they were exempt from multiple state insurance laws. Under current law, plans offered by any insurer or multiple employer[16] group, such as an association, are subject to the entire body of state insurance law for any state in which those products are offered.

Proposal

The President's budget proposes an initiative to establish "Association Health Plans." Such plans could allow small employers, civic groups and community organizations to band together and use their purchasing power to obtain health coverage for their employees, members, and their families.

Reports

For a description of Association Health Plan legislation during the 109th Congress, see CRS Report RL31963, *Association Sponsored Health Plans: Legislation in the 109th Congress*, by Jean Hearne.

Health Insurance: Creating a Competitive Marketplace Across State Lines

Background

States have primary jurisdiction over the regulation of health insurance carriers and products. States have passed laws on numerous topics in this area: benefit mandates, patient protections, rating laws, grievance and appeals processes, just to name a few. This has resulted in health insurance requirements totaling in the thousands. Insurance carriers and other health insurers, particularly those that operate in multiple states, have sought relief from these requirements. They argue that reducing the number of applicable state laws will lead to more plan options at affordable prices in the private market. One possible approach to reducing state regulation of health insurance is for multi-state carriers to designate one state as the "primary" state with respect to applicable insurance laws. Another approach is to allow qualified insurers to offer coverage that does not meet any state benefit mandates. Both approaches could provide flexibility to carriers to design cheaper, less-generous health insurance products, but maintain some level of existing consumer protections.

Proposal

The President's budget proposes an initiative to create a competitive marketplace across state lines that maintains strong consumer protections.

Reports

For information on issues related to offering insurance products across state lines, see CRS Report RS22476, *Standardizing State Health Insurance Regulation*, by Jean Hearne and Bernadette Fernandez and CRS Report RL31963, *Association Sponsored Health Plans: Legislation in the 109th Congress*, by Jean Hearne.

Health Insurance: Reforming Medical Liability Law

Background

The rising cost of medical malpractice insurance is a public policy concern because of its potential impact on the availability of health care providers and services. As malpractice insurance becomes increasingly expensive, some physicians claim that premium increases have forced them to limit the services they provide, move their practice locations, or leave medicine altogether. They cite "frivolous" lawsuits and unreasonably large jury awards as the causes of the malpractice insurance "crisis." However, lawyer and consumer groups counter that the insurance industry is to blame for the rapid rise in malpractice insurance premiums. These groups contend that bad investment choices, in addition to the underwriting cycle, have led to dwindling profits for insurers, who then try to recoup their losses through expensive insurance products. There is a third perspective, which has not generated the same level of attention or controversy, that sees the overall medical error rate as the root of the problem.

Proposal

The President's budget proposes an initiative to reform medical liability law, with the expectation it will increase access to quality, affordable health care while reducing non-meritorious lawsuits against doctors and other health care providers.

Reports

For more information on reforming medical liability, see CRS Report RL33358, *Medical Malpractice: An Overview*, by Bernadette Fernandez and Baird Webel.

Health Insurance: Fostering Affordable Choices

Background

Under current law, uninsured individuals in need of medical care must either self-pay for health care services or forego them. For very large inpatient hospital costs, uninsured individuals are sometimes able to negotiate a price reduction. The unpaid portion of the bills are written off as bad debt or charity care. Certain hospitals provide a disproportionate share of charity care and uncompensated care to people who are not able to pay. Under Medicaid, states are required to make special payments to hospitals that provide a disproportionate amount (relative to other hospitals) of uncompensated care and care to Medicaid beneficiaries.

Proposal

The President's budget proposes to have the Secretary of HHS work with Congress on establishing a more efficient distribution of institutional payments, redirecting some portion toward health insurance for people with poor health or limited income. The proposal seeks to focus on helping the uninsured purchase private insurance in order to improve the likelihood that people would receive the care they need in the most appropriate setting. Such health care reforms would be state-based and budget neutral.

Reports

For background information on Medicaid DSH payments, see CRS Report 97-483, *Medicaid Disproportionate Share Payments*, by Jean Hearne.

Congressional Action

FY2008 Budget Resolution

The House and Senate adopted their respective budget resolutions for FY2008 in March of 2007. A conference agreement was adopted by both chambers on May 17. Although it is not binding, the budget resolution provides a framework for subsequent legislative action.

Senate

On March 15, 2007, the Senate Budget Committee reported an FY2008 budget resolution (S.Con.Res. 21), which was amended and passed by the Senate on March 23. Relevant provisions include:

- Up to $50 billion over five years for SCHIP reauthorization, with language specifying that it should be a top priority for the remainder of FY2007. The resolution provides a deficit-neutral reserve fund of up to $20 billion for this purpose. It also provides a $30 billion increase in spending for the budget function that includes SCHIP ($15 billion of which might be paid for with Medicare savings assumed in the resolution,[17] and $15 billion of which is paid for out of an FY2012 surplus assumed in the resolution[18]). The resolution specifies that an increase in the federal tobacco tax could be among the policy changes considered to achieve offsets for the remaining $20 billion.

- Deficit-neutral reserve funds for: (1) comparative effectiveness research, (2) small business health insurance, (3) health care reform (if an SCHIP reauthorization bill is enacted), (4) long-term care, (5) health information technology, (6) mental health parity, (7) delayed implementation of a proposed rule that would affect Medicaid and SCHIP financing (see the "Revise Payments for Government Providers" proposal described earlier), (8) the use of Medicare data to evaluate a variety of health care issues in federal programs and the private health care system, and (9) improving health insurance.
- Up to $383 million in FY2008 discretionary funding for the health care fraud and abuse control program at HHS.

House

On March 23, 2007, the House Budget Committee reported its own budget resolution (H.Con.Res. 99), which was passed by the House on March 29. Relevant provisions include:

- A deficit/surplus-neutral reserve fund of up to $50 billion over five years for expanding coverage and improving children's health through SCHIP and Medicaid.
- A deficit/surplus-neutral reserve fund for extending Medicaid transitional medical assistance through FY2008.
- Up to $183 million in FY2008 discretionary funding for the health care fraud and abuse control program at HHS. In addition, all House committees are directed to review programs within their jurisdiction for waste, fraud, and abuse in spending and to provide annual recommendations for improved performance.
- A finding that the most significant factor affecting entitlement programs is a rapid increase in health care costs that is not unique to Medicare and Medicaid, and a "sense of the House" that the growing cost of entitlements should be dealt with in a way that addresses the causes of cost growth in the broader health care system.
- A sense of the House that legislation consistent with PAYGO that makes health insurance more affordable and accessible (with attention to the special needs of small businesses), and lowers costs and improves health care quality, should be adopted.

Conference Agreement

On May 17, 2007, the House and Senate adopted a conference agreement on the budget resolution (H.Rept. 110-153 accompanying S.Con.Res. 21). Relevant provisions in the FY2008 budget resolution include:

- A reserve fund of up to $50 billion for SCHIP legislation that is deficit-neutral in the Senate and deficit/surplus-neutral in the House.
- Deficit-neutral reserve funds for: (1) health information technology; (2) comparative effectiveness research; (3) the use of Medicare data to evaluate a variety of health care issues in federal programs and the private health care system; (4) small business health insurance; (5) legislation to improve health care, provide quality health insurance for the uninsured and underinsured, and protect individuals with current

health coverage (if an SCHIP reauthorization bill is enacted); (6) long-term care; (7) mental health parity; (8) delayed implementation of administrative proposals that would affect Medicaid and SCHIP financing, graduate medical education, rehabilitation services, and school-based services (see the "Revise Payments for Government Providers," "Eliminate Graduate Medical Education," "Clarify Rehabilitation Services," and "School-Based Services" proposals described earlier); (9) a demonstration project regarding Medicaid coverage of low-income individuals with HIV; (10) extending Medicaid transitional medical assistance.

- Up to $383 million in FY2008 discretionary funding for the health care fraud and abuse control program at HHS.
- Two "sense of the Congress" provisions regarding health care cost growth and affordable health coverage.

Appropriations

In general, spending for Medicaid and SCHIP is not controlled through the annual appropriations process. Medicaid is an entitlement program, meaning that its spending level is based on the underlying benefit and eligibility criteria established in law.[19] SCHIP is capped grant program, with annual appropriations specified in law through FY2007 (as described below, legislation to reauthorize the program is pending). However, the annual appropriations process does provide an opportunity for Congress to place limitations on the availability of funds for specified activities.[20] For example, the Labor, Health and Human Services, and Education appropriations bill regularly contains restrictions that limit the circumstances under which federal funds can be used to pay for abortions.[21]

Spending for other health insurance provisions is more complicated, and must be examined on a case-by-case basis. As with Medicaid and SCHIP, some spending (including tax expenditures) may be based on underlying statute. Other spending may occur through the annual appropriations process (e.g., certain state grants associated with the health coverage tax credit).

Other Legislation

In the 110th Congress, a number of Medicaid and SCHIP issues have seen legislative action. As described earlier, a war supplemental appropriations bill enacted on May 25, 2007 (H.R. 2206, P.L. 110-28), contains SCHIP funding to cover projected FY2007 shortfalls, delays implementation of Medicaid administrative proposals related to intergovernmental transfers (payments for government providers) and graduate medical education for one year, and requires the use of tamper-resistant pads for Medicaid prescriptions executed after September 30, 2007. In addition, the bill allows any state operating a Medicaid Pharmacy Plus waiver that would otherwise expire on June 30, 2007, to continue operating the waiver through December 31, 2009.[22]

Legislation was also enacted to temporarily extend Medicaid transitional medical assistance through September 30, 2007 (S. 1701, P.L. 110-48). Another bill to extend TMA and the QI-1 program through December 31, 2007, apply an asset verification pilot to

Medicaid for five years, and delay implementation of the new Medicaid tamper-resistant prescription pad requirement for six months (H.R. 3668, P.L. 110-90) was enacted at the end of September.

On the issue of SCHIP reauthorization, numerous bills have been introduced. The Children's Health Insurance Program (CHIP) Reauthorization Act of 2007 was marked up by the Senate Finance Committee on July 19, introduced as S. 1893 on July 26, and passed by the Senate as an amendment to H.R. 976 on August 2. The Children's Health and Medicare Protection (CHAMP) Act of 2007 was introduced as H.R. 3162 on July 24. After moving through the House Ways and Means and House Energy and Commerce Committees, H.R. 3162 was reported by the House Rules Committee early on August 1 and passed by the House later that day.

A bicameral agreement on SCHIP reauthorization passed the House on September 25 and the Senate on September 27 as an amendment to H.R. 976. President Bush vetoed the legislation on October 3.[23] A continuing resolution that contains short-term funding for SCHIP (H.J.Res. 52, P.L. 110-92) was enacted at the end of September.

S. 1893/H.R. 976 — The Children's Health Insurance Program Reauthorization Act of 2007

Major elements of H.R. 976, as passed by the Senate on August 2, include:[24]

- national allotment appropriations totaling $61.4 billion over five years (an increase of $36.2 billion over the current law baseline of $25.2 billion), distributed to states and territories using a new formula;
- a new incentive bonuses pool (for making payments to states exceeding certain Medicaid/SCHIP enrollment levels), which would receive an FY2008 appropriation of $3 billion and deposits of certain unspent SCHIP funds through FY2012;
- a new contingency fund (for making payments to states for certain shortfalls of federal SCHIP funds), which would receive deposits through a separate appropriation each year through FY2012 and make payments of up to 12.5% of the available national allotment for SCHIP;
- additional grants for outreach and enrollment totaling $100 million each year through FY2012;
- provisions to remove barriers to enrollment, including a new option for meeting citizenship documentation requirements;
- provisions to eliminate barriers to providing premium assistance;
- provisions to strengthen quality of care and health outcomes of children;
- miscellaneous provisions, including improved data collection; and
- tobacco tax changes.

An August 24 estimate from CBO and JCT[25] indicates that the Senate bill would increase net outlays by $35.2 billion over 5 years and by $71.0 billion over 10 years.[26] These costs would be offset by an increase in the federal tobacco tax and other changes, which CBO and JCT estimate would increase net revenue by $36.1 billion over 5 years and by $72.8 billion over 10 years.

H.R. 3162 — The Children's Health and Medicare Protection Act of 2007

H.R. 3162, as passed by the House on August 1, contains SCHIP provisions to reauthorize and increase funding levels for the program; improve enrollment and retention; change certain benefit and coverage requirements; and address access, quality, and program integrity issues.[27] It also contains a variety of Medicaid provisions, numerous changes to the Medicare program, and an increase in the federal tobacco tax.

An August 1 estimate from CBO[28] indicates that the SCHIP title of H.R. 3162 would increase outlays by $47.4 billion over 5 years and by $128.7 billion over 10 years, and that the Medicaid title of the bill would increase outlays by $4.4 billion over 5 years and by $4.6 billion over 10 years. Including Medicare and miscellaneous provisions, CBO estimates that the entire bill would increase outlays by $25.6 billion over 5 years and by $58.0 billion over 10 years. These costs would be offset by an increase in the federal tobacco tax and other changes, which CBO estimates would increase revenue by $28.1 billion over 5 years and by $58.1 billion over 10 years.

Bicameral Agreement on SCHIP Reauthorization

Major elements of the bicameral agreement on SCHIP reauthorization, which passed the House and Senate as an amendment to H.R. 976 but was vetoed on October 3, include:[29]

- national allotment appropriations totaling $61.4 billion over five years (an increase of $36.2 billion over the current law baseline of $25.2 billion), distributed to states and territories using a new formula that builds on provisions in the House and Senate reauthorization bills;
- a new contingency fund (for making payments to states for certain shortfalls of federal SCHIP funds), which would receive deposits through a separate appropriation each year through FY2012 and make payments of up to 20% of the available national allotment for SCHIP;
- new performance bonus payments (for states exceeding certain Medicaid/SCHIP enrollment levels), which are funded with an FY2008 appropriation of $3 billion and deposits of certain unspent SCHIP funds through FY2012;
- additional grants for outreach and enrollment totaling $100 million each year through FY2012;
- provisions to remove barriers to enrollment, including a new option for meeting citizenship documentation requirements;
- provisions to eliminate barriers to providing premium assistance;
- provisions to strengthen quality of care and health outcomes of children;
- program integrity and miscellaneous provisions, including some that affect the Medicaid program; and
- tobacco tax changes.

A September 24 estimate from CBO and JCT[30] indicates that the SCHIP agreement would increase net outlays by $34.9 billion over 5 years and by $71.5 billion over 10 years.[31] These costs would be offset by an increase in the federal tobacco tax and other changes, which CBO and JCT estimate would increase net revenue by $36.3 billion over 5 years and by $72.8 billion over 10 years.

and Accountability Act (HIPAA) of 1996: Overview and Guidance on Frequently Asked Questions, by Hinda R. Chaikind, Jean Hearne, Bob Lyke, and C. Stephen Redhead.

[7] 69 Federal Register 78720, Final Regulations for Health Coverage Portability for Group Health Plans and Group Health Insurance Issuers Under HIPAA Titles I and IV, December 30, 2004.

[8] For example, see HHS, Office of Inspector General (OIG), Review of Medicaid Transportation Claims Made by the New York City Department of Education, A-02-03-01023, September 2005; HHS, OIG, Audit of LaPorte Consortium's Administrative Costs Claimed for Medicaid School-Based Services, A-06-02-00051, January 2006; and Government Accountability Office, Medicaid in Schools: Improper Payments Demand Improvements in HCFA Oversight, GAO/HES/OSI-00-69, April 2000.

[9] K. Allen, *States' Efforts to Maximize Federal Reimbursements Highlight Need for Improved Federal Oversight*, Government Accountability Office, Testimony Before the U.S. Senate, Committee on Finance, GAO-05-836T, June 28, 2005. (Hereafter cited as "GAO Testimony, June 2005.")

[10] HHS, Office of Inspector General, Audit of Medicaid Claims for Iowa Rehabilitation Treatment Services Family-Centered Program, A-07-02-03023, July 2004.

[11] GAO Testimony, June 2005.

[12] Department of Health and Human Services, "Federal Financial Participation in State Assistance Expenditures; Federal Matching Shares for Medicaid, the State Children's Health Insurance Program, and Aid to Needy Aged, Blind, or Disabled Persons for October 1, 2006 Through September 30, 2007," 70 *Federal Register* 71856, November 30, 2005, and 71 *Federal Register* 28041, May 15, 2006.

[13] Some of the details of this description are based on a briefing by OMB officials on February 5, 2007.

[14] Sources include HHS, Fiscal Year 2008 Budget in Brief; OMB, Budget of the United States Government, Fiscal Year 2008; and Department of the Treasury, General Explanations of the Administration's Fiscal Year 2008 Revenue Proposals, available at [http://www.treas.gov/offices/tax-policy/library/bluebk07.pdf].

[15] Cafeteria plans are employer-established benefit plans under which employees may choose between receiving cash (typically additional take-home pay) and certain normally nontaxable benefits (such as employer-paid health insurance) without being taxed on the value of the benefits if they select the latter.

[16] Under federal law, the term for groups of two or more employers that purchase insurance together is multiple employer welfare arrangement (MEWA).

[17] Senate Budget Committee, *Chairman's Mark: FY2008 Budget*, March 14, 2007, p. 12, available at [http://budget.senate.gov/democratic/documents/2007/ Budres chairmansmark031407.pdf].

[18] *Congressional Record*, March 21, 2007, pp. S3468-S3471.

[19] See CRS Report RS20129, Entitlements and Appropriated Entitlements in the Federal Budget Process, by Bill Heniff Jr.

[20] See CRS Report 98-518, Earmarks and Limitations in Appropriations Bills, by Sandy Streeter.

[21] See CRS Report RL34076, Labor, Health and Human Services, and Education: FY2008 Appropriations, by Pamela W. Smith.

[22] For information on these waivers, see CRS Report RS21054, *Medicaid and SCHIP Section 1115 Research and Demonstration Waivers*, by Evelyne P. Baumrucker.

[23] Message to the House of Representatives (October 3, 2007), available at [http://www.whitehouse.gov/news/releases/2007/10/20071003-2.html].

[24] See CRS Report RL34107, S. 1893/H.R. 976: The Children's Health Insurance Program Reauthorization Act of 2007, by Evelyne Baumrucker et al., and CRS Report RL34129, Medicaid and SCHIP Provisions in H.R. 3162 and S. 1893/H.R. 976, by Evelyne Baumrucker et al.

[25] CBO, letter to the Honorable Max Baucus (August 24, 2007), available at [http://www.cbo.gov/ftpdocs/85xx/doc8584/08-28-CHIP.pdf].

[26] As described above, the Senate bill would specify national allotment funding for five years. In FY2012, this funding would consist of two semi-annual allotments of $1.75 billion each plus a one-time appropriation of $12.5 billion to accompany the first semi-annual allotment. For years beyond FY2012, CBO is required to assume that national allotment funding continues at the level prescribed by existing law, which appears to be $3.5 billion under the Senate bill. In contrast, the SCHIP baseline under current law assumes an appropriation of $5.04 billion for years beyond FY2007. As a result of this difference, CBO's cost estimate for national allotments in the Senate bill shows *savings* in years beyond FY2012. For more information on budget baselines and scorekeeping, see CRS Report 98-560, *Baselines and Scorekeeping in the Federal Budget Process*, by Bill Heniff Jr.

[27] See CRS Report RL34122, H.R. 3162: Provisions in the Children's Health and Medicare Protection Act of 2007, by Richard Rimkunas et al., and CRS Report RL34129, Medicaid and SCHIP Provisions in H.R. 3162 and S. 1893/H.R. 976, by Evelyne Baumrucker et al.

[28] CBO, Estimated Effect on Direct Spending and Revenues of H.R. 3162, the Children's Health and Medicare Protection Act, for the Rules Committee (August 1, 2007), available at [http://www.cbo.gov/ftpdocs/85xx/doc8519/HR3162.pdf].

[29] See CRS Report RL34129, Medicaid and SCHIP Provisions in H.R. 3162 and S. 1893/H.R. 976, by Evelyne Baumrucker et al.

[30] CBO, letter to the Honorable Max Baucus (September 25, 2007), available at [http://www.cbo.gov/ftpdocs/86xx/doc8655/hr976.pdf].

[31] For an explanation of why CBO's cost estimate for national allotments in the agreement shows savings in years beyond FY2012, see earlier footnote on the Senate bill.

In: State Children's Health Insurance Program (SCHIP) ISBN: 978-1-60456-333-7
Editor: Mary T. Ewing, pp. 99-128

Chapter 3

STATE CHILDREN'S HEALTH INSURANCE PROGRAM (SCHIP): A BRIEF OVERVIEW*

Elicia J. Herz, Chris L. Peterson and Evelyne P. Baumrucker

ABSTRACT

The Balanced Budget Act of 1997 (BBA 97; P.L. 105-33) established the State Children's Health Insurance Program (SCHIP) under a new Title XXI of the Social Security Act. In general, this program allows states to cover targeted low-income children with no health insurance in families with income that is above Medicaid eligibility levels. As of August 2007, the highest upper income eligibility limit under SCHIP was 350% of the federal poverty level, in one state, New Jersey.

Under SCHIP, states may enroll targeted low-income children in an SCHIP-financed expansion of Medicaid, create a new separate state SCHIP program, or devise a combination of both approaches. States choosing the Medicaid option must provide all Medicaid mandatory benefits and all optional services covered under the state plan, and must follow the nominal Medicaid cost-sharing rules. In general, separate state programs must follow certain coverage and benefit options outlined in SCHIP law. While some cost-sharing provisions vary by family income, the total annual aggregate cost-sharing (including premiums, copayments, and other similar charges) for a family may not exceed 5% of total income in a year. Preventive services are exempt from cost-sharing.

Nearly $40 billion was appropriated for SCHIP for FY1998 through FY2007. Annual allotments among the states are determined by a formula that is based on a combination of the number of low-income children and low-income uninsured children in the state, adjusted by a cost factor that reflects the average health service industry wages in the state compared to the national average. Like Medicaid, SCHIP is a federal-state matching program. While the Medicaid federal medical assistance percentage (FMAP) ranged from 50% to 75.89% in FY2007, the enhanced SCHIP FMAP ranged from 65% to 83.12% across states.

All states, the District of Columbia, and five territories have SCHIP programs. As of June 2007, 15 use Medicaid expansions, 18 use separate state programs, and 23 use a combination approach. At the national level, approximately 6.7 million children were

---

* Excerpted from CRS Report RL30473, dated August 20, 2007.

enrolled in SCHIP during FY2006 (latest official data). In addition, 12 states reported enrolling about 701,000 adults in SCHIP through program waivers.

Spending was slow in the early years of SCHIP, but that trend changed in more recent years and has led some states to exhaust their federal SCHIP funds. The Deficit Reduction Act of 2005 (DRA; P.L. 109-171) provided a new appropriation of $283 million to address anticipated FY2006 shortfalls in federal SCHIP funding, although two states (Illinois and Massachusetts) still experienced shortfalls. The NIH Reform Act of 2006 (P.L. 109-482) included provisions to delay FY2007 shortfalls until the first part of May. Under P.L. 110-28, Congress appropriated up to $650 million to cover shortfalls in 12 states in FY2007. Before the August recess, Congress passed legislation (H.R. 3162 in the House and S. 1893/H.R. 976 in the Senate) that would provide additional funding for SCHIP for FY2008 and additional years, and would make a number of other changes to both SCHIP and Medicaid.

The Balanced Budget Act of 1997 (BBA 97; P.L. 105-33) established the State Children's Health Insurance Program (SCHIP) under a new Title XXI of the Social Security Act. The program offers federal matching funds to states and territories to provide health insurance to certain low-income children. Although specific requirements apply to eligibility, benefits, and beneficiary cost-sharing, as described below, these rules can be modified via waiver authority provided in Section 1115 of the Social Security Act.[1]

ELIGIBILITY

In general, Title XXI defines a targeted low-income child as one who is under the age of 19 years with no health insurance, and who would not have been eligible for Medicaid under the rules in effect in the state on March 31, 1997. States can set the upper income level for targeted low-income children up to 200% of the federal poverty level (FPL),[2] or 50 percentage points above the applicable pre-SCHIP Medicaid income level.

Within these general rules, states may provide assistance to qualifying children in two basic ways. They may cover such children under their Medicaid programs and/or they may create a separate SCHIP program for this purpose. (More details on available benefits under each approach are described in the next section.) When states provide Medicaid coverage to targeted low-income children, Medicaid rules typically apply. When states provide coverage to targeted low-income children through separate SCHIP programs, Title XXI rules typically apply. In both cases, the federal share of program costs comes from federal SCHIP funds (also described in further detail below).

Title XXI does not establish an *individual* entitlement to benefits. Instead, Title XXI entitles *states* with approved state SCHIP plans to pre-determined federal allotments based on a distribution formula set in the law (explained further below). However, targeted low-income children covered under a SCHIP-financed expansion of Medicaid are entitled to the benefits offered under that program as dictated by Medicaid law. No such individual entitlement exists for targeted low-income children covered in separate SCHIP programs.

Table 1. SCHIP Enrollment Data for the 50 States and the District of Columbia, FY2006

State and Program Type	Upper Income Level for Children (% FPL) as of 8/8/07	Number of Children Ever Enrolled during FY2006			Number of Adults Ever Enrolled in SCHIP Demonstrations (and Upper Income Level by Group) during FY2006			
		Medicaid Expansions	Separate SCHIP Programs	Total Children	Pregnant Women	Parents	Childless Adults	Total Adults
Alabama (S)	200%	—	84,257	84,257				
Alaska (M)	175%	22,227	—	22,227				
Arizona (S)	200%	—	96,669	96,669	—	24,769 (200%)	84,969 (100%)a	109,738
Arkansas (C)	200%	86,778	3,440	90,218				b
California (C)	250%c	214,216	1,177,189	1,391,405				
Colorado (S)	200%	—	69,997	69,997	2,625 (200%)	—	—	2,625
Connecticut (S)	300%	—	23,110	23,110				
Delaware (C)	200%	172	10,579	10,751				
District of Columbia (M)	300%	6,332	—	6,332				
Florida (C)	200%	1,877	301,718	303,595				
Georgia (S)	235%	—	343,690	343,690				
Hawaii (M)	300%	22,031	—	22,031				
Idaho (C)	185%	17,858	6,869	24,727	d	277 (185%)	105 (185%)	382
Illinois (C)	200%	139,565	177,216	316,781	—	209,622 (185%)	1,492 (185%)e	211,114
Indiana (C)	200%	97,213	36,483	133,696				
Iowa (C)	200%	17,756	31,819	49,575				
Kansas (S)	200%	—	48,934	48,934				
Kentucky (C)	200%	41,943	22,918	64,861				
Louisiana (M)	200%	142,389	—	142,389				
Maine (C)	200%	22,167	8,947	31,114				
Maryland (C)	300%	112,123	23,911	136,034				
Massachusetts (C)	300%	126,120	64,520	190,640				
Michigan (C)	200%	61,214	57,287	118,501	—	—	101,919 (35%)	101,919
Minnesota (C)	280%	97	5,246	5,343	—	34,313 (200%)	—	34,313

Table 1. (Continued).

State and Program Type	Upper Income Level for Children (% FPL) as of 8/8/07	Number of Children Ever Enrolled during FY2006			Number of Adults Ever Enrolled in SCHIP Demonstrations (and Upper Income Level by Group) during FY2006			
		Medicaid Expansions	Separate SCHIP Programs	Total Children	Pregnant Women	Parents	Childless Adults	Total Adults
Mississippi (S)	200%	—	83,359	83,359				
Missouri (M)	300%	106,577	—	106,577				
Montana (S)	150%	—	17,304	17,304				
Nebraska (M)	185%	44,981	—	44,981				
Nevada (S)	200%	—	39,317	39,317				
New Hampshire (C)	300%	671	11,722	12,393				
New Jersey (C)	350%	49,994	92,811	142,805	205 (200%)	88,401 (115%)	—	88,606
New Mexico (M)	235%	25,155	—	25,155	—	2,756 (200%)	3,031(200%)	5,787
New York (C)	250%	51,576	636,786	688,362				
North Carolina (C)	200%	53,180	194,811	247,991				
North Dakota (C)	140%	1,889	4,429	6,318				
Ohio (M)	200%	218,529	—	218,529				
Oklahoma (M)	200%	116,012	—	116,012				
Oregon (S)	185%	—	59,039	59,039	d	7,306 (185%)	6,444 (185%)	13,750
Pennsylvania (S)	300%	—	188,765	188,765				
Rhode Island (C)	250%	24,028	1,464	25,492	354 (250%)	20,771 (185%)	—	21,125
South Carolina (M)	150%	68,870	—	68,870				
South Dakota (C)	200%	11,254	3,330	14,584				
Tennessee (C)	250%	—	— f	—				
Texas (S)	200%	—	585,461	585,461				
Utah (S)	200%	—	51,967	51,967				
Vermont (S)	300%	—	6,314	6,314				
Virginia (C)	200%	65,536	72,106	137,642	939 (185%)	—	—	939

Table 1. (Continued).

State and Program Type	Upper Income Level for Children (% FPL) as of 8/8/07	Number of Children Ever Enrolled during FY2006			Number of Adults Ever Enrolled in SCHIP Demonstrations (and Upper Income Level by Group) during FY2006			
		Medicaid Expansions	Separate SCHIP Programs	Total Children	Pregnant Women	Parents	Childless Adults	Total Adults
Washington (S)	250%	—	15,000	15,000				
West Virginia (S)	220%	—	39,855	39,855				
Wisconsin (M)	185%	56,627	—	56,627	—	110,298 (185%)	—	110,298
Wyoming (S)	200%	—	7,715	7,715				
TOTALS		2,026,957	4,706,354	6,733,311	4,123	498,513	197,960	700,596

Sources: Table prepared by CRS based on several sources. For SCHIP upper income levels for children, unpublished set of tables provided by CMS via e-mail on August 8, 2007. For program type and number of children ever enrolled, see *FY 2006 Number of Children Ever Enrolled Year - SCHIP by Program Type*, at [http://www.cms.hhs.gov/NationalSCHIPPolicy/downloads/FY2006StateTotalTable.pdf], plus more recent unpublished information from CMS on the number of children enrolled for Arkansas, New Jersey and Virginia. For the number of adults enrolled in SCHIP demonstrations, *Adult SCHIP Chart FY2006 (030107).xls*, provided by CMS via e-mail on March 8, 2007. For upper income eligibility limits for adults in SCHIP, see the CRS Congressional Distribution Memorandum, *Medicaid and SCHIP Adult Coverage under the Section 1115 Waiver Authority*, by Evelyne P. Baumrucker (available upon request); additional information obtained directly from states when the upper income eligibility levels for adults were below the maximum permitted.

Notes: S — Separate child health program. M — Medicaid expansion program. C — Combination program. FPL — federal poverty level.

[a] Arizona started phasing down its use of SCHIP funds for childless adults during FY2005. Since the December 2005 quarter, Arizona has covered childless adults using only Medicaid funds (personal communication with Arizona state officials, June 5, 2007).

[b] Arkansas and Nevada did not start enrollment in their demonstrations until FY2007. Arkansas covers parents up to 200% FPL and Nevada covers pregnant women up to 185% FPL and parents up to 200% FPL.

[c]. California also provides coverage up to 300% in four select counties and for infants covered under the Access for Infants and Mothers (AIM) program.

[d] Idaho and Oregon did not report for their pregnant women populations (in both states, covered up to 185% FPL).

[e] Childless adults are not a separate eligibility category in Illinois' SCHIP but may be covered through the state's programs for hemophiliacs and its high risk pool.

[f]. Using SCHIP funds to expand its existing Medicaid Section 1115 waiver demonstration, Tennessee began enrolling children in October 1997 through FY2002. In that year, enrolment reached 10,216. Eligibility for this Medicaid expansion program was limited to older children in families with income up to 100% FPL. As of October 1, 2002, all such children had to be covered under regular Medicaid, that is, they were no longer eligible for SCHIP coverage. Thus, Tennessee has no enrollment in its SCHIP Medicaid expansion program subsequent to FY2002. New groups became eligible for a separate SCHIP program in FY2007, so there was no FY2006 enrollment.

States may cover targeted low-income children by expanding their Medicaid programs in the following ways: (1) by establishing a new optional eligibility group for such children as authorized in Title XXI, and/or (2) by liberalizing the financial rules[3] for any of several existing Medicaid eligibility categories. Many states with Medicaid-expansion SCHIP programs chose the latter, opting to cover targeted low-income children under existing Medicaid eligibility pathways, especially Medicaid's poverty-related child groups, rather than by establishing the Title XXI optional coverage group.[4] Such a strategy reduces the administrative burden of creating and implementing a new coverage group.[5]

States may also provide coverage to targeted low-income children by creating a separate SCHIP program. States define the group of targeted low-income children who may enroll in separate SCHIP programs. Title XXI allows states to use the following factors in determining eligibility: geography (e.g., sub-state areas or statewide), age (e.g., subgroups under 19), income, resources, residency, disability status (so long as any standard relating to that status does not restrict eligibility), access to or coverage under other health insurance (to establish whether such access/coverage precludes SCHIP eligibility), and duration of SCHIP enrollment.

As of August 2007, the highest upper income eligibility limit under SCHIP was 350% of the FPL (see table 1).[6] New York has submitted a state plan amendment (SPA) to expand SCHIP eligibility to children up to 400% FPL, but it has not yet been approved by the Administration. Twenty-four states had established upper income limits at 200% FPL. Another 18 states plus the District of Columbia exceeded 200% FPL. Eight states set maximum income levels below 200% FPL.[7]

BENEFITS

As noted above, when designing their SCHIP programs, states may cover targeted low-income children under their Medicaid program, create a new separate SCHIP program, or devise a combination of both approaches.

States that use Medicaid-expansion SCHIP programs must provide the full range of mandatory Medicaid benefits, as well as all optional services specified in their state Medicaid plans. As an alternative to providing all of the mandatory and selected optional benefits under traditional Medicaid, the Deficit Reduction Act of 2005 (P.L. 109-171; DRA) gives states the option to enroll state-specified groups, including children in SCHIP Medicaid expansions, in new benchmark and benchmark-equivalent benefit plans. These plans are nearly identical to the benefit packages offered through separate SCHIP programs (described below). For any child under age 19 in one of the major mandatory and optional Medicaid eligibility groups, including targeted low-income children, the benefits available through the Early and Periodic Screening, Diagnostic, and Treatment (EPSDT) Program must be provided. Under EPSDT, children receive well-child care, immunizations, and other screening services, as well as medical care necessary to correct or ameliorate identified defects, illnesses, or conditions, including optional services states may not otherwise cover in their Medicaid programs.

States that choose to create separate SCHIP programs may elect any of three benefit options: (1) a benchmark benefit package, (2) benchmark equivalent coverage, or (3) any other health benefits plan that the Secretary of Health and Human Services determines will provide appropriate coverage to the targeted population of uninsured children.[8]

A benchmark benefit package is one of the following three plans: (1) the standard Blue Cross/Blue Shield preferred provider option plan offered under the Federal Employees Health Benefits Program (FEHBP), (2) the health coverage that is offered and generally available to state employees in the state involved, and (3) the health coverage that is offered by a health maintenance organization (HMO) with the largest commercial (non-Medicaid) enrollment in the state involved.

Benchmark-equivalent coverage is defined as a package of benefits that has the same actuarial value as one of the benchmark benefit packages. A state choosing to provide benchmark-equivalent coverage must cover each of the benefits in the "basic benefits category." The benefits in the basic benefits category are inpatient and outpatient hospital services, physicians' surgical and medical services, lab and x-ray services, and well-baby and well-child care, including age-appropriate immunizations. Benchmark-equivalent coverage must also include at least 75% of the actuarial value of coverage under the benchmark plan for each of the benefits in the "additional service category." These additional services include prescription drugs, mental health services, vision services, and hearing services. States are encouraged to cover other categories of service not listed above. Abortions may not be covered, except in the case of a pregnancy resulting from rape or incest, or when an abortion is necessary to save the mother's life.

COST-SHARING

Cost-sharing refers to the out-of-pocket payments made by beneficiaries of a health insurance plan. Cost-sharing may include monthly premiums, enrollment fees, deductibles, copayments, coinsurance and other similar charges.

Federal law permits states to impose cost-sharing for some beneficiaries and some services under SCHIP. States that cover targeted low-income children under Medicaid must follow the nominal cost-sharing rules of the Medicaid program. Under these rules, the majority of such children are exempt. Children who are 18 years of age and enrolled in Medicaid expansions under SCHIP may be subject to service-related cost-sharing (e.g., copayments) at state option.

DRA[9] provides states with a new option for premiums and service-related cost-sharing that may be applied to targeted low-income children under SCHIP Medicaid-expansion programs. For children in families with income under 100% FPL, no premiums are allowed and service-related cost-sharing is limited to nominal amounts. For children in families with income between 100%-150% FPL, no premiums may be imposed; however, service-related cost-sharing may be applied up to 10% of the cost of the item or service rendered. For children in families with income above 150% FPL, premiums are allowed (no limit is specified), and service-related cost-sharing may be applied up to 20% of the cost of the item or service rendered. For all individuals, the total aggregate amount of all cost-sharing cannot exceed 5% of family income (on a quarterly or monthly basis as specified by the state). Preventive services for children are exempt from DRA cost-sharing. The nominal Medicaid cost-sharing amounts in regulation will be indexed by medical care inflation. Special rules apply to cost-sharing for prescription drugs, and for emergency room copayments for non-emergency care. DRA also allows states to condition continuing Medicaid eligibility on the payment of premiums. Providers may also be allowed to deny care for failure to pay service-related cost-sharing.

If a state implements SCHIP through a separate state program, premiums or enrollment fees for program participation may be imposed, but the maximum allowable amount is dependent on family income. For all families with incomes under 150% FPL and enrolled in separate state programs, premiums may not exceed the amounts set forth in federal Medicaid regulations. Additionally, these families may be charged service-related cost-sharing, but such cost-sharing is limited to (1) nominal amounts defined in federal Medicaid regulations for the subgroup with income below 100% FPL, and (2) slightly higher amounts defined in SCHIP regulations for families with income between 100%-150% FPL. For a family with income above 150% FPL, cost-sharing may be imposed in any amount, provided that cost-sharing for higher-income children is not less than cost-sharing for lower-income children.

Under SCHIP law, the total annual aggregate cost-sharing (including premiums, deductibles, copayments, and any other charges) for all children in separate SCHIP programs may not exceed 5% of total family income for the year. In addition, states are required to inform families of these limits and provide a mechanism for families to stop paying once the cost-sharing limits have been reached.

Preventive services are exempt from cost-sharing for all SCHIP families regardless of income. The Centers for Medicare and Medicaid Services (CMS) defines preventive services to include the following: all healthy newborn inpatient physician visits, including routine screening (inpatient and outpatient); routine physical examinations; laboratory tests; immunizations and related office visits; and routine preventive and diagnostic dental services (for example, oral examinations, prophylaxis and topical fluoride applications, sealants, and x-rays).

FINANCING

Federal financing of SCHIP includes three major components: (1) total federal appropriations and the allotment of those funds among the states and territories, (2) reallocation of unspent federal funds, and (3) other factors affecting federal financing including the federal matching rate and caps on administrative expenses.

Federal Appropriations and Allotment among the States and Territories

BBA 97 appropriated a total of approximately $40 billion for SCHIP for FY1998-FY2007.[10] The funding level by fiscal year varies across time. The total annual appropriation for each of FY1998-FY2001 was a little more than $4.2 billion. This annual total dropped to under $3.2 billion in FY2002-FY2004. Then the appropriation rose to about $4.1 billion for FY2005 and FY2006, with a further increase to roughly $5.0 billion in FY2007. The drop in funding for FY2002-FY2004, sometimes referred to as the "SCHIP dip," was written into SCHIP's authorizing legislation due to budgetary constraints applicable at the time the legislation was drafted.

Allotment of funds among the states is determined by a formula set in law. This formula is based on a combination of the number of low-income children and the number of *uninsured* low-income children in the state, adjusted by a cost factor that reflects average wages in the states' health service industry compared to the national average.

Annual allotments are basically separate, sequential funding accounts. For each state and territory, the account for a given fiscal year is made available at the beginning of that year, and remains available for up to three years. For example, the FY2004 original allotments were available to states until the end of FY2006. Typically, SCHIP payments are taken out of the earliest active account. Once that fiscal year allotment is fully expended and the next year's allotment becomes available (active), states can begin to access the next fiscal year's allotment.

Reallocation of Unspent Federal Funds

At the end of the applicable three-year period of availability, unspent allotments are subject to reallocation among the states. The rules regarding reallocation vary by fiscal year. Generally, the year-specific rules divide states into two groups for the purpose of reallocation:

- those states that fully exhaust the applicable original allotment by the three-year deadline, called *redistribution states* (shown in table 2 by fiscal year), and
- those states that did *not* exhaust the applicable original allotment by the three-year deadline, called *retention states*.

(Territories are treated differently; see the "SCHIP Legislative History" section near the end of this report for more details.)

Table 2. States Exhausting Particular SCHIP Allotments

State	Exhausted FY1998 allotment by FY2001	Exhausted FY1999 allotment by FY2002	Exhausted FY2000 allotment by FY2003	Exhausted FY2001 allotment by FY2004	Exhausted FY2002 allotment by FY2005	Exhausted FY2003 allotment by FY2006	Exhausted FY2004 allotment by FY2007
Alabama					Yes	Yes	Yes
Alaska	Yes	Yes	Yes	Yes	Yes	Yes	Yes
Arizona				Yes	Yes	Yes	Yes
Arkansas						Yes	Yes
California						Yes	Yes
Colorado						Yes	Yes
DC						Yes	Yes
Florida				Yes	Yes	Yes	Yes
Georgia				Yes	Yes	Yes	Yes
Hawaii						Yes	Yes
Idaho							Yes
Illinois					Yes	Yes	Yes
Indiana	Yes	Yes				Yes	Yes
Iowa					Yes	Yes	Yes

Table 2. (Continued).

State	Exhausted FY1998 allotment by FY2001	Exhausted FY1999 allotment by FY2002	Exhausted FY2000 allotment by FY2003	Exhausted FY2001 allotment by FY2004	Exhausted FY2002 allotment by FY2005	Exhausted FY2003 allotment by FY2006	Exhausted FY2004 allotment by FY2007
Kansas			Yes	Yes	Yes	Yes	Yes
Kentucky	Yes	Yes	Yes	Yes	Yes	Yes	Yes
Louisiana					Yes	Yes	Yes
Maine	Yes	Yes	Yes	Yes	Yes	Yes	Yes
Maryland	Yes	Yes	Yes	Yes	Yes	Yes	Yes
Massachusetts	Yes	Yes	Yes	Yes	Yes	Yes	Yes
Michigan					Yes	Yes	Yes
Minnesota			Yes	Yes	Yes	Yes	Yes
Mississippi			Yes	Yes	Yes	Yes	Yes
Missouri	Yes	Yes			Yes	Yes	Yes
Montana					Yes	Yes	Yes
Nebraska				Yes	Yes	Yes	Yes
New Hampshire							Yes
New Jersey		Yes	Yes	Yes	Yes	Yes	Yes
New York	Yes	Yes	Yes	Yes	Yes	Yes	Yes
North Carolina	Yes	Yes		Yes	Yes	Yes	Yes
North Dakota						Yes	Yes
Ohio					Yes	Yes	Yes
Oklahoma						Yes	Yes
Oregon							Yes
Pennsylvania	Yes				Yes	Yes	Yes
Rhode Island	Yes	Yes	Yes	Yes	Yes	Yes	Yes
South Carolina	Yes	Yes	Yes			Yes	Yes
South Dakota				Yes	Yes	Yes	Yes
Utah						Yes	Yes
Vermont							Yes
Virginia						Yes	Yes
West Virginia			Yes	Yes	Yes	Yes	Yes
Wisconsin		Yes	Yes	Yes	Yes	Yes	Yes
Wyoming						Yes	Yes
US	12	13	14	19	28	40	44

Source: Congressional Research Service (CRS) analysis of data from the Centers for Medicare and Medicaid Services.

In the first reallocation legislation for FY1998 and FY1999 (P.L. 106-554), redistribution states (12 in FY1998 and 13 in FY1999) were given access to unspent funds from other states equal to their excess spending above their original allotments during the applicable three-year period. After a set-aside of 1.05% of the total unspent funds for territories that fully exhausted their original allotments (all five), the remaining unused funds were divided among the retention states in proportion to their contribution to the total pool of unspent funds. In contrast, under the second reallocation legislation for FY2000 and FY2001 (P.L. 108-74), a different rule was used. A set-aside of 1.05% of the total unspent funds was made for territories that fully exhausted their original allotments (again, all five). Then, retention states kept one-half of their unused funds. The remaining unspent funds were then distributed among redistribution states (14 for FY2000 and 19 for FY2001) in proportion to their contribution to the total pool of excess spending.[11]

Because no law was enacted specifying otherwise, the reallocation process followed BBA 97 requirements for unspent FY2002 funds. Under this law, unspent allotments are subject to redistribution among only those states that fully expend their allotments by the applicable three-year deadline, by a method to be determined by the Secretary of Health and Human Services. Six states that were projected to exhaust *all* of their available federal SCHIP accounts (excluding any possible FY2002 redistributed funds) in FY2005, based on their estimated FY2005 expenditures, received FY2002 redistribution money equal to that estimated shortfall. After eliminating these states' initial projected shortfall, the remaining balance of unspent FY2002 funds was then divided among a total of 28 redistribution states, including the six initial shortfall states, based on each such state's percentage of the total excess spending above the FY2002 allotments during the three-year period of availability of these funds.[12] Also according to BBA 97, reallocation pots expire at the end of one year. In the case of reallocated FY2002 funds, the expiration date was the end of FY2005.

For FY2006, the Secretary was required to distribute both unspent FY2003 original allotments and the new appropriation of $283 million from DRA for covering projected shortfalls. The only limitation in attempting to cover states' shortfalls was that the DRA funds could not pay for adult coverage. Without the DRA appropriation, 12 states were projected to face shortfalls, even with the $173 million available from the redistribution of unspent FY2003 original allotments. Based on states' projections at the time, the $283 million appropriation would have nearly eliminated the shortfalls among these 12 states. However, since then, two states (Illinois and Massachusetts) increased their FY2006 SCHIP spending such that they experienced shortfalls totaling approximately $100 million, almost all of that from Illinois.

In FY2007, $147 million in unspent FY2004 original allotments was available for redistribution. In the closing hours of the 109th Congress, a bill was passed to specify how those funds would be redistributed. The National Institutes of Health (NIH) Reform Act of 2006 (H.R. 6164, P.L. 109-482) required that the funds go to states "in the order in which such [shortfall] States realize monthly funding shortfalls ... for fiscal year 2007." The purpose was to delay any state facing a shortfall as far into the year as possible with the available funds. CRS projections indicated that this particular provision would delay shortfalls until the end of March. To delay shortfalls even further, the SCHIP provisions of H.R. 6164 called for an initial redistribution of up to half of unspent FY2005 original allotments as of March 31, 2007 (capped at $20 million per state) — after 2½ years of availability. For a state to forgo unspent FY2005 funds on that date, H.R. 6164 required not only that the state have unspent FY2005 balances but that the state's *total* SCHIP balances (from the FY2005-FY2007 original allotments) as of March 31, 2007, were at least double what the state projected to spend in federal SCHIP funds in FY2007. This was projected to provide an additional $138 million for shortfall states, delaying any state facing a shortfall of federal SCHIP funds until May 2007. The shortfalls remaining for the rest of the fiscal year were projected at just over $600 million in 12 states. Under P.L. 110-28, Congress appropriated up to $650 million to cover state shortfalls for the remainder of FY2007.

Other Factors Affecting Federal Financing

Like Medicaid, SCHIP is a federal-state matching program. For each dollar of state spending, the federal government makes a matching payment drawn from SCHIP accounts. A state's share of program spending for Medicaid is equal to 100% minus the federal medical assistance percentage (FMAP). The enhanced SCHIP FMAP is equal to a state's Medicaid FMAP increased by the number of percentage points that is equal to 30% multiplied by the number of percentage points by which the FMAP is less than 100%.[13] For example, in states with a Medicaid FMAP of 60%, the enhanced FMAP equals the Medicaid FMAP increased by 12 percentage points (60% + [30% multiplied by 40 percentage points] = 72%.) In this example, the state share is 100% - 72% = 28%.

In other words, the enhanced FMAP means a state's share of expenditures is 30% lower than under the regular FMAP. In the previous example, with the federal government paying 60% of Medicaid expenditures, the state's share was 40%. Under the enhanced FMAP in SCHIP, the state's share is 28% (i.e., 40% x 0.7).

Compared with the Medicaid FMAP, which ranges from 50% to 75.89% in FY2007, the enhanced FMAP for SCHIP ranges from 65% to 83.12%. All SCHIP assistance for targeted low-income children, including coverage provided under Medicaid, is eligible for the enhanced FMAP. The Medicaid FMAP and the enhanced SCHIP FMAP are subject to a ceiling of 83% and 85%, respectively.

There is a limit on federal spending for SCHIP administrative expenses, which include activities such as data collection and reporting, outreach and education, and other activities. For federal matching purposes, a 10% cap applies to state non-benefit expenses. This cap is tied to the dollar amount that a state draws down from its annual allotment to cover benefits and these non-benefit costs under SCHIP, as opposed to 10% of a state's total annual allotment. In other words, no more than 10% of the federal funds that a state draws down for SCHIP benefit and non-benefit expenditures combined can be used for non-benefit costs including administrative expenses.

General Program Characteristics

All 50 states, the District of Columbia, and five territories have SCHIP programs. As of June 2007, 15 use Medicaid expansions (including all five territories), 18 use separate state programs, and 23 use a combination approach. Three states received authority under the Balanced Budget Act of 1997 to operate previously existing comprehensive state-based plans as their separate SCHIP program. Among other types of separate SCHIP programs, data from 2005[14] indicate that most of the benchmark and benchmark-equivalent plans are based on the state employees' health plan, and most secretary-approved plans are modeled after Medicaid.

SCHIP programs across states are evolving rapidly, as evidenced by the numerous changes states have made to their original state plans over time. As of June 2007, 285 amendments to original state plans had been approved and 10 more were in review.[15] Most states have multiple amendments. The content of the plan amendments varies among states. For example, some states use amendments to extend coverage beyond income levels defined in their original state plans. Others define new copayment standards for program participants. Still others modify benefit packages.

In addition to the amendment process, states that want to make changes to their SCHIP programs that go beyond what the law will allow may do so through what is called a Section 1115 waiver (named for the section of the Social Security Act that defines the circumstances under which such waivers may be granted). The Secretary of Health and Human Services may waive certain statutory requirements for conducting research and demonstration projects under SCHIP that allow states to adapt their programs to specific needs. On August 4, 2001, the Bush Administration announced the Health Insurance Flexibility and Accountability (HIFA) Demonstration Initiative. Using Section 1115 waiver authority, this initiative is designed to encourage states to extend Medicaid and SCHIP to the uninsured, with a particular emphasis on statewide approaches that maximize private health insurance coverage options and target populations with income below 200% FPL.

For example, states have used this waiver authority to (1) provide services to individuals not traditionally eligible for SCHIP (e.g., parents of Medicaid or SCHIP-eligible children, caretaker relatives, legal guardians, and non-pregnant childless adults[16]); (2) extend access to premium assistance programs beyond current law constraints; (3) provide access to pregnancy-related services, including prenatal care and labor and delivery, and 60 days of postpartum care for the mother for populations not otherwise eligible for SCHIP (e.g., adult pregnant women); and (4) limit benefit packages for certain groups (e.g., provide access to "bare bones" benefit packages for specified groups, such as employees of small businesses). In addition to waiver authority, states may provide prenatal and labor/delivery services to unborn children through a state plan option that can be used to provide assistance to pregnant women aged 19 and older, and to pregnant individuals who do not qualify for Medicaid or SCHIP because of their immigration status, for example. As of March 2007, 16 states were granted Section 1115 demonstrations under the HIFA initiative, and 13 had approval to finance at least some of their adult coverage groups with unspent SCHIP funds. As of June 2007, 17 states offered pregnancy-related services using SCHIP funds. Of those, 11 states extended coverage through the unborn child state plan option, and 6 states used Section 1115 waiver authority.

Under SCHIP, states may purchase "family coverage" under an employer-sponsored health insurance plan if it is cost-effective relative to the amount paid to cover only the targeted low-income children and does not substitute for coverage under group health plans otherwise provided to the children. In addition, states using SCHIP funds for employer-based plan premiums must ensure that (1) SCHIP minimum benefits are provided, (2) SCHIP cost-sharing ceilings are met, and (3) the children to be enrolled have not had group coverage for a specified period of time (typically four to six months). Because of these requirements, implementation of premium assistance programs under SCHIP is not widespread. Also, as part of the HIFA initiative, states have used both Medicaid and SCHIP funds to pay premium costs for waiver enrollees who have access to employer-sponsored insurance (ESI). ESI programs approved under this waiver authority are not subject to the comprehensiveness, cost-effectiveness, and waiting period tests otherwise applicable to SCHIP's family coverage option. As of March 2007, 10 states reported operating a premium assistance program under SCHIP or Medicaid through waiver authority. (Other states may also be providing premium assistance through state plan amendments.)

TRENDS IN ENROLLMENT AND EXPENDITURES

Early enrollment estimates indicated that nearly 1 million children (982,000) were enrolled in SCHIP under 43 operational state programs as of December 1998.[17] Nearly two million children (1,979,450) were enrolled in SCHIP during FY1999 under 53 operational state programs.[18] The latest official numbers show that SCHIP enrollment reached a total of 6.7 million children in FY2006 (see table 1). Of this total, about 4.7 million were covered in separate state programs, and 2.0 million were targeted low-income children under Medicaid.

Ten states also reported enrollment of about 701,000 adults in SCHIP in FY2006 (see table 1). A substantial share of these adults (about 71%) were parents. A little over one-fourth were childless adults, and the remainder were pregnant women. Finally, in FY2006, adult enrollment exceeded child enrollment in three states (Arizona, Minnesota, and Wisconsin).

Expenditures under SCHIP have been the subject of much debate and controversy almost since the program's inception. Despite the fact that most states began enrolling children in SCHIP in late 1997 or 1998, new programs often take time to get off the ground and participation rates in the early years of SCHIP rose more slowly than expected. As a consequence, spending was slow to ramp up too, as evidenced by the fact that a minority of states (12 to 19, depending on the year) fully expended their original FY1998-FY2001 allotments by the applicable three-year deadlines (see table 2). It was not until FY2005, when the redistribution of unspent FY2002 funds took place, that more than half of the states (28) succeeded in qualifying for a portion of these unused funds because they spent all their own FY2002 allotments within the three-year period of availability. All but seven states exhausted their FY2004 allotments before FY2007. But only selected shortfall states actually received the unspent FY2004 funds, as described above.

Table 3 provides a historical snapshot of SCHIP funding and expenditures for FY1998-FY2005. A total of $30.5 billion of the total federal SCHIP appropriation of nearly $40 billion was made available to states and territories during this period. By the end of FY2005, nearly 77% ($23.4 billion) of these funds was spent. However, an additional $1.4 billion available to 11 states actually expired by the close of FY2005; these expired funds were comprised of unspent FY1998 to FY2002 reallocated monies. The column displaying net funds gained or lost through the reallocation process indicates that 31 states forfeited more funds to redistribution than they received. California (-$1.5 billion) and Texas (-$808 million) had the largest absolute net losses, while New York ($1.8 billion)[19] and New Jersey ($531 million) had the largest absolute net gains.

Table 4 displays available SCHIP funds and reported expenditures for FY2006. During FY2006, several SCHIP accounts were active:

- reallocated FY2003 funds and the new DRA appropriation of $283 million to cover shortfalls, available only in FY2006, and
- original allotments for FY2004, FY2005, and FY2006, each available for a three-year period.

As noted previously, 12 states (plus the five territories) received additional funds through the reallocation of unspent FY2003 funds and/or the DRA appropriation. After these distributions, and because actual expenditures ended up below states' projections, FY2006 shortfalls of federal SCHIP funds were averted in 10 of the 12 states projected to face shortfalls when DRA was developed. Illinois and Massachusetts experienced FY2006 shortfalls, but stopped claiming SCHIP funds before their balances were entirely depleted, which is why balances remain for them in table 4. Illinois estimated its FY2006 shortfall of federal SCHIP funds at approximately $95 million, and Massachusetts estimated its shortfall at approximately $7 million. The options these states tended to use in response to these shortfalls were (1) to delay claiming until the beginning of FY2007, when the new original allotment was available (although this would add to their FY2007 shortfall), and/or (2) to receive Medicaid funding for eligible claims, although at the regular FMAP rather than the enhanced SCHIP FMAP. Nationally, the end-of-FY2006 balances of federal SCHIP funds totaled approximately $4.6 billion, including $147 million in unspent FY2004 original allotments, which were redistributed to FY2007 shortfall states.

Table 3. Status of FY1998-FY2005 Federal SCHIP Funds, by State and Territory (millions of dollars)

States and territories	FY1998-FY2005 original SCHIP allotments	Net funds gained (forfeited) through reallocation of FY1998-FY2002 original allotments[a]	Federal SCHIP expenditures through the end of FY2005	Amount of expired FY1998-FY2002 reallocated SCHIP funds through the end of FY2005
Alabama	$541.1	($72.9)	$378.3	
Alaska	$61.0	$97.5	$134.3	$8.6
Arizona	$856.1	$25.0	$856.6	
Arkansas	$357.5	($134.0)	$130.5	$11.2
California	$5,454.4	($1,454.9)	$3,009.3	
Colorado	$349.9	($54.9)	$193.0	
Connecticut	$263.3	($82.9)	$109.5	
Delaware	$69.7	($25.0)	$23.5	
DC	$78.5	($24.3)	$37.7	
Florida	$1,780.4	$49.6	$1,426.5	
Georgia	$952.9	($36.9)	$835.4	
Hawaii	$80.7	($23.9)	$38.1	
Idaho	$141.5	($20.3)	$83.3	
Illinois	$1,087.1	($228.0)	$818.2	
Indiana	$492.1	$66.6	$439.0	
Iowa	$221.8	($10.8)	$190.8	
Kansas	$219.3	$31.6	$201.7	
Kentucky	$381.4	$239.9	$429.4	$98.5
Louisiana	$637.1	($127.3)	$423.2	
Maine	$94.0	$49.7	$115.8	$5.9
Maryland	$383.3	$389.9	$684.9	$8.1
Massachusetts	$386.5	$216.5	$501.9	$31.3
Michigan	$798.0	($152.6)	$521.3	
Minnesota	$255.5	$39.4	$273.9	
Mississippi	$386.4	$80.8	$450.9	
Missouri	$411.8	$41.2	$415.9	
Montana	$96.5	($5.2)	$70.0	
Nebraska	$125.9	$0.1	$125.4	
Nevada	$252.1	($59.2)	$117.5	
New Hampshire	$80.3	($30.0)	$28.6	
New Jersey	$660.0	$530.6	$1,140.9	

Table 3. (Continued).

States and territories	FY1998-FY2005 original SCHIP allotments	Net funds gained (forfeited) through reallocation of FY1998-FY2002 original allotments[a]	Federal SCHIP expenditures through the end of FY2005	Amount of expired FY1998-FY2002 reallocated SCHIP funds through the end of FY2005
New Mexico	$374.1	($144.3)	$88.9	$33.1
New York	$2,067.0	$1,788.2	$2,417.5	$951.1
North Carolina	$710.5	$165.1	$765.2	
North Dakota	$44.9	($7.5)	$28.4	
Ohio	$955.4	($14.2)	$804.7	
Oklahoma	$509.0	($170.7)	$255.3	
Oregon	$335.7	($112.0)	$134.9	
Pennsylvania	$934.4	($33.1)	$705.5	
Rhode Island	$71.7	$114.3	$185.9	
South Carolina	$451.1	$144.0	$359.1	$152.2
South Dakota	$58.9	($1.0)	$50.4	
Tennessee	$549.7	($189.1)	$68.0	$97.3
Texas	$3,469.5	($808.1)	$1,856.8	
Utah	$209.3	($11.4)	$146.1	
Vermont	$31.9	($6.2)	$16.8	
Virginia	$525.4	($133.6)	$286.2	
Washington	$414.1	($142.3)	$109.8	$11.5
West Virginia	$167.8	$24.7	$150.9	
Wisconsin	$354.8	$141.5	$437.2	
Wyoming	$51.7	($18.7)	$22.0	
Puerto Rico	$261.0	$90.9	$299.3	
Guam	$10.0	$3.5	$13.5	
Virgin Islands	$7.4	$2.6	$8.6	
American Samoa	$3.4	$1.2	$6.2	
N. Mariana Islands	$3.1	$1.1	$8.3	
Total	$30,528	$0	$23,431	$1,409

Source: Congressional Research Service (CRS) analysis of data from the Centers for Medicare and Medicaid Services.

Note: Data are not additive across columns.

For example, original allotments for FY2004 and FY2005 remain available to states beyond FY2005, while other accounts have closed or expired.

[a]. These reallocations were first active in FY2001-FY2005, respectively.

Table 4. Status of FY2006 Federal SCHIP Funds, by State and Territory (millions of dollars)

State	FY2006 SCHIP original allotments	Available balances from FY2004 and FY2005 original allotments	Net funds gained (forfeited) through reallocation of FY2003 allotments and from DRA appropriationa	A Total amount available in FY2006b	B FY2006 spending	C = A-B End-of-FY2006 balance
Alabama	$64.2	$90.0		$154.1	$87.4	$66.7
Alaska	$9.1	$15.6		$24.7	$19.5	$5.2
Arizona	$107.4	$24.5		$131.9	$109.0	$22.9
Arkansas	$43.8	$81.8		$125.6	$49.7	$76.0
California	$646.7	$990.2		$1,636.9	$1,150.9	$486.0
Colorado	$58.0	$102.1		$160.0	$60.2	$99.8
Connecticut	$34.5	$64.5	($6.4)	$99.1	$20.5	$78.6
Delaware	$9.0	$16.9	($4.3)	$25.9	$7.0	$18.9
DC	$9.6	$16.6		$26.1	$7.8	$18.3
Florida	$249.3	$403.5		$652.9	$214.1	$438.7
Georgia	$129.5	$80.6		$210.1	$192.3	$17.8
Hawaii	$12.4	$18.7		$31.1	$13.7	$17.4
Idaho	$20.6	$37.7	($0.2)	$58.3	$18.5	$39.8
Illinois	$169.2	$40.9	$117.5	$327.6	$324.3	$3.3
Indiana	$73.0	$119.7		$192.7	$78.8	$113.9
Iowa	$27.0	$20.2	$6.1	$53.3	$47.9	$5.5
Kansas	$27.5	$49.1		$76.6	$48.6	$28.0
Kentucky	$57.8	$93.3		$151.1	$77.1	$74.0
Louisiana	$77.1	$86.6		$163.8	$96.5	$67.2
Maine	$11.9	$21.9		$33.9	$24.5	$9.3
Maryland	$48.7	$80.3	$13.7	$142.7	$138.0	$4.7
Massachusetts	$59.4	$69.8	$21.9	$151.1	$151.1	$0.0
Michigan	$117.2	$124.2		$241.4	$175.5	$65.9
Minnesota	$39.4	$21.0	$20.1	$80.4	$66.1	$14.3
Mississippi	$49.9	$16.3	$73.6	$139.8	$103.3	$36.4
Missouri	$56.3	$37.1		$33.8	$17.3	$16.5
Montana	$12.6	$21.3		$33.8	$17.3	$16.5
Nebraska	$16.8	$0.6	$15.7	$33.2	$21.5	$11.7
Nevada	$41.9	$71.6	($3.9)	$113.4	$27.5	$86.0

Table 4. (Continued).

State	FY2006 SCHIP original allotments	Available balances from FY2004 and FY2005 original allotments	Net funds gained (forfeited) through reallocation of FY2003 allotments and from DRA appropriationa	A Total amount available in FY2006b	B FY2006 spending	C = A-B End-of-FY2006 balance
New Hampshire	$9.2	$17.3	($4.5)	$26.5	$9.9	$16.6
New Jersey	$89.5	$49.8	$105.6	$244.8	$242.1	$2.7
New Mexico	$42.2	$74.9	($32.8)	$117.1	$31.4	$85.7
New York	$272.5	$486.6		$759.1	$328.5	$430.5
North Carolina	$110.3	$110.3	$2.8	$223.4	$177.1	$46.3
North Dakota	$6.3	$9.0		$15.4	$10.7	$4.7
Ohio	$124.6	$136.5		$261.1	$169.8	$91.3
Oklahoma	$57.4	$83.1		$140.4	$81.1	$59.3
Oregon	$46.9	$85.3	($3.5)	$132.2	$58.4	$73.8
Pennsylvania	$134.1	$195.9		$330.0	$164.4	$165.6
Rhode Island	$9.8	$0.2	$66.1	$76.1	$69.7	$6.5
South Carolina	$55.5	$83.7		$139.3	$49.1	$90.1
South Dakota	$7.8	$7.5	$0.5	$15.9	$10.6	$5.3
Tennessee	$80.4	$136.9	($58.4)	$217.3	$0.0	$217.3
Texas	$454.7	$780.8	($23.8)	$1,235.6	$269.4	$966.2
Utah	$32.2	$51.8		$84.0	$45.3	$38.8
Vermont	$4.8	$8.7	($0.1)	$13.5	$4.8	$8.7
Virginia	$72.3	$105.6	($35.5)	$179.7	$36.2	$143.5
Washington	$64.7	$115.0	($35.5)	$179.7	$36.2	$143.5
West Virginia	$23.3	$41.6		$64.9	$33.7	$31.2
Wisconsin	$55.8	$59.1		$114.9	$88.2	$26.7
Wyoming	$5.9	$11.1		$16.9	$6.4	$10.6
Puerto Rico	$39.0	$52.6	$4.4	$95.9	$37.8	$58.2
Guam	$1.5	$0.0	$0.2	$1.7	$3.4	($1.7)
Virgin Islands	$1.1	$1.4	$0.1	$2.6	$1.9	$0.7
American Samoa	$0.5	$0.0	$0.1	$0.6	$0.8	($0.2)

Table 4. (Continued).

State	FY2006 SCHIP original allotments	Available balances from FY2004 and FY2005 original allotments	Net funds gained (forfeited) through reallocation of FY2003 allotments and from DRA appropriationa	A Total amount available in FY2006b	B FY2006 spending	C = A-B End-of-FY2006 balance
N. Mariana Islands	$0.5	$0.0	$0.1	$0.5	$0.5	$0.1
National total	$4,082.4	$5,521.1	$283.0	$10,059.9	$5,453.7	$4,606.2

Source: Congressional Research Service (CRS) analysis of data from the Centers for Medicare and Medicaid Services.

[a]. Redistributed FY2003 funds and the Deficit Reduction Act of 2005 (DRA) appropriation of $283 million for SCHIP are active only during FY2006. States with blank cells in this column exhausted their FY2003 allotments by the three-year deadline and did not face shortfalls in FY2006. In prior reallocations, all such states received a portion of unspent funds available for redistribution. The unspent FY2003 funds went only to states expected to have shortfalls in FY2006.

[b]. This column shows the sum of only the positive numbers in the previous three columns. In the third column, the negative numbers in parentheses refer to amounts unspent and forfeited at the end of FY2005, and thus were no longer available to these states at the beginning of FY2006. For states with negative values in the third column, this column is equal to the sum of the first and second columns.

FORTHCOMING SCHIP ISSUES

SCHIP has federal appropriations for the current fiscal year, but none are slated for FY2008 and beyond. Before the August recess, Congress passed legislation (H.R. 3162 in the House and S. 1893/H.R. 976 in the Senate) that would provide additional funding for SCHIP for FY2008 and additional years, and would make a number of other changes to both SCHIP and Medicaid. For a detailed description of the proposed changes in each bill, see CRS Report RL34129, *Medicaid and SCHIP Provisions in H.R. 3162 and S. 1893/H.R. 976.*

SCHIP LEGISLATIVE HISTORY

Below is a summary of major SCHIP changes enacted in public laws beginning with the legislation authorizing the program in 1997:

Balanced Budget Act of 1997 (BBA 97), P.L. 105-33:

1. *Creation of SCHIP.* — Under BBA 97, the State Children's Health Insurance Program was established, effective August 5, 1997. A number of provisions specified eligibility criteria; coverage requirements for health insurance; federal allotments and the state allocation formula; payments to states and the enhanced FMAP formula; the process for submission, approval and amendment of state SCHIP plans; strategic objectives and performance goals, and plan administration; annual reports and evaluations; options for expanding coverage of children under Medicaid; and diabetes grant programs.
2. *CBO Scoring.* — In making its cost estimates, the Congressional Budget Office (CBO) is required to assume that programs in existence on or before the enactment of BBA97 (which would include SCHIP) that lack future appropriations but with current-year outlays of at least $50 million will continue operating at the last appropriated level. SCHIP's last appropriated level is approximately $5 billion in FY2007. Thus, legislation that simply appropriates $5.0 billion annually beyond FY2007 would not be scored by CBO as increasing federal government spending above its current baseline.

District of Columbia Appropriations Act of 1998, P.L. 105-100:

1. *Increased Appropriation.* This law increased the FY1998 SCHIP appropriation from $4.275 billion to $4.295 billion.

Omnibus Consolidated and Emergency Supplemental Appropriation Act, FY1999, P.L. 105-277:

1. *Increased Appropriation for Territories.* For FY1999, an additional appropriation of $32 million for the territories was provided, bringing the FY1999 total appropriation to $4.307 billion.

2. *Freeze Each State's Share of Appropriation.* Each state's percentage of the total appropriation available to states for the FY1998 SCHIP allotments was also used for determining the FY1999 allotments.
3. *Change in Allotment Formula Affecting Some Native American Children.* For FY1998 and FY1999, the law changed the annual state allotment formula by stipulating that children with access to health care funded by the Indian Health Service and no other health insurance would be counted as uninsured (rather than as insured as required under the previously existing law).

The Medicare, Medicaid and SCHIP Balanced Budget Refinement Act of 1999 (BBRA 99), incorporated by reference in the Consolidated Appropriations Act for Fiscal Year 2000, P.L. 106-113:

1. *Stabilizing the SCHIP Allotment Formula.* Annual federal allotments to each state are determined in part by states' success in covering previously uninsured low-income children under SCHIP. Under prior law, the more successful a state was in enrolling children in SCHIP, especially early in the program, the greater the potential reduction in subsequent annual allotments. To limit the amount a state's allocation can fluctuate from one year to the next, BBRA 99 modified the allotment distribution formula and established new floors and ceilings.
2. *Targeted, Increased Allotments.* Additional allotments for the commonwealths and territories were provided for FY2000-FY2007.
3. *Improved Data Collection.* The law provided new funding for the collection of data to produce reliable, annual state-level estimates of the number of uninsured children. These data changes will improve research and evaluation efforts. They will also affect state-specific counts of the number of low-income children and the number of such children who are uninsured that feed into the formula that determines annual state-specific allotments from federal SCHIP appropriations.
4. *Federal Evaluation.* New funding was also provided for a federal evaluation[20] to identify effective outreach and enrollment practices for both SCHIP and Medicaid, barriers to enrollment, and factors influencing beneficiary drop-out.
5. *Additional Reports and a Clearinghouse.* The law also required (a) an inspector general audit[21] and GAO report on enrollment of Medicaid-eligible children in SCHIP,[22] (b) states to report annually the number of deliveries to pregnant women and the number of infants who receive services under the Maternal and Child Health Services Block Grant or who are entitled to SCHIP benefits, and (c) the Secretary of Health and Human Services to establish a clearinghouse for the consolidation and coordination of all federal databases and reports regarding children's health.

Agriculture Risk Protection Act of 2000, P.L. 106-224:

1. *Information Sharing.* This law allows schools operating federally subsidized school meal programs to take a more active role in identifying children eligible for, and enrolling such children in, the Medicaid and SCHIP programs. It permits schools to share income and other relevant information collected when determining eligibility for free and reduced-price school meals with state Medicaid and SCHIP agencies, as

long as there is a written agreement that limits use of the information and parents are notified and given a chance to "opt out."

2. *Demonstration Project.* The law also establishes a demonstration project in one state in which administrative funds under the Special Supplemental Nutrition Program for Women, Infants and Children (WIC) may be used to help identify children eligible for, and enroll such children in, the Medicaid and SCHIP programs.

Children's Health Act of 2000, P.L. 106-310:

1. *Rights of Institutionalized Children.* The law requires that general hospitals, nursing facilities, intermediate care facility and other health care facilities receiving federal funds, including SCHIP, protect the rights of each resident, including the right to be free from physical or mental abuse, corporal punishment, and any restraints or involuntary seclusions imposed for the purposes of discipline or convenience. Restraints and seclusion may be imposed in such facilities only to ensure the physical safety of the resident, a staff member or others. Additional requirements govern reporting of resident deaths, promulgation of regulations regarding staff training, and enforcement.
2. *Children's Rights in Community-Based Settings.* The law also includes requirements for protecting the rights of residents of certain non-medical, community-based facilities for children and adolescents, when that facility receives funding under this act or under Medicaid. (Existing regulations do not clarify if and how these rights apply to such facilities funded by SCHIP.) For such individuals and facilities, restraints and seclusion may only be imposed in emergency circumstances and only to ensure the physical safety of the resident, a staff member or others, and less restrictive interventions have been determined to be ineffective. Additional requirements govern reporting of resident deaths, promulgation of regulations regarding staff training, and enforcement.

Medicare, Medicaid and SCHIP Benefits Improvement and Protection Act of 2000 (BIPA), incorporated by reference into the Consolidated Appropriations Act 2001, P.L. 106-554:

1. *Special Redistribution Rules for Unspent FY1998 and FY1999 Allotments.* For each of these years separately, a pool of unspent funds is created from the unused allotment amounts of those states that did not fully expend their original allotments within the applicable three-year time frame. From this pool, 1.05% is set aside for the territories that fully exhaust their original allotments. Each such territory receives a percentage of the available 1.05% pool equal to that territory's original allotment divided by the sum of original allotments for such territories. Then the states that *did* fully expend their original allotments within the three-year deadline receive access to redistributed funds from the remaining pool equal to the amount by which their three-year spending exceeds their original allotments.[23] The remaining states that did *not* use all their original allotments for the year retain access to a portion of the remaining funds in the pool, equal to the ratio of such a state's unspent original allotment to the total amount of unspent funds for that fiscal year. These latter states

are permitted to use up to 10% of their retained FY1998 funds for outreach activities. This allowance is over and above spending for such activities under the general administrative cap described above. The deadline for spending all redistributed and retained funds from FY1998 and FY1999 is September 30, 2002, although this date was extended by P.L. 108-74 as described below. (See the text for additional information on redistribution of unspent SCHIP funds.)

2. *Presumptive Eligibility.* Under Medicaid presumptive eligibility rules, states are allowed to temporarily enroll children whose family income appears to be below Medicaid income standards, until a final formal determination of eligibility is made. BIPA clarified states' authority to conduct presumptive eligibility determinations, as defined in Medicaid law, under separate (non-Medicaid) SCHIP programs.
3. *Authority to Pay SCHIP Medicaid Expansion Costs from Title XXI Appropriation.* Under prior law, states' allotments under SCHIP paid only the federal share of costs associated with separate (non-Medicaid) SCHIP programs. The federal share of costs associated with covering targeted low-income children under Medicaid was paid for by Medicaid. State SCHIP allotments were reduced by the amounts paid by Medicaid for such costs. BIPA authorized the payment of the costs of targeted low-income children under Medicaid, and the costs of benefits provided during periods of presumptive eligibility, from the SCHIP appropriation rather than the Medicaid appropriation, and as a conforming amendment, eliminated the requirement that state SCHIP allotments be reduced by these (former) Medicaid payments. Also, for FY1998-FY2000 only, BIPA authorized the transfer of unexpended SCHIP appropriations to the Medicaid appropriation account for the purpose of reimbursing payments made on behalf of targeted low-income children under Medicaid.

Public Health Security and Bioterrorism Preparedness and Response Act of 2002, P.L. 107-188:

1. *Waiver of Provider Requirements and Medicare+Choice Payment Limits.* The law authorizes the Secretary to temporarily waive conditions of participation and other certification requirements for any entity that furnishes health care items or services to Medicare, Medicaid, or SCHIP beneficiaries in an emergency area during a declared disaster or public health emergency. During such an emergency, the Secretary may waive: (a) participation, state licensing (as long as an equivalent license from another state is held and there is no exclusion from practicing in that state or any state in the emergency area), and pre-approval requirements for physicians and other practitioners; (b) sanctions for failing to meet requirements for emergency transfers between hospitals; (c) sanctions for physician self-referral; and (d) limitations on payments for health care and services furnished to individuals enrolled in Medicare+Choice (M+C) plans when services are provided outside the plan. To the extent possible, the Secretary must ensure that M+C enrollees do not pay more than would have been required had they received care within their plan network.
2. *Notification to Congress.* The law also requires the Secretary to provide Congress with certification and written notice at least two days prior to exercising this waiver authority. It also provides for this waiver authority to continue for 60 days, and permits the Secretary to extend the waiver period.

3. *Evaluation.* The Secretary is further required, within one year after the end of the emergency, to provide Congress with an evaluation of this approach and recommendations for improvements under this waiver authority.

Health Care Safety Net Amendments of 2002, P.L. 107-251:

1. *Study of Migrant Farm Workers.* This law requires the Secretary to conduct a study of the problems experienced by farm workers and their families under Medicaid and SCHIP, specifically, barriers to enrollment, and lack of portability of Medicaid and SCHIP coverage for farm workers eligible in one state who move to other states on a periodic basis. The Secretary must also identify possible strategies to increase enrollment and access to benefits for these families. Strategies to be examined must include (a) use of interstate compacts to establish portability and reciprocity, (b) multi-state demonstration projects, (c) use of current law flexibility for coverage of residents and out-of-state coverage, (d) development of programs of national migrant family coverage, (e) use of incentives to private coverage alternatives, and (f) other solutions as deemed appropriate. In conducting the study, the Secretary must consult with several groups. The Secretary must submit a report on this study to the President and Congress in October 2003. This report shall address findings and conclusions and provide recommendations for appropriate legislative and administrative action.

State Children's Health Insurance Program Allotments Extension Act, P.L. 108-74:

1. *Extension of Available SCHIP Reallocated Funds from FY1998 and FY1999.* This law extends the availability of FY1998 and FY1999 reallocated funds through the end of FY2004 (rather than the end of FY2002).
2. *Revision of Methods for Reallocation of Unspent FY2000 and FY2001, and Extension of the Availability of Such Funds.* The law also establishes a new method for reallocating unspent funds from FY2000 and FY2001 allotments. For each of these years separately, a pool of unspent funds is created from the unused allotment amounts of those states that did not fully expend their original allotments within the applicable three-year time frame. From this pool, 1.05% is set aside for the territories that fully exhaust their original allotments. Each such territory receives a percentage of the available 1.05% pool equal to that territory's original allotment divided by the sum of original allotments for such territories. For each year separately, each state that does *not* spend its full original allotment by the three-year deadline retains 50% of its unspent funds. Then the remaining pool is allocated to each state that fully expends (exceeds) its original allotment by the three-year deadline. The redistribution amount for each such state is based on the proportion of its excess spending relative to the total amount of excess spending for all such states. Reallocated funds for FY2000 and FY2001 are available until the end of FY2004 and FY2005, respectively.
3. *Authority for Qualifying States to Use Certain Funds for Medicaid Expenditures.* For specific expenditures occurring after August 15, 2003, the law permits certain states to apply federal SCHIP funds toward the coverage of certain children enrolled in

regular Medicaid (not a SCHIP Medicaid expansion). Specifically, qualifying states may spend their available balances from FY1998-FY2001 (up to a maximum of 20% of those original allotments) for services delivered to Medicaid beneficiaries under age 19 who are not otherwise eligible for SCHIP and have family income that exceeds 150% of the FPL. For such services, these federal SCHIP funds can be used to pay the difference between the SCHIP enhanced federal matching rate and the regular Medicaid federal matching rate the state receives for these children. Qualifying states include those that on or after April 15, 1997 had an income eligibility standard of at least 185% of the FPL for at least one category of children, other than infants. (Other qualifications apply to states with statewide waivers under Section 1115 of the Social Security Act.) Under this law, the qualifying states included Connecticut, Minnesota, New Hampshire, Tennessee, Vermont, Washington, and Wisconsin. (See below for changes to this section of this law.)

Technical Corrections with Respect to the Definition of Qualifying State, P.L. 108-127:

1. *Change in the Income Standard and Applicable Dates.* This law modified P.L. 108-74 by changing the income eligibility standard affecting some qualifying states from 185% to 184% of the FPL. It also modified applicable dates with respect to certain states with Section 1115 waivers that covered children in families with income of at least 185% of the FPL. The effect of these changes was to add four states (i.e., Hawaii, Maryland, New Mexico, and Rhode Island) to the set of qualifying states, thus allowing them to also use certain funds for Medicaid expenditures (see above description for P.L. 108-74).

Deficit Reduction Act of 2005, P.L. 109-171:

1. *Additional allotments to eliminate FY2006 funding shortfalls.* This law appropriated $283 million for shortfall states and territories in FY2006. A shortfall state was defined as a state that the Secretary estimated would have expenditures in FY2006 that exceed the sum of all available SCHIP funds in that year (i.e., reallocated unspent FY2003 funds, balances remaining from FY2004 and FY2005 original allotments, and FY2006 original allotments), based on the most recent SCHIP data as of December 31, 2005. From the new FY2006 appropriation, after a 1.05% set-aside for the territories, each FY2006 shortfall state received an allotment intended to cover its projected shortfall. On October 1, 2006, any remaining unspent additional allotments revert to the Treasury. The additional FY2006 appropriation is restricted to payments for benefits provided to targeted low-income children only.
2. *Prohibition against covering non-pregnant, childless adults with SCHIP funds.* The Secretary of HHS is prohibited from approving new 1115 waivers, on or after October 1, 2005, that would use SCHIP funds to provide coverage to non-pregnant, childless adults. The Secretary may continue to approve projects that expand SCHIP to caretaker relatives of Medicaid- or SCHIP-eligible children, and to pregnant adults. Existing waivers that use SCHIP funds to cover non-pregnant, childless adults (including extensions, amendments, and renewals of such waivers) that were approved before enactment of DRA are allowed to continue.

3. *Continued authority for qualifying states to use SCHIP funds for certain Medicaid expenditures.* The law allows qualifying states to use any available FY2001, FY2004, and FY2005 SCHIP funds (i.e., original allotments and/or reallocated funds, as applicable) for coverage of certain children enrolled in regular Medicaid (not an SCHIP Medicaid expansion) for such Medicaid payments made on or after October 1, 2005, up to the 20% allowance. See the discussion of P.L. 108-74 and P.L. 108-127 for more details.

National Institutes of Health Reform Act of 2006, P.L. 109-482:[24]

1. *Prioritizing Redistribution of Unspent FY2004 Original Allotments.* The Secretary of HHS is required to redistribute unspent FY2004 original allotments to states in the order in which they are projected to exhaust their federal SCHIP funds.
2. *Early, Partial Redistribution of Unspent FY2005 Original Allotments.* An initial redistribution is required of up to half of states' unspent FY2005 original allotments as of March 31, 2007 (capped at $20 million per state) — after 2½ years of availability. For a state to forgo unspent FY2005 funds on that date, the state's *total* SCHIP balances (from the FY2005-FY2007 original allotments) as of March 31, 2007, must be at least double what the state projects to spend in federal SCHIP funds in FY2007. These funds would also be targeted to shortfall states in the order in which those shortfalls are experienced. The initial redistribution of unspent FY2005 funds does not replace the regular redistribution at the end of the allotment's three-year period of availability. Thus, among the states that forgo half of their unspent FY2005 funds on March 31, 2007, any amount still unspent at the end of FY2007 will be redistributed to other states after having been available for three years.
3. *Limitations on Spending.* The FY2004 and FY2005 redistributed funds available in FY2007 may only be used to cover populations eligible in a state's SCHIP program as of October 1, 2006. The FY2004 and FY2005 redistributed funds may pay only the regular FMAP, rather than the enhanced SCHIP FMAP, for non-pregnant adults enrolled in SCHIP. The Secretary is authorized to alter the amount of FY2004 and FY2005 redistributed funds received by states on the basis of actual end-of-FY2007 expenditures, to account for how actual expenditures may differ from the projections on which the initial redistributions are based, with some limitations. The territories do not receive any FY2004 and FY2005 redistributed funds in FY2007.
4. *Continued authority for qualifying states to use SCHIP funds for certain Medicaid expenditures.* The law allows qualifying states to use any available FY2006 and FY2007 SCHIP funds (in addition to the FY2005 funds) for coverage of certain children enrolled in regular Medicaid (not an SCHIP Medicaid expansion), up to the 20% allowance. See the discussion of P.L. 108-74 and P.L. 108-127 for more details.

U.S. Troop Readiness, Veterans' Care, Katrina Recovery, and Iraq Accountability Appropriations Act, 2007, P.L. 110-28:

1. *Elimination of remainder of SCHIP funding shortfalls, tiered match, and other limitation on expenditures.* This law required the Secretary of HHS to allot to certain shortfall states the amount determined by the Secretary to eliminate each such state's

estimated FY2007 shortfall, not to exceed a total of $650 million for all such states. Shortfall states are defined as those for which projected FY2007 federal expenditures would exceed the sum of (1) the amount of the state's unspent FY2005 and FY2006 allotments still available by the end of FY2006, (2) the state's FY2007 allotment, and (3) the amounts of redistributed FY2004 and FY2005 funds available to the state in FY2007 (if any). It also eliminated the requirement in NIHRA that redistributed FY2004 and FY2005 funds pay only the regular FMAP for non-pregnant adults in SCHIP.

2. *Prohibition.* P.L. 110-28 also prohibited the Secretary of HHS from taking an administrative action to finalize or otherwise implement Medicaid administrative proposals related to intergovernmental transfers (payments for government providers) and graduate medical education for one year from the date of enactment of this law.
3. *Requirement for use of tamper-resistant prescription pads under the Medicaid Program.* The law requires the use of tamper-resistant pads for Medicaid prescriptions executed after September 30, 2007. It also allows any state operating a Medicaid Pharmacy Plus waiver that would otherwise expire on June 30, 2007, to continue operating the waiver through December 31, 2009.

REFERENCES

[1] See CRS Report RS21054, Medicaid and SCHIP Section 1115 Research and Demonstration Waivers, by Evelyne P. Baumrucker.

[2] In 2007, the poverty guideline in the 48 contiguous states and the District of Columbia is $20,650 for a family of four. ("Annual Update of the HHS Poverty Guidelines," 72 Federal Register 3147, January 24, 2007.)

[3] Under Medicaid law, Section 1902(r)(2) authority may be used to liberalize income and resource methodologies for a number of groups, including, for example, poverty-related children (i.e., those under age 6 in families with income up to 133% FPL and those between ages 6 and 18 in families with income up to 100% FPL). That same authority can be used to liberalize financial rules for SCHIP purposes. Family coverage is provided under Section 1931. This section has its own provisions for liberalizing income and resource standards.

[4] Personal communication with Judy Rhoades, Centers for Medicare and Medicaid Services, June 5, 2003.

[5] Because individuals can have other health insurance and still be covered by Medicaid, this approach also allows states to bring into Medicaid otherwise ineligible higher-income children regardless of their other health insurance status. Under this strategy, for example, states can provide Medicaid benefits to additional children whose existing health insurance is limited (sometimes referred to as under-insured). When states liberalize the financial rules for existing Medicaid eligibility groups, the federal share of the costs for services provided to the subset without other health insurance — the targeted low-income children — is paid for out of SCHIP funds (described in further

detail below). The federal share of the costs for services delivered to the remaining children with other health insurance is paid for by Medicaid.

[6] For determining financial eligibility for SCHIP and Medicaid, certain types and/or amounts of income are not counted. These are called "income disregards." For example, specified dollar amounts may be subtracted from gross income to calculate net income, which is then compared to the applicable income criterion.

[7] States may apply resource, or asset, tests in determining financial eligibility, but are not required to do so. In states with a resource test, individuals must have resources for which the dollar value is less than a specified standard amount in order to qualify for coverage. States determine what items constitute countable resources and the dollar value assigned to those countable resources. Assets may include, for example, cars, savings accounts, real estate, trust funds, tax credits, etc. In 2005, asset/resource tests were an eligibility criteria in only four states — Idaho, Missouri, Oregon and Texas (see N. Kaye, et al., Charting SCHIP III: An Analysis of the Third Comprehensive Survey of State Children's Health Insurance Programs, National Academy for State Health Policy (NASHP), September 2006, [http://www.chipcentral.org/Files/Charting _CHIP_III_9-21-6.pdf], pp. 42-43).

[8] When the law establishing SCHIP was enacted, existing programs financed entirely by the state in Florida, New York, and Pennsylvania were designated as meeting the minimum benefit requirements under SCHIP (i.e., these programs were grandfathered into SCHIP).

[9] P.L. 109-432 modified DRA by specifying cost-sharing rules for individuals in families with income under 100% FPL. For additional information, see CRS Report RS22578, Medicaid Cost-Sharing under the Deficit Reduction Act of 2005 (DRA), by Elicia J. Herz.

[10] From the original appropriated amounts specified in BBA 97, the law set aside 0.25% of SCHIP funds for five territories (Puerto Rico, Guam, Virgin Islands, American Samoa, and the Northern Mariana Islands). Later, funds were added to the total annual appropriation and earmarked for the territories for each year beginning in FY1999. For FY1998-FY2002 only, $60 million annually was set aside for special diabetes grants.

[11] Finally, P.L. 108-74 also permits certain states to spend their available balances from FY1998-FY2001 (up to a maximum of 20% of those original allotments) for services delivered to Medicaid beneficiaries under age 19 who are not otherwise eligible for SCHIP and have family income that exceeds 150% of the FPL. Subsequently, P.L. 108-127 modified the definition of a state that qualifies to make such expenditures. In addition, P.L. 109-171 (DRA) continued this authority with respect to FY2004 and FY2005 funds. See the "SCHIP Legislative History" section below for details.

[12] All five territories also exceeded their FY2002 original allotments by the three-year deadline. As with prior redistributions (see the "SCHIP Legislative History" section below for more details), 1.05% of all unspent FY2002 funds was set aside for the territories. Each received an amount equal to its original allotment for FY2002 divided by the sum of FY2002 allotments among the territories.

[13] The federal medical assistance percentage (FMAP) and the enhanced federal medical assistance percentage (enhanced FMAP) are calculated and published annually by the Secretary of DHHS. FMAP is a measure of the per capita income in each state, squared,

compared to that of the nation as a whole. This formula is designed to provide a higher FMAP to states with lower per capita income.

[14] CRS analysis of unpublished data from a 2005 survey of state SCHIP programs conducted by the National Academy for State Health Policy (NASHP). For more information about this survey, see [http://www.chipcentral.org/Files/ Charting_CHIP_III_9-21-6.pdf].

[15] The source for this information can be found online at [http://www.cms.hhs.gov/LowCostHealthInsFamChild/downloads/SCHIPStatePlanActivityMap.pdf], as of June 1, 2007.

[16] The Deficit Reduction Act of 2005 (P.L. 109-171) prohibits the use of SCHIP funds for coverage of non-pregnant childless adults in any new waivers approved after February 8, 2006.

[17] U.S. Health Care Financing Administration, A Preliminary Estimate of the Children's Health Insurance Program Aggregate Enrollment Numbers Through Dec. 31, 1998 (background only), April 20, 1999.

[18] U.S. Health Care Financing Administration, The State Children's Health Insurance Program, Annual Enrollment Report, Oct. 1, 1998-Sept. 30, 1999 (no date).

[19] Even though New York gained access to a lot of additional federal dollars through reallocations during this period, $951 million in SCHIP funds for this state still expired by the end of FY2005.

[20] Implementation of the State Children's Health Insurance Program: Momentum is Increasing After a Modest Start, First Annual Report, Cambridge, MA: Mathematica Policy Research, Inc., January 2001. For additional reports describing results from other components of the national evaluation of SCHIP, go to [http://aspe.os.dhhs.gov/health/schip/background.htm].

[21] The OIG has issued two audit reports: Department of Health and Human Services, Office of Inspector General, State Children's Health Insurance Program: Assessment of State Evaluations Reports, OEI-05-00-00240, February 2001, and Department of Health and Human Services, Office of Inspector General, State Children's Health Insurance Program: Ensuring Medicaid Eligibles are not Enrolled in SCHIP, OEI-05-00-00241, February 2001.

[22] U.S. General Accounting Office, Children's Health Insurance: Inspector General Reviews Should Be Expanded to Further Inform the Congress, GAO-02-512, March 2002.

[23] For example, if a state's FY1998 allotment was $10 million, and the state's FY1998, FY1999 and FY2000 spending totaled $12 million, the state would receive access to a redistribution of $2 million.

[24] For additional detail on the legislation and its projected impact on SCHIP, see CRS Report RS22553, SCHIP Provisions of H.R. 6164 (NIH Reform Act of 2006), by Chris L. Peterson.

In: State Children's Health Insurance Program (SCHIP) ISBN: 978-1-60456-333-7
Editor: Mary T. Ewing, pp. 129-150

Chapter 4

MEDICAID AND SCHIP: FY2007 BUDGET ISSUES*

April Grady, Jean Hearne and Elicia J. Herz

ABSTRACT

Each year, the President is required to submit a comprehensive federal budget proposal to Congress no later than the first Monday in February. Once it is submitted, the Congressional Budget Office (CBO) analyzes the proposal using its own economic assumptions and estimation techniques. Then, the House and Senate Budget Committees each develop a budget resolution after reviewing the President's budget, the views of other committees, and information from CBO. Differences between the houses are supposed to be resolved by April 15, but this deadline is rarely met. Although it is not binding, the resolution provides a framework for subsequent legislative action on the budget (e.g., annual appropriations bills).

The President's FY2007 budget contains a number of proposals that would affect Medicaid and the State Children's Health Insurance Program (SCHIP). Some are program expansions, and others are designed to reduce federal spending. While certain proposals would require legislative action, others would be implemented administratively (e.g., via regulatory changes, issuance of program guidance, etc.).

On March 9, 2006, the Senate Budget Committee reported a budget resolution, S.Con.Res. 83, which was subsequently amended and passed by the Senate on March 16. The resolution did not include reconciliation instructions for the Senate Finance Committee, which has jurisdiction over Medicaid and SCHIP. It did include a deficit-neutral reserve fund for the uninsured and funding for four of the President's Medicaid and SCHIP proposals.

On March 29, 2006, the House Budget Committee reported its own budget resolution, H.Con.Res. 376, which was subsequently amended and passed by the House on May 18. The resolution did not include reconciliation instructions for the House Energy and Commerce Committee, which has jurisdiction over Medicaid and SCHIP. Its spending levels for Medicaid and SCHIP are based on CBO's baseline projections under current law and policies, with no reduction in Medicaid assumed.

Although no agreement was reached by the House and Senate on a FY2007 budget resolution, current law spending for Medicaid and SCHIP is unaffected. As entitlement

* Excerpted from CRS Report RL33272, dated December 28, 2006.

programs, their spending levels are based on the underlying benefit and eligibility criteria established in law (in the case of SCHIP, these criteria include a statutory annual funding cap). However, legislation that would increase Medicaid or SCHIP spending above current law could encounter procedural roadblocks in the House or Senate if funding is not assumed in a budget resolution or in a "deeming resolution." The annual appropriations process also provides an opportunity for Congress to place limitations on the availability of federal funds for specified Medicaid and SCHIP activities.

Before the 109th Congress adjourned, it passed two bills — H.R. 6111 and H.R. 6164 — that addressed a variety of Medicaid and SCHIP issues, including some of the proposals in the President's FY2007 budget.

INTRODUCTION

Each year, the President is required to submit a comprehensive federal budget proposal to Congress no later than the first Monday in February. Once it is submitted, the Congressional Budget Office (CBO) analyzes the proposal using its own economic assumptions and estimation techniques. Then, the House and Senate Budget Committees each develop a budget resolution after reviewing the President's budget, the views of other committees, and information from CBO. Differences between the houses are supposed to be resolved by April 15, but this deadline is rarely met. Although it is not binding, the resolution provides a framework for subsequent legislative action on the budget (e.g., annual appropriations bills).

This report provides information on Medicaid and State Children's Health Insurance Program (SCHIP) budget issues for FY2007. It will be updated to reflect relevant activity until the President's FY2008 budget is released.

MEDICAID AND SCHIP IN THE PRESIDENT'S FY2007 BUDGET

The President's FY2007 budget contains a number of proposals that would affect Medicaid and SCHIP. Some are program expansions, and others are designed to reduce federal spending. For each of the proposals, this report provides:

- background information;
- a description of the proposal based on available information;[1] and
- a list of relevant Congressional Research Service (CRS) reports.

The proposals generally are presented in the order in which they appear in the Department of Health and Human Services' (HHS) *Fiscal Year 2007 Budget in Brief*. The description of each proposal includes HHS and CBO estimates of its cost or savings in FY2007 and over the FY2007-FY2011 period. These estimates are summarized in table 1. CRS staff contact information by Medicaid and SCHIP topic area is provided in table 2, at the end of the report.

Legislative Versus Administrative Proposals

As shown in table 1, some of the President's proposals would require legislative action, while others would be implemented administratively (e.g., via regulatory changes, issuance of program guidance, etc.).

In their analyses of the President's budget, both CBO and executive branch agencies such as HHS and the Office of Management and Budget (OMB) provide baseline (current law) estimates of Medicaid and SCHIP spending along with estimated costs and savings of proposed changes. However, CBO and the executive branch differ in their treatment of legislative and administrative proposals.

In executive branch documents describing the President's budget, implementation of proposed administrative changes is assumed in estimates of baseline Medicaid and SCHIP spending, and estimates for legislative proposals are presented separately.[2] In general, CBO only adjusts its baseline estimates to account for administrative changes as they are implemented — rather than as they are proposed — and only provides separate estimates for legislative proposals. For this reason and others, CBO and executive branch estimates of Medicaid and SCHIP spending will differ.

Among the administrative proposals in the President's FY2007 budget, two have received widespread attention — limiting the extent to which states may tax certain health care providers to obtain additional federal Medicaid dollars, and a plan to cap Medicaid payments to government providers to no more than the cost of furnishing services. In May and June of 2006, respectively, members of the House and Senate sent separate letters to HHS Secretary Leavitt urging him to not implement changes to Medicaid via administrative action. Both letters cited the importance of review and input from Congress in modifying Medicaid.[3] As described later, before adjourning, the 109th Congress passed legislation (H.R. 6111) that prevents the President's provider tax proposal from being implemented.

The Congress also passed legislation to address transitional medical assistance (H.R. 6111) and FY2007 SCHIP shortfalls (H.R. 6164), two issues for which legislative proposals were included in the President's FY2007 budget.

Table 1. Cost (Savings) of Medicaid and SCHIP Proposals in the President's FY2007 Budget

Proposal	Outlays in millions			
	HHS estimate		CBO estimate	
	FY2007	FY2007-FY2011	FY2007	FY2007-FY2011
Medicaid	($1,487)	($14,015)	($948)	($4,545)
Legislative proposals	($158)	($1,772)	($948)	($4,545)
Transitional medical assistance (Medicaid impact)	$180	$360	$129	$526
Vaccines for Children	$140	$700	$115	$715
Expand third party liability[a]	($90)	($525)	($105)	($265)
Reduce targeted case management match	($208)	($1,187)	($250)	($1,485)
Amend drug rebate formula	$0	$0	$0	$0
Restructure pharmacy reimbursement	($130)	($1,285)	($275)	($2,325)
Optional managed formulary for prescription drugs	($15)	($177)	($10)	($200)
Administrative cost allocation	($280)	($1,770)	($280)	($1,770)

Table 1. (Continued).

Proposal	Outlays in millions			
	HHS estimate		CBO estimate	
	FY2007	FY2007-FY2011	FY2007	FY2007-FY2011
Refugee exemption extension	$42	$134	$5	$17
Health Insurance Portability and Accountability Act modifications	$0	$0	—	—
Modify SCHIP redistribution to address FY2007 shortfalls (Medicaid impact)	—	—	($290)	($235)
Cover the Kids (Medicaid impact)	$203	$1,978	$13	$477
Administrative proposals[b]	($1,329)	($12,243)	—	—
Eliminate pay and chase for pharmacy	($105)	($430)	—	—
Phase down provider tax	$0	($2,070)	—	—
Issue provider tax regulation	$0	$0	—	—
Cap government providers	($384)	($3,812)	—	—
Stricter reimbursement for rehabilitative services	($225)	($2,286)	—	—
Eliminate school-based administration and transportation	($615)	($3,645)	—	—
Clarify disproportionate share hospital provisions in regulation	$0	$0	—	—
SCHIP	$704	$440	$570	$483
Legislative proposals	$704	$440	$570	$483
Transitional medical assistance (SCHIP impact)	—	—	($3)	($3)
Modify SCHIP redistribution to address FY2007 shortfalls (SCHIP impact)	$635	$110	$570	$460
Health Insurance Portability and Accountability Act modifications	$0	$0	—	—
Cover the Kids (SCHIP impact)	$69	$330	$3	$26
Total Medicaid and SCHIP	($783)	($13,575)	($378)	($4,062)
Health Care Fraud and Abuse Control account (Medicaid and SCHIP financial management)	$10	$26	—	—

Source: Department of Health and Human Services, *Fiscal Year 2007 Budget in Brief*, available at [http://www.hhs.gov/budget/07budget/2007BudgetInBrief.pdf] and Congressional Budget Office, *Preliminary Analysis of the President's Budget Request for 2007* (Mar. 3, 2005), available at [http://www.cbo.gov/showdoc.cfm?index=7055 and sequence=0 and from=7].

Note: Numbers in parentheses represent savings. Estimates for proposals that do not show a dollar figure were not provided in the documents cited above.

[a]. CBO noted that it did not have enough information to estimate the part of the proposal that would expand the use of liens for certain liability settlements.

[b]. In executive branch documents describing the President's budget, implementation of proposed administrative changes is assumed in estimates of baseline Medicaid and SCHIP spending, and estimates for legislative proposals are presented separately. In general, CBO only adjusts its baseline estimates to account for administrative changes as they are implemented — rather than as they are proposed — and only provides separate estimates for legislative proposals.

Medicaid: Transitional Medical Assistance

Background

States are required to continue Medicaid benefits for certain low-income families who would otherwise lose coverage because of changes in their income. This continuation of benefits is known as transitional medical assistance (TMA). Federal law permanently requires four months of TMA for families who lose Medicaid eligibility due to increased child or spousal support collections. It also permanently requires four months of TMA for families who lose Medicaid eligibility due to an increase in earned income or hours of employment.

However, Congress expanded work-related TMA benefits in 1988, requiring states to provide at least six, and up to 12, months of TMA coverage to families losing Medicaid eligibility due to increased hours of work or income from employment, as well as to families who lose eligibility due to the loss of a time-limited earned income disregard (such disregards allow families to qualify for Medicaid at higher income levels for a set period of time). Congress has acted on numerous occasions to extend these expanded TMA requirements (which are outlined in Section 1925 of the Social Security Act) beyond their original sunset date of September 30, 1998. They are currently set to expire on December 31, 2006.

Proposal

The President's budget seeks legislation to extend expanded TMA requirements through September 30, 2007. HHS estimates that the proposal would cost Medicaid $180 million in FY2007, and $360 million over the FY2007-FY2011 period (the budgetary effects extend beyond FY2007 because families are still entitled to up to 12 months of TMA if they qualify on or before the expiration date). CBO estimates that the proposal would cost Medicaid $129 million in FY2007, and $526 million over the FY2007-FY2011 period. CBO also estimates that the proposal would save SCHIP $3 million in both FY2007 and over the FY2007-FY2011 period.

Congressional Action

Before adjourning, the 109th Congress passed H.R. 6111, which extends expanded TMA requirements through June 30, 2007.

Reports

See CRS Report RL31698, Transitional Medical Assistance (TMA) Under Medicaid, by April Grady.

Medicaid: Vaccines for Children

Background

The Vaccines for Children (VFC) program is funded by federal Medicaid appropriations and administered by the Centers for Disease Control and Prevention (CDC). Under Section 1928 of the Social Security Act, children who are (1) Medicaid recipients, (2) uninsured, (3) American Indians or Alaska Natives, or (4) "underinsured" because their health insurance does not cover qualified pediatric immunizations are entitled to receive VFC vaccines free of charge. Currently, children in the first three categories may receive VFC vaccines from any program-registered provider (as defined in Section 1928(c) of the Social Security Act), while underinsured children may only receive VFC vaccines at federally qualified health centers (FQHCs) or rural health clinics.

In 2002, there were approximately 42,000 active VFC provider sites (30,000 private and 12,000 public).[4] In 2000, an estimated 57% of children receiving VFC vaccines were

to compute the rebates are intended to ensure that Medicaid pays the lowest price that the manufacturers offer for the drugs. Rebate calculations depend on the type of drug. For single source and innovator multiple source drugs, basic rebate amounts are determined by comparing the average manufacturer price (AMP) for a drug (the average price paid by wholesalers) to the "best price," which is the lowest price offered by the manufacturer in the same period to any wholesaler, retailer, nonprofit, or public entity. The basic rebate is the greater of 15.1% of the AMP or the difference between the AMP and the best price. Additional rebates are required if the weighted average prices for all of a given manufacturer's single source and innovator multiple source drugs rise faster than inflation. For non-innovator multiple source drugs, basic rebates are equal to 11% of the AMP.

Proposal

The President's budget seeks legislation to eliminate the "best price" from the rebate formula for single source and innovator multiple source drugs, changing the best price-based formula to a flat rebate. This change is intended to be made in a budget neutral manner. HHS explanatory materials describe the proposal as a way to simplify drug rebate calculations and allow private purchasers to negotiate lower drug prices. HHS estimates that the proposal would have no cost impact in FY2007 or over the FY2007-FY2011 period. CBO estimates that the proposal would have no cost impact in FY2007 or over the FY2007-FY2011 period.

Reports

For a general background on Medicaid prescription drug coverage and pricing including a description of drug rebates, see CRS Report RL30726, *Prescription Drug Coverage Under Medicaid*, by Jean Hearne.

Medicaid: Restructure Pharmacy Reimbursement

Background

Under current law, state Medicaid programs set the prices paid to pharmacies for Medicaid outpatient drugs. Federal reimbursements for those drugs, however, are limited to a federal upper limit (FUL). The FUL that applies to drugs available from multiple sources (generic drugs, for the most part) is calculated by the Centers for Medicare and Medicaid Services (CMS) to be equal to 150% of the lowest published average wholesale price (AWP) for the least costly therapeutic equivalent. The upper limit that applies to brand-name and other drugs is equal to the acquisition cost as estimated by the states. Recently, the President signed the Deficit Reduction Act of 2005 (DRA 2005) which will change the FUL formula for multiple source drugs. Beginning January 1, 2007, the FUL for these drugs will be equal to 250% of the average manufacturer's price (AMP, the average price paid by wholesalers to manufacturers).

Proposal

The President's budget seeks legislation that would build on changes made by DRA 2005 to achieve additional savings in the Medicaid program. The proposal would reduce the FULs on multiple source drugs from 250% of the AMP to 150% of the AMP. HHS estimates that the proposal would save $130 million in FY2007, and $1.285 billion over the FY2007-

FY2011 period. CBO estimates that the proposal would save $275 million in FY2007, and $2.325 billion over the FY2007-FY2011 period.

Reports

For more information on the Medicaid provisions of DRA 2005, see CRS Report RL33131; *Budget Reconciliation FY2006: Medicaid, Medicare, and State Children's Health Insurance Program (SCHIP) Provisions*, by Evelyne P. Baumrucker, et al. and CRS Report RL33251, *Side-by-Side Comparison of Medicare, Medicaid, and SCHIP Provisions in the Deficit Reduction Act of 2005*, by Karen Tritz, et al. Additional background information on Medicaid prescription drugs can be found in CRS Report RL30726, *Prescription Drug Coverage Under Medicaid*, by Jean Hearne.

Medicaid: Optional Managed Formulary for Prescription Drugs

Background

Federal statute allows state Medicaid programs to establish formularies, or lists of preferred pharmaceuticals to be made available to Medicaid beneficiaries. When health care insurers or providers cover only those drugs on the list and deny payment for others, the list is referred to as a "closed formulary." Medicaid formularies are seldom as restrictive as the closed formularies found in the private market for insurance because of two requirements: (1) states are required to provide any non-formulary drug (with the exception of drugs in specific categories, described below) that is specifically requested and approved through a prior authorization process, and (2) states are required to cover all drugs offered by manufacturers entering into rebate agreements with the Secretary of HHS.

States, on the other hand, are permitted to exclude certain categories of drug products from Medicaid coverage. These include drugs used: (a) to treat anorexia, weight loss or weight gain; (b) to promote fertility; (c) for cosmetic purposes or hair growth; (d) for the relief of coughs and colds; (e) for smoking cessation; and (f) prescription vitamins and mineral products (except prenatal vitamins and fluoride preparations; (g) non-prescription drugs; (h) barbiturates; (i) benzodiazepines; and (j) drugs requiring tests or monitoring that can only be provided by the drug manufacturer. Formularies may also exclude a drug for which there is no significant therapeutic advantage over other drugs that are included in the formularies as long as there is a written explanation of the reason for its exclusion and the explanation is available to the public. As of January 1, 2006, federal law also prohibits federal Medicaid funds from being used to pay for drugs for the treatment of sexual or erectile dysfunction.

Proposal

The President's budget seeks legislation to allow states to use private sector management techniques to leverage greater discounts through negotiations with drug manufacturers. Supporting material describes these management techniques as common cost control tools for private insurers. No other description of the management techniques is provided. HHS estimates that the proposal would save $15 million in FY2007, and $177 million over the FY2007-FY2011 period. CBO estimates that the proposal would save $10 million in FY2007, and $200 million over the FY2007-FY2011 period.

Reports

For a general background on Medicaid prescription drug benefits, formularies, and other cost control mechanisms used in administering those benefits, see CRS Report RL30726, *Prescription Drug Coverage Under Medicaid*, by Jean Hearne.

Medicaid: Administrative Cost Allocation

Background

Because of the overlap in eligible populations, states often undertake administrative activities that benefit more than one program. Under the former Aid to Families with Dependent Children (AFDC) cash welfare program, AFDC and Medicaid program eligibility were linked, and many AFDC families also qualified for food stamps. As a result, states often collected necessary information for all three programs during a single eligibility interview or performed other shared administrative tasks and charged the full amount of the cost to AFDC as a matter of convenience. Since the federal government reimbursed states for 50% of administrative expenditures for all three programs, total federal spending was not affected by the way in which states allocated the programs' common administrative costs.

When Congress replaced AFDC with the Temporary Assistance for Needy Families (TANF) block grant program in 1996, the 50% federal match for expenditures related to cash welfare assistance ended and the automatic link between cash welfare and Medicaid eligibility was severed. Later, HHS clarified that states are required to allocate common administrative costs for TANF, Medicaid, and food stamps based on the relative benefits derived by each program. A remaining issue of controversy stems from the fact that TANF block grants are calculated in part on the basis of pre-1996 federal welfare spending, including any amounts received by states as reimbursement for common administrative costs. As a result, TANF block grants are higher in many states than they would be if common administrative costs attributable to Medicaid and food stamps were excluded from block grant calculations. To compensate, Congress has permanently reduced federal reimbursement for food stamp administrative costs in most states by a flat dollar amount that reflects the administrative costs attributable to food stamps that are included in each state's TANF block grant (the annual reductions total nearly $200 million). Congress has not reduced federal reimbursement for Medicaid administrative costs in a similar manner.

Proposal

The President's budget seeks legislation to recoup Medicaid administrative costs assumed in states' TANF block grants. HHS estimates that the proposal would save $280 million in FY2007, and $1.770 billion over the FY2007-FY2011 period. CBO estimates that the proposal would save $280 million in FY2007, and $1.770 billion over the FY2007-FY2011 period.

Reports

See CRS Report RS22101, State Medicaid Program Administration: A Brief Overview, by April Grady.

Medicaid: Refugee Exemption Extension

Background

Under current law, most legal immigrants who entered the country on or after August 22, 1996, and some who entered prior to that date, are not eligible for Supplemental Security Income (SSI) benefits — and thus, SSI-related Medicaid — until they have resided in the country for five years or have obtained citizenship. Refugees and asylees are currently exempted from this ban for the first seven years they reside in the United States.

Proposal

The President's budget seeks legislation to extend the exemption for refugees and asylees from seven years to eight years, allowing additional time for individuals to complete the citizenship process without losing SSI and SSI-related Medicaid eligibility. HHS estimates that the proposal would cost $42 million in FY2007, and $134 million over the FY2007-FY2011 period. CBO estimates that the proposal would cost $5 million in FY2007, and $17 million over the FY2007-FY2011 period.

Reports

For general background information, see CRS Report RL31269, *Refugee Admissions and Resettlement Policy*, by Andorra Bruno; CRS Report RL31630, *Federal Funding for Unauthorized Aliens' Emergency Medical Expenses*, by Alison M. Siskin; and CRS Report RL31114, *Noncitizen Eligibility for Major Federal Public Assistance Programs: Policies and Legislation*, by Ruth Wasem.

Medicaid: Eliminate Pay and Chase for Pharmacy

Background

As described earlier (under the "expand third party liability" proposal), if a state has determined that probable third party liability exists at the time a claim for reimbursement is filed, it generally must reject the claim and return it to the provider for a determination of the amount of third party liability (referred to as "cost avoidance"). If probable liability has not been established or the third party is not available to pay the individual's medical expenses, the state must pay the claim and then attempt to recover the amount paid (referred to as "pay and chase"). States are generally required to cost avoid claims unless they have an approved waiver that allows them to use the pay and chase method.

Proposal

The President's budget would, through administrative action, require states to use cost avoidance by eliminating the pay and chase waiver option for pharmacy claims. HHS estimates that the proposal would save $105 million in FY2007, and $430 million over the FY2007-FY2011 period. CBO did not provide an estimate for the proposal (see earlier discussion under "Legislative Versus Administrative Proposals").

Medicaid: Phase Down Provider Tax

Background

Under federal law and regulations, a state's ability to use provider-specific taxes to fund its state share of Medicaid expenditures is limited. If states establish provider-specific taxes, those taxes generally cannot exceed 25% of the state (or non-federal) share of Medicaid expenditures and the state cannot provide a guarantee to the providers that the taxes will be returned to them. However, if the taxes returned to a provider are less than 6% of the provider's revenues (a ceiling created in regulation by HHS), the prohibition on guaranteeing the return of tax funds is not violated. As a result, a state could impose a provider tax of 6% of revenues, return those revenues to the provider in the form of a Medicaid "payment," and receive a federal match for those amounts. In effect, the state has temporarily borrowed funds from the provider for the purpose of inflating federal matching funds.

Proposal

The President's budget seeks a regulatory change to phase down the allowable provider tax rate from 6% to 3%. HHS estimates that the proposal would have no budget impact in FY2007, and would save $2.070 billion over the FY2007-FY2011 period. CBO did not provide an estimate for the proposal (see earlier discussion under "Legislative Versus Administrative Proposals").

Congressional Action

Before adjourning, the 109th Congress passed H.R. 6111, which prevents the President's provider tax proposal from being implemented via administrative action. H.R. 6111 fixed the provider tax ceiling in statute at 6%, except for the period January 1, 2008-September 31, 2011, during which the rate is fixed at 5.5%.

Reports

For background information on provider taxes, see CRS Report 97-483, *Medicaid Disproportionate Share Payments*, by Jean Hearne.

Medicaid: Issue Provider Tax Regulation

Background

See the "phase down provider tax" proposal above.

Proposal

The President's budget seeks to clarify, through regulation, existing policies used to determine whether or not provider taxes comply with statute and regulations. HHS estimates that the proposal would have no cost impact in FY2007 or over the FY2007-FY2011 period. CBO did not provide an estimate for the proposal (see earlier discussion under "Legislative Versus Administrative Proposals").

Reports

For background information on provider taxes, see CRS Report 97-483, *Medicaid Disproportionate Share Payments*, by Jean Hearne.

Medicaid: Cap Government Providers

Background

Aggregate Medicaid payments to specific groups of institutional providers (e.g., hospitals and nursing facilities) cannot exceed a reasonable estimate of what would have been paid under Medicare payment principles. This is called the Medicaid upper payment limit (UPL) rule. In many states, Medicare payment rates for hospital and nursing home care are higher than corresponding Medicaid payment rates. The UPL based on Medicare payment principles has enabled some states to draw down additional federal dollars that exceed what they would have received based on Medicaid payment rates. These additional funds are paid to government providers which are sometimes required by states to transfer all or a portion of the extra payments received (i.e., some or all of the difference between the Medicare and Medicaid payment rates) back to the state through an intergovernmental transfer (IGT). Instead of financing more or improved Medicaid services, in some cases states have used the additional federal dollars for non-health services, or to make up part of the state share of Medicaid costs to draw down another round of federal dollars.

During 2000-2002, Congress and the Clinton and Bush Administrations revised UPL rules by changing permissible accounting methods used to claim federal matching payments. These changes significantly reduced the excess federal dollars states received under approved UPL plans that involved IGTs. However, these reforms did not eliminate all such excess payments because no changes were made to the Medicaid UPL standard which remains tied to the Medicare payment rate, nor to federal statute or regulations governing IGTs. Administration officials have taken additional steps to curb what they have identified as improper state financing mechanisms, especially certain intergovernmental transfers. In late 2003, CMS began requesting detailed information regarding the sources of the state share of Medicaid costs from states applying for Medicaid waivers and submitting Medicaid state plan amendments. In some cases, these proposals were modified to minimize the use of improper IGTs (i.e., IGTs that use "recycling mechanisms" under which payments to providers are returned to the state, artificially inflating the federal matching rate).

Proposal

The President's budget would, through administrative action: (1) recover federal payments resulting from improper IGTs and (2) cap payments to government providers to no more than the cost of providing services to Medicaid beneficiaries, rather than to Medicare payment principles. HHS estimates that the proposal would save \$384 million in FY2007, and \$3.812 billion over the FY2007-FY2011 period. CBO did not provide an estimate for the proposal (see earlier discussion under "Legislative Versus Administrative Proposals").

Reports

See CRS Report RL31021, Medicaid Upper Payment Limits and Intergovernmental Transfers: Current Issues and Recent Regulatory and Legislative Action, by Elicia J. Herz.

Medicaid: Stricter Reimbursement Policies for Rehabilitation Services

Background

Since the inception of Medicaid in 1965, states have been authorized to cover "other diagnostic, screening, preventive, or *rehabilitative* services" as an optional Medicaid service.[6] In subsequent legislation (OBRA 90, P.L. 101-508), Congress clarified the benefit as "including any medical or remedial service (provided in a facility, a home, or other setting) recommended by a physician or other licensed practitioner of the healing arts within the scope of their practice under state law, for the maximum reduction of physical or mental disability and restoration of an individual to the best possible functional level." The rehabilitation benefit allows states to cover a broad range of services to individuals with various types of conditions and disabilities. Under the rehabilitation benefit, states often cover ongoing mental health and/or substance abuse services, early intervention services for children with disabilities, rehabilitation for individuals with physical disabilities, school-based rehabilitation, and services for children in foster care and juvenile justice programs.

Both the Government Accountability Office (GAO) and the HHS Office of the Inspector General (OIG) have reported that the Medicaid rehabilitation benefit has been used by some states to bill Medicaid for activities that are not allowable as rehabilitation services, and/or to pay rehabilitation providers using methods that did not meet the statutory requirement for being "efficient and economical."[7,8] Further, CMS financial management officials reported to GAO that they believed that states "were inappropriately filing claims for services that were the responsibility of other state programs."[9]

Proposal

The President's budget seeks to clarify, through regulation, which services may be claimed as Medicaid rehabilitation services. HHS estimates that the proposal would save $225 million in FY2007, and $2.286 billion over the FY2007-FY2011 period. CBO did not provide an estimate for the proposal (see earlier discussion under "Legislative Versus Administrative Proposals").

Medicaid: Eliminate School-Based Administration and Transportation

Background

Medicaid pays for covered medical services provided to Medicaid-eligible children with Individualized Family Service Plans (IFSP) and Individualized Education Plans (IEP), pursuant to the Individuals with Disabilities Education Act (IDEA). In its budget documents, the Administration notes that Medicaid claims for services provided in school settings have been prone to abuse and overpayments, especially with respect to transportation and administrative activities. Over the past few years, several GAO and HHS OIG studies have reached similar conclusions.[10]

For transportation services, examples of inappropriate Medicaid billing include (1) no verification that transportation was in fact provided, (2) a Medicaid-covered school health service other than transportation was not provided on the day that transportation was billed, and (3) child/family plans did not include a recommendation for transportation services, or there was no IEP or IFSP.

School districts may perform administrative functions for Medicaid purposes, including for example, outreach, eligibility intake, information and referrals, health service coordination and monitoring, and interagency coordination. Examples of inappropriate Medicaid billing include (1) payments based on inaccurate time studies used to allocate the cost of these administrative activities across funding sources including Medicaid, (2) expenditures for school employees who do not perform Medicaid administrative activities, (3) expenditures for operating costs such as nursing supplies, non-Medicaid outreach supplies, and education-related expenditures, (4) expenditures for personnel funded by other federal programs, and (5) payments for personnel who render only direct medical services.

Proposal

The President's budget would, through administrative action, prohibit federal reimbursement for IDEA-related school-based administration and transportation costs. HHS estimates that the proposal would save $615 million in FY2007, and $3.645 billion over the FY2007-FY2011 period. CBO did not provide an estimate for the proposal (see earlier discussion under "Legislative Versus Administrative Proposals").

Reports

See CRS Report RS22397, The Link Between Medicaid and the Individuals with Disabilities Education Act (IDEA): Recent History and Current Issues, by Elicia J. Herz, and CRS Report RL31722, Individuals with Disabilities Education Act (IDEA) and Medicaid, by Richard N. Apling and Elicia J. Herz.

Medicaid: Clarify DSH Provisions in Regulation

Background

States and the District of Columbia are required to recognize, in establishing hospital payment rates, the situation of hospitals that serve a disproportionate number of Medicaid beneficiaries and other low-income patients with special needs. Under broad federal guidelines, each state determines which hospitals receive disproportionate share hospital (DSH) payments and the payment amounts to be made to each qualifying hospital. The federal government shares in the cost of state DSH payments at the same federal matching percentage as for most other Medicaid services. Total federal reimbursement for each state's DSH payments are capped at a statewide ceiling, referred to as the state's DSH allotment, and DSH payments to each hospital are capped at a hospital-specific ceiling.

Proposal

The President's budget seeks to clarify, through regulation, provisions related to the allowable uses of DSH funds. HHS estimates that the proposal would have no cost impact in FY2007 or over the FY2007-FY2011 period. CBO did not provide an estimate for the proposal (see earlier discussion under "Legislative Versus Administrative Proposals").

Reports

For background information on Medicaid DSH payments, see CRS Report 97-483, *Medicaid Disproportionate Share Payments*, by Jean Hearne.

SCHIP: Modify Redistribution to Address 2007 Shortfalls

Background

The Balanced Budget Act of 1997 established SCHIP. In general, this program allows states to cover targeted low-income children with no health insurance in families with income that is above Medicaid eligibility levels. States may choose among three benefit options when designing their SCHIP programs. They may enroll targeted low-income children in Medicaid, create a separate state program, or devise a combination of both approaches. All states, the District of Columbia, and five territories have SCHIP programs. Nearly $40 billion has been appropriated for SCHIP for FY1998-FY2007. The authorized appropriation for FY2007 is $5.0 billion. Annual allotments among the states are determined by a formula that is based on a combination of the number of low-income children, and low-income uninsured children in the state, and includes a cost factor that represents the average health service industry wages in the state compared to the national average.

States have three years to spend each annual allotment (e.g., states have until the end of FY2007 to spend their FY2005 allotments). At the end of the applicable three-year period, unspent funds are reallocated among states based on year-specific rules. In the early years of the SCHIP, both states that did and did not fully exhaust their original allotments received unspent funds. For more recent years, only those states that fully exhaust their original allotments receive unspent funds. Some states have experienced shortfalls in SCHIP funds, meaning at the end of a given fiscal year, they have spent all federal SCHIP funds available to them at that point in time, including original allotments and reallocations of unspent funds from other states.

Proposal

The President's budget seeks legislation to better target SCHIP funds in a more timely manner to address potential state shortfalls in FY2007. HHS estimates the cost of the proposal at $635 million in FY2007, with a net cost of $110 million over the FY2007-FY2011 period. CBO estimates the SCHIP cost of the proposal at $570 million in FY2007, with a net cost of $460 million over the FY2007-FY2011 period. CBO also estimates that the proposal would save Medicaid $290 million in FY2007, with a net savings of $235 million over the FY2007-FY2011 period.

Congressional Action

Before adjourning, the 109th Congress passed H.R. 6164, which requires a redistribution of certain unspent FY2004 and FY2005 SCHIP funds to delay state shortfalls in FY2007.

Reports

For more information, see CRS Report RS22553, *SCHIP Provisions of H.R. 6164 (NIH Reform Act of 2006)*, by Chris L. Peterson; CRS Report RL30473, *State Children's Health Insurance Program (SCHIP): A Brief Overview*, by Elicia J. Herz, Bernadette Fernandez, and Chris L. Peterson; CRS Report RL32807, *SCHIP Financing: Funding and Projections and State Redistribution Issues*, by Chris L. Peterson; CRS Report RL33366, *SCHIP Original Allotments: Description and Analysis*, by Chris L. Peterson; and CRS Report RL33251, *Side-by-Side Comparison of Medicare, Medicaid, and SCHIP Provisions in the Deficit Reduction Act of 2005*, by Karen Tritz, et al.

Medicaid and SCHIP: HIPAA Modifications

Background

The Health Insurance Portability and Accountability Act of 1996 (HIPAA, P.L. 104-191) established a number of rules for employer-based health insurance plans to improve access to and portability of plans for people enrolled or enrolling into those plans. One of those provisions requires employer-based health plans to allow for new enrollment into the plan during periods outside of the typical annual open enrollment period for certain special reasons. Examples of those reasons include when an eligible employee (or their dependent) exhausts COBRA continuation coverage, or when an employee gains a new dependent through birth or adoption. Another HIPAA provision limits the ability of private health insurance plans to exclude coverage for pre-existing conditions during what are known as "preexisting condition exclusion periods." The allowable length of such pre-existing condition exclusion periods depends on the amount of time the new enrollee had been covered by prior "creditable" health insurance coverage.[11] A beneficiary can prove they have had prior creditable coverage by providing certificates issued by insurers at the end of each year. Because HIPAA was created in law before SCHIP was established, SCHIP was not included on the list of types of health insurance that can be considered as prior creditable coverage.

Proposal

The President's budget seeks two legislative changes relating to HIPAA. The first would define a determination of Medicaid or SCHIP eligibility as a qualifying event allowing for a special enrollment period into employer-based health insurance plans. This provision is intended to improve Medicaid and SCHIP programs' ability to coordinate coverage with private employer-offered coverage. The second proposal would require SCHIP programs to issue certificates of creditable coverage. This provision is intended to improve the reach of HIPAA's portability provisions by recognizing SCHIP coverage as prior creditable coverage. Both of these interpretations have previously been promulgated in a final regulation implementing HIPAA's portability for group health plan provisions.[12] HHS estimates that the proposal would have no cost impact in FY2007 or over the FY2007-FY2011 period. CBO did not provide an estimate for the proposal in its preliminary analysis.

Reports

For general information on HIPAA, see CRS Report RL31634, *The Health Insurance Portability and Accountability Act (HIPAA) of 1996: Overview and Guidance on Frequently Asked Questions*, by Hinda R. Chaikind, Jean Hearne, Bob Lyke, and Stephen Redhead.

Medicaid and SCHIP: Cover the Kids

Background

According to the latest available official statistics, in FY2004, the number of children ever enrolled in SCHIP reached nearly 6.2 million. In FY2003, the number of children ever enrolled in Medicaid during that year reached 27.4 million. There have been ongoing concerns about take-up rates among children who meet eligibility standards but are not covered by these two programs. Estimates of the number of children eligible but not enrolled in Medicaid or SCHIP have varied considerably over time. By 2002, national survey data showed that 2.8 million children under age 19 were uninsured but eligible for SCHIP, and an additional 3.4 million were uninsured but eligible for Medicaid.[13]

Outreach can be financed under the Medicaid and SCHIP programs. Under Medicaid, the federal matching rate for administrative expenses which include outreach activities is set at 50% for all states. There is a limit on federal spending for SCHIP administrative expenses, which also include outreach. For federal matching purposes, a 10% cap applies to state administrative expenses. This cap is tied to the dollar amount that a state draws down from its annual SCHIP allotment to cover benefits, as opposed to 10% of a state's total annual allotment.

Proposal

The Cover the Kids outreach program would provide annual grants to states, working with schools and community organizations to enroll eligible children in Medicaid and SCHIP. The grant is not part of the Medicaid or SCHIP budget proposals, but rather is a component of the State Grants and Demonstrations budget proposals under the jurisdiction of CMS (which is responsible for oversight of Medicaid and SCHIP). The grant would cost $100 million in FY2007, and $500 million over the FY2007-FY2011 period. HHS estimates that the impact of the grant on Medicaid spending would result in additional costs of $203 million in FY2007, and $1.978 billion over the FY2007-FY2011 period. Likewise, HHS estimates that the impact of the grant on SCHIP spending would be $69 million in FY2007, and $330 million over the FY2007-FY2011 period. CBO estimates that the proposal would increase Medicaid spending by $13 million in FY2007, and $477 million over the FY2007-FY2011 period. CBO also estimates that the proposal would increase SCHIP spending by $3 million in FY2007, and $26 million over the FY2007-FY2011 period.

Health Care Fraud and Abuse Control Account

Background

The Health Insurance Portability and Accountability Act of 1996 established a national Health Care Fraud and Abuse Control (HCFAC) account within the federal Hospital Insurance (HI, also known as Medicare Part A) trust fund. The HCFAC account funds the Medicare Integrity Program within CMS and certain health care fraud and abuse activities within the Federal Bureau of Investigation (FBI). Additional HCFAC funds are earmarked specifically for Medicare and Medicaid activities of the HHS OIG, and remaining "wedge" funds are divided among other HHS agencies (including CMS) and the Department of Justice. Annual mandatory minimum and maximum HCFAC appropriations are specified in statute.

Proposal

The President's budget seeks legislation to increase HCFAC funding with a discretionary appropriation. While the proposal would not directly affect Medicaid or SCHIP spending, it would fund Medicaid and SCHIP financial management activities at CMS and supplement HCFAC funding for other agencies with Medicaid and SCHIP oversight responsibilities (e.g., HHS OIG). HHS estimates that the CMS portion of the proposal would cost $10 million in

FY2007, and $26 million over the FY2007-FY2011 period. CBO did not provide an estimate for the proposal in its preliminary analysis.

Reports

For information on HCFAC and related changes made by DRA 2005, see CRS Report RL33251, *Side-by-Side Comparison of Medicare, Medicaid, and SCHIP Provisions in the Deficit Reduction Act of 2005*, by Karen Tritz, et al.

CONGRESSIONAL ACTION

On March 9, 2006, the Senate Budget Committee reported a budget resolution, S.Con.Res. 83, which was subsequently amended and passed by the Senate on March 16. The resolution did not include reconciliation instructions for the Senate Finance Committee, which has jurisdiction over Medicaid and SCHIP. It did include a deficit-neutral reserve fund for the uninsured, and a March 8 Senate Budget Committee document indicates that it included funding for four of the President's Medicaid and SCHIP proposals:[14]

- TMA extension ($523 million over five years);
- Vaccines for Children proposal allowing health departments to provide vaccines ($715 million);
- Cover the Kids initiative ($874 million);[15] and
- SCHIP funding boost in 2007 and 2008 ($225 million).

On March 29, 2006, the House Budget Committee reported its own budget resolution, H.Con.Res. 376, which was subsequently amended and passed by the House on May 18. The resolution did not include reconciliation instructions for the House Energy and Commerce Committee, which has jurisdiction over Medicaid and SCHIP. The report accompanying the resolution as reported by the House Budget Committee (H.Rept. 109-402) indicates that spending levels for Medicaid and SCHIP were based on CBO's baseline projections under current law and policies, and that no reduction in Medicaid was assumed.[16]

Although no agreement was reached by the House and Senate on a FY2007 budget resolution, current law spending for Medicaid and SCHIP is unaffected. As entitlement programs, their spending levels are based on the underlying benefit and eligibility criteria established in law (in the case of SCHIP, these criteria include a statutory annual funding cap).[17] However, legislation that would increase Medicaid or SCHIP spending above current law could encounter procedural roadblocks in the House or Senate if funding is not assumed in a budget resolution or in a "deeming resolution."[18]

The annual appropriations process also provides an opportunity for Congress to place limitations on the availability of federal funds for specified Medicaid and SCHIP activities.[19] For example, when the House reported its proposal for FY2007 Labor, Health and Human Services, and Education, and Related Agencies (L-HHS-ED) appropriations on June 20, 2006 (H.R. 5647, H.Rept. 109-515), it included a provision that would prohibit HHS from using any of the funds in its FY2007 budget to implement the President's proposal to phase down or reduce provider taxes below 6% through administrative action.[20] Annual L-

HHS-ED appropriations also regularly contain restrictions that limit — for one year at a time — the circumstances under which federal funds can be used to pay for abortions.

Before the 109th Congress adjourned, it passed two bills that addressed a variety of Medicaid and SCHIP issues, including some of the proposals in the President's FY2007 budget. As described earlier, H.R. 6164 requires a redistribution of certain unspent FY2004 and FY2005 SCHIP funds to delay state shortfalls in FY2007. In addition, H.R. 6111 prevents the President's provider tax proposal from being implemented via administrative action and extends expanded TMA requirements through June 30, 2007. H.R. 6111 also addressed Medicaid issues that were not part of the President's budget, including technical corrections to the Deficit Reduction Act of 2005 (P.L. 109-171) and FY2007 DSH allotments for Hawaii and Tennessee.

Table 2. CRS Staff Contact Information by Medicaid and SCHIP Topic Area

Topic	Staff member	Phone number
Medicaid		
Administration	April Grady	7-9578
Benefits and eligibility		
Aged	Julie Stone	7-1386
Children, families, immigrants, other non-disabled adults	Evelyne Baumrucker	7-8913
	Jean Hearne	7-7362
	Elicia Herz	7-1377
Individuals with disabilities, medically needy	Julie Stone	7-1386
Expenditures	April Grady	7-9578
Dual eligibles	Julie Stone	7-1386
Financing		
Disproportionate share hospital payments	Jean Hearne	7-7362
Federal medical assistance percentage	April Grady	7-9578
General issues	April Grady	7-9578
	Jean Hearne	7-7362
	Elicia Herz	7-1377
Intergovernmental transfers	Jean Hearne	7-7362
	Elicia Herz	7-1377
Upper payment limits	Elicia Herz	7-1377
Integrity (waste, fraud, and abuse)	April Grady	7-9578
Long-term care	Julie Stone	7-1386
Managed care	Elicia Herz	7-1377
Prescription drugs	Jean Hearne	7-7362
Provider payment issues	Jean Hearne	7-7362
Territories	Evelyne Baumrucker	7-8913
	Jean Hearne	7-7362
	Elicia Herz	7-1377
Section 1115	Evelyne Baumrucker	7-8913
Section 1915(c)	Carol O'Shaughnessy	7-7329
	Julie Stone	7-1386
SCHIP		
Financing	Evelyne Baumrucker	7-8913
	Chris Peterson	7-4681
General issues	Evelyne Baumrucker	7-8913
	Elicia Herz	7-1377
Section 1115 waivers	Evelyne Baumrucker	7-8913

REFERENCES

[1] Sources include Department of Health and Human Services (HHS), *Fiscal Year 2007 Budget in Brief*, available at [http://www.hhs.gov/budget/07budget/ 2007 BudgetInBrief.pdf]; HHS, Centers for Medicare and Medicaid Services, *Fiscal Year 2007 Justification of Estimates for Appropriations Committees*; Office of Management and Budget, *Budget of the United States Government, Fiscal Year 2007*, available at [http://www.whitehouse.gov/ omb/budget/fy2007]. CBO cost estimates are from *Preliminary Analysis of the President's Budget Request for 2007* (Mar. 3, 2005), available at [http://www.cbo.gov/showdoc.cfm? index=7055 and sequence=0 and from=7].

[2] For a description of adjustments made to arrive at baseline FY2007 Medicaid expenditures, see HHS, Centers for Medicare and Medicaid Services, *Fiscal Year 2007 Justification of Estimates for Appropriations Committees*, pp. 138-145.

[3] See CQ HealthBeat News, GOP Lawmakers Warn Leavitt of Medicaid Cuts in President's Budget Proposal, May 18, 2006, and CQ HealthBeat News, Senators Warn Administration Against Cutting Medicaid Payments on Its Own, June 30, 2006.

[4] Centers for Disease Control and Prevention, *VFC Program Data*, available at [http://www.cdc.gov/nip/vfc/st_immz_proj/data/data.htm].

[5] Institute of Medicine, *Calling the Shots: Immunization Finance Policies and Practices* (Washington: National Academy Press, 2000), pp. 77-85.

[6] Section 1905(a)(13) of the Social Security Act.

[7] K. Allen, *States' Efforts to Maximize Federal Reimbursements Highlight Need for Improved Federal Oversight*, Government Accountability Office, Testimony Before the U.S. Senate, Committee on Finance, GAO-05-836T, June 28, 2005. (Hereafter cited as "GAO Testimony, June 2005.")

[8] HHS, Office of Inspector General, Audit of Medicaid Claims for Iowa Rehabilitation Treatment Services Family-Centered Program, A-07-02-03023, July 2004.

[9] GAO Testimony, June 2005.

[10] For example, see HHS, Office of Inspector General (OIG), Review of Medicaid Transportation Claims Made by the New York City Department of Education, A-02-03-01023, Sep. 2005; HHS, OIG, Audit of LaPorte Consortium's Administrative Costs Claimed for Medicaid School-Based Services, A-06-02-00051, Jan. 2006; and Government Accountability Office, Medicaid in Schools: Improper Payments Demand Improvements in HCFA Oversight, GAO/HES/OSI-00-69, Apr. 2000.

[11] Not all prior health insurance coverage is considered to be creditable. For a discussion of creditable coverage, see CRS Report RL31634, *The Health Insurance Portability and Accountability Act (HIPAA) of 1996: Overview and Guidance on Frequently Asked Questions*, by Hinda R. Chaikind, Jean Hearne, Bob Lyke, and C. Stephen Redhead.

[12] 69 Federal Register 78720, Final Regulations for Health Coverage Portability for Group Health Plans and Group Health Insurance Issuers Under HIPAA Titles I and IV, Dec. 30, 2004.

[13] Statistics taken from T. Selden, J. Hudson, and J. Banthin, "Tracking Changes in Eligibility and Coverage Among Children, 1996-2000," *Health Affairs*, vol. 23, no. 5 (Sept./Oct. 2004), pp. 39-50.

[14] Senate Budget Committee, *Chairman's Mark: FY2007 Budget* (Mar. 8, 2006), available at [http://budget.senate.gov/republican/pressarchive/MarkSummary.pdf].

[15] In addition to the Medicaid and SCHIP costs, this amount presumably includes the state grant costs of the proposal that are not borne directly by Medicaid or SCHIP.

[16] Medicaid and SCHIP are part of the Health (550) budget function.

[17] See CRS Report RS20129, Entitlements and Appropriated Entitlements in the Federal Budget Process, by Bill Heniff Jr. and CRS Report RL33291, Congressional Budget Actions in 2006, by Bill Heniff Jr.

[18] See CRS Report RL31443, The "Deeming Resolution": A Budget Enforcement Tool, by Robert Keith.

[19] See CRS Report 98-518, Earmarks and Limitations in Appropriations Bills, by Sandy Streeter.

[20] For more on FY2007 L-HHS-ED appropriations, see CRS Report RL33576, *Labor, Health and Human Services, and Education: FY2007 Appropriations*, by Paul M. Irwin.

In: State Children's Health Insurance Program (SCHIP) ISBN: 978-1-60456-333-7
Editor: Mary T. Ewing, pp. 151-157

Chapter 5

WHAT HAPPENS IF SCHIP IS NOT "REAUTHORIZED"?*

Chris L. Peterson

ABSTRACT

The Balanced Budget Act of 1997 created the State Children's Health Insurance Program (SCHIP) and provided nearly $40 billion in appropriations over the 10-year period FY1998 to FY2007. Legislative action would be necessary to provide new funds for SCHIP for FY2008 and beyond, but SCHIP's statutory provisions do not need to be reauthorized as they will remain on the books unless Congress expressly repeals the current law. In the absence of an FY2008 SCHIP allotment, states with unexpended FY2006 and FY2007 federal SCHIP balances could continue to operate their programs with those funds in FY2008. Fourteen states and the District of Columbia are projected to be able to cover all of their federal FY2008 SCHIP spending even without an FY2008 SCHIP allotment. Among the 36 states projected to exhaust their federal SCHIP funds in FY2008, some may be able to access Medicaid funding, though at a reduced matching rate compared to SCHIP. However, 13 states would be in shortfall immediately, entering FY2008 with no prior-year SCHIP balances. An amount equal to approximately 18 days of these states' federal SCHIP expenditures is projected to be available from the redistribution of unspent FY2005 allotments. This report may be updated in December 2007 with states' more recent projections.

The Balanced Budget Act of 1997 created the State Children's Health Insurance Program (SCHIP), a direct spending program, and appropriated approximately $40 billion from FY1998 to FY2007. SCHIP needs to be "reauthorized" in the sense that Congress must take legislative action if it wishes to provide the program with new FY2008 funding. However, the statutory provisions governing SCHIP do not need to be reauthorized, as they do not expire or sunset as of the end of FY2007, and so would remain on the books. Legislation has passed

* Excerpted from CRS Report RS22712, dated September 17, 2007.

both the House (H.R. 3162) and Senate (S. 1893/H.R. 976), described in other CRS reports, that would provide federal SCHIP appropriations at least through FY2012.

Even if Congress does not appropriate funds for SCHIP for FY2008, legal authority for the program provisions would continue in effect, unless Congress were expressly to repeal the current law. Thus, states would have access to some (though, in some cases, very limited) federal SCHIP funds in FY2008. This is because (1) federal SCHIP allotments are currently available to states for three years, and (2) any allotments unspent after three years are available for redistribution to other states. Thus, under current law, states will continue to have access to any unspent FY2006 and FY2007 SCHIP allotments they might have; in addition, any unspent FY2005 allotments will be available for redistribution to other states.

FY2006 and FY2007 Allotments Available in FY2008

According to current-law projections from the Centers for Medicare and Medicaid Services (CMS), based on states' August 2007 estimates of SCHIP spending in FY2007 and FY2008, 36 states would exhaust all federal SCHIP funds at some point in FY2008 without a new appropriation (that is, those states showing shortfalls in the last column of table 1). Comparing these states' available FY2008 funding to their projected spending, their shortfall of federal SCHIP funds would total $4.66 billion.

The District of Columbia and 14 states — Colorado, Connecticut, Delaware, Florida, Idaho, Indiana, Nevada, New Hampshire, New York, Tennessee, Texas, Vermont, Washington and Wyoming — are projected to have enough federal SCHIP funds to last the entirety of FY2008 (states with amounts in Column D of table 1).

Of the 36 states that would experience a shortfall of federal SCHIP funds in FY2008, 13 (Alaska, Georgia, Illinois, Iowa, Maine, Maryland, Massachusetts, Minnesota, Mississippi, Nebraska, New Jersey, Rhode Island, and Wisconsin) would face shortfalls immediately in FY2008, which begins October 1, 2007. Their immediate shortfall would result because these states are projected to exhaust all of their federal SCHIP allotments in *FY2007[1]* and therefore have no prior-year balances in FY2008. Four other states — California, Missouri, North Carolina, and North Dakota — are projected to have so little in prior-year balances that they would also likely exhaust their federal SCHIP funds in October 2007.

Redistributed FY2005 Allotments Available in FY2008

At the end of FY2007, states' FY2005 allotments will have been available for three years, with the unspent amounts available for redistribution to other states in FY2008. Current projections indicate that four states will have unspent FY2005 funds at the end of FY2007 totaling $108 million.[2] It is unlikely these funds will be available on October 1, 2007. The redistribution of FY2005 funds will likely occur once final expenditure reports are filed. In recent years, CMS has given states until November 30 to submit expenditure reports for the previous fiscal year. However, CMS could require states to file those reports earlier in order to redistribute the FY2005 funds sooner. CMS is not required to give states a minimum amount of time to file those reports.

Current law permits the Secretary of Health and Human Services (HHS) to redistribute the unspent funds among states that had exhausted the FY2005 allotment using "an appropriate procedure."[3] In previous years in which the Secretary had this flexibility and states faced shortfalls, the Secretary redistributed unspent funds first to shortfall states.[4] For FY2007, the Secretary was required to redistribute FY2004 funds to shortfall states "in the order in which states realize funding shortfalls."[5] If, for example, the Secretary redistributed the currently projected $108 million in unspent FY2005 funds proportionally among the 13 states with no other federal SCHIP funds, the funds could cover approximately 18 days of their projected FY2008 SCHIP spending.

Medicaid Fallback Financing for Certain States

When states exhaust their federal SCHIP funds, some have the ability to draw down federal Medicaid funds as a fallback option. This can occur in one of two ways.

First, states that have an SCHIP-financed expansion of Medicaid may access federal Medicaid funds at the regular Medicaid matching rate, although this match rate is lower than the SCHIP matching rate.[6] States that have an SCHIP program entirely separate from Medicaid cannot revert to Medicaid funds when their SCHIP funds are exhausted, except as discussed below. Table 1 shows whether a state's SCHIP program is a Medicaid expansion (M), is separate from Medicaid (S), or both (C, for combination). Most SCHIP enrollees are in a separate SCHIP program,[7] although historical analyses have shown that "states that were projected to have shortfalls [in FY2005, FY2006, or FY2007] ... were more likely to have a Medicaid component to their SCHIP program."[8]

In general, Section 1115 of the Social Security Act provides the Secretary with broad authority to waive certain statutory requirements in Medicaid and/or SCHIP. Some states have approval under Section 1115 waiver authority, in the event of a shortfall, to draw federal Medicaid funds for the portion of their SCHIP program that is *not* a Medicaid expansion. Arizona, Hawaii, Massachusetts, Oregon, and Rhode Island are known to have such provisions in their approved waivers.

Federal Requirements before Terminating SCHIP

There are laws and regulations that pertain to states' ability to terminate SCHIP-financed coverage. None specifically mentions doing so as a result of the absence of a federal allotment for a given fiscal year. HHS may issue guidance for states terminating coverage because of the absence of federal funding, although nothing prohibits states from continuing to operate their SCHIP programs at 100% state cost, with the opportunity to receive a federal match from future SCHIP funds.[9] This section briefly discusses some of the pertinent laws and regulations for states terminating individuals' SCHIP-financed coverage, which vary for Medicaid-expansion programs (in which case Medicaid limitations apply, based on Title XIX of the Social Security Act) and separate-SCHIP programs (in which case SCHIP limitations apply, based on Title XXI).

Separate SCHIP Programs

Under Title XXI, "An approved [SCHIP program] shall continue in effect unless and until the State amends the plan," with such an amendment contingent on approval by the Secretary.[10] Thus, even in the absence of any federal SCHIP funding, a state would ultimately need to submit a State Plan Amendment (SPA) to terminate coverage in its separate SCHIP program.

The law states that "[a]ny plan amendment that eliminates or restricts eligibility or benefits under the plan may not take effect unless the State certifies that it has provided prior public notice of the change, in a form and manner provided under applicable State law."[11] Federal regulations also require that if "eligibility is denied, suspended or terminated," a state "must provide enrollees and applicants timely written notice."[12] In addition, if eligibility is suspended or terminated, the state must provide "sufficient notice to enable the child's parent or caretaker to take any appropriate actions that may be required to allow coverage to continue without interruption."[13] Neither federal statute nor regulation appears to provide a specific length of time.

Having met these requirements, the state may terminate individuals' eligibility without prior Secretary approval, as long as the SPA is transmitted to the Secretary within 60 days of the state having implemented the policy.[14] A SPA is considered approved unless the Secretary notifies the state in writing within 90 days after receiving the SPA that it is disapproved (and the reasons for disapproval) or that specified additional information is needed.[15]

Medicaid-Expansion SCHIP Programs

Under Title XIX, the effective date of a SPA that terminates or suspends coverage to an enrollment group, such as SCHIP-financed enrollees, "may be a date requested by the State if CMS approves it."[16] Enrollees must receive "timely and adequate notice of proposed action to terminate, discontinue, or suspend their eligibility."[17] Again, there appears to be no specific length of time required.

Assumptions Required for Budget Purposes

Under current law, SCHIP has no federal appropriations for FY2008 onward. However, for budget enforcement purposes, funding for SCHIP through FY2012 will remain in the baseline budget projections and the budget resolution (S.Con.Res. 21, H.Rept. 110-153) at least until the end of 2007. In developing its baseline budget projections, the Congressional Budget Office is required to assume that the program continues at the last-appropriated level, which is currently approximately $5 billion in FY2007. The FY2008 budget resolution also assumed the continuation of the program at the FY2007 level. Therefore, at least until the end of 2007, legislation providing that level of funding for each year covering FY2008-FY2012 ($25 billion over the period) presumably would not be subject to points of order under PAYGO rules or rules enforcing the levels associated with the budget resolution.

Table 1. Projected FY2008 Federal SCHIP Financing Under Current Law (Without FY2008 Allotment), in Millions of Dollars

State	Projected balances of unspent FY2006 and FY2007 allotments available in FY2008	States' projected FY2008 federal SCHIP spending (provided in August 2007)	Projected unspent balances at the end of FY2008	Projected shortfalls at the end of FY2008
A	B	C	D = B - C, if any	E = C - B, if any
Alabama (S)	$44.75	$112.55		$67.79
Alaska (M)		$23.01		$23.01
Arizona (S)	$35.50	$138.44		$102.95
Arkansas (C)	$53.00	$117.19		$64.19
California (C)	$94.61	$1,226.26		$1,131.65
Colorado (S)	$102.43	$70.69	$31.75	
Connecticut (S)	$74.43	$35.67	$38.75	
Delaware (C)	$17.31	$10.18	$7.13	
DC (M)	$18.05	$9.57	$8.48	
Florida (C)	$448.59	$259.74	$188.85	
Georgia (S)		$370.42		$370.42
Hawaii (M)	$13.87	$19.93		$6.06
Idaho (C)	$36.78	$31.11	$5.67	
Illinois (C)		$465.15		$465.15
Indiana (C)	$118.38	$98.75	$19.63	
Iowa (C)		$69.17		$69.17
Kansas (S)	$18.44	$51.42		$32.99
Kentucky (C)	$65.26	$83.03		$17.77
Louisiana (M)	$43.01	$130.97		$87.96
Maine (C)		$32.94		$32.94
Maryland (C)		$162.44		$162.44
Massachusetts (C)		$275.09		$275.09
Michigan (C)	$36.12	$182.46		$146.34
Minnesota (C)		$90.26		$90.26
Mississippi (S)		$116.76		$116.76
Missouri (M)	$4.39	$126.23		$121.84
Montana (S)	$14.02	$24.28		$10.25
Nebraska (M)		$35.51		$35.51
Nevada (S)	$89.65	$37.94	$51.70	
New Hampshire (C)	$14.86	$13.33	$1.53	
New Jersey (C)		$334.05		$334.05
New Mexico (M)	$78.21	$105.95		$27.74
New York (C)	$437.28	$412.08	$25.20	
North Carolina (C)	$9.02	$194.65		$185.64
North Dakota (C)	$0.70	$13.47		$12.77
Ohio (M)	$59.01	$228.80		$169.79
Oklahoma (M)	$32.00	$124.36		$92.36
Oregon (S)	$61.04	$105.17		$44.12
Pennsylvania (S)	$154.36	$230.08		$75.72
Rhode Island (C)		$77.02		$77.02
South Carolina (M)	$117.24	$120.86		$3.62
South Dakota (C)	$2.77	$13.95		$11.18
Tennessee (C)	$177.87	$66.38	$111.49	
Texas (S)	$1,012.72	$800.25	$212.47	
Utah (S)	$34.81	$56.09		$21.28
Vermont (S)	$9.80	$4.39	$5.41	
Virginia (C)	$65.92	$124.62		$58.70

Table 1. (Continued).

State	Projected balances of unspent FY2006 and FY2007 allotments available in FY2008	States' projected FY2008 federal SCHIP spending (provided in August 2007)	Projected unspent balances at the end of FY2008	Projected shortfalls at the end of FY2008
Washington (S)	$144.59	$29.65	$114.93	
West Virginia (S)	$23.25	$41.32		$18.06
Wisconsin (M)		$101.63		$101.63
Wyoming (S)	$9.80	$9.08	$0.72	
TOTAL $3,773.83		$7,614.31	$823.73	$4,664.21
Projected amount available from redistribution of unspent FY2005 funds				$108.2
Total projected state shortfalls if no FY2008 allotment (in millions)				$4,556.0

Source: Centers for Medicare and Medicaid Services (CMS) "FY07-08SF-Cht.xls," provided on September 14, 2007, based on states' projections of FY2007 and FY2008 SCHIP spending as of August 2007. SCHIP program types from table 1 of CRS Report RL30473, *State Children's Health Insurance Program (SCHIP): A Brief Overview*, by Elicia J. Herz and Chris L. Peterson.

Notes: S — Separate child health program. M — Medicaid expansion program. C — Combination program.

REFERENCES

[1] States exhausting their federal SCHIP funds in FY2007 will receive appropriations to cover their FY2007 shortfalls. The appropriation (not to exceed $650 million) was enacted on May 25, 2007, as part of the U.S. Troop Readiness, Veterans' Care, Katrina Recovery, and Iraq Accountability Appropriations Act, 2007 (P.L. 110-28).

[2] Based on states' August 2007 projections of expenditures, states forgoing unspent FY2005 funds would be Connecticut ($0.7 million), Tennessee ($33.4 million), Texas ($56.8 million), and Washington ($17.2 million).

[3] § 2104(f) of the Social Security Act.

[4] This was the Secretary's approach for the redistribution of unspent FY2002 funds in FY2005 and the redistribution of unspent FY2003 funds in FY2006. In all other redistributions, Congress prescribed the way in which the funds would be redistributed.

[5] § 2104(h)(1)(C) of the Social Security Act, as added by the National Institutes of Health Reform Act of 2006 (NIHRA, P.L. 109-482, enacted on January 15, 2007).

[6] The federal government matching rate for Medicaid expenditures — the Medicaid federal medical assistance percentage (FMAP) — ranges across states from 50% to 75.89% in FY2007. The enhanced SCHIP FMAP ranges from 65% to 83.12%. The difference between the percentages results from the states' share of expenditures being 30% smaller in SCHIP compared to Medicaid.

[7] See table 1 of CRS Report RL30473, *State Children's Health Insurance Program (SCHIP): A Brief Overview*, by Elicia J. Herz and Chris L. Peterson.

[8] Kathryn G. Allen, "Children's Health Insurance: States' SCHIP Enrollment and Spending Experiences and Considerations for Reauthorization," Government Accountability Office, statement before the House Energy and Commerce Subcommittee on Health, March 1, 2007, p. 32, at [http://www.gao.gov/new.items/d07558t.pdf].

[9] States may receive federal reimbursement for SCHIP claims even if the expenditures were incurred before a particular SCHIP allotment was available (42 CFR § 457.614(a)).
[10] § 2106(e).
[11] § 2106(b)(3)(B)(i).
[12] 42 CFR § 457.340(e)(2) and 42 CFR § 457.1180.
[13] 42 CFR § 457.340(e)(2).
[14] § 2106(b)(3)(B)(ii).
[15] § 2106(c)(2).
[16] 42 CFR 430.20(b)(3).
[17] 42 CFR 435.919(a).

In: State Children's Health Insurance Program (SCHIP) ISBN: 978-1-60456-333-7
Editor: Mary T. Ewing, pp. 159-165

Chapter 6

SCHIP PROVISIONS OF H.R. 6164 (NIH REFORM ACT OF 2006)*

Chris L. Peterson

ABSTRACT

The State Children's Health Insurance Program (SCHIP) is a federal-state matching program providing health insurance to targeted low-income children (and some adults) in families with income above Medicaid eligibility levels. Because SCHIP is a capped-grant program, it is possible for states to exhaust all of the federal SCHIP funds available to them in a given year. According to data available in late December 2006, 14 states are projected to exhaust their federal SCHIP funds in FY2007 (i.e., have a federal SCHIP shortfall). On January 15, 2007, the President signed into law H.R. 6164 (National Institutes of Health Reform Act of 2006, P.L. 109-482). The SCHIP provisions of H.R. 6164 require a redistribution of certain unspent FY2004 and FY2005 SCHIP original allotments to shortfall states in FY2007. The goal is to delay as long as possible the date in FY2007 on which any state faces a shortfall. Congress may address the remaining FY2007 shortfalls as part of reauthorization that provides SCHIP with appropriations needed beginning in FY2008. The SCHIP provisions of H.R. 6164 delay shortfalls to the first part of May 2007, according to current CRS projections. Although the provisions redistribute an additional $124 million for projected FY2007 shortfalls, the shortfalls remaining for the rest of the fiscal year are projected at $745 million. This report summarizes the SCHIP provisions of H.R. 6164 and their impact on SCHIP financing in FY2007.

The Balanced Budget Act of 1997 (BBA 97, P.L. 105-33) established the State Children's Health Insurance Program (SCHIP). In general, this program allows states to cover targeted low-income children with no health insurance in families with incomes above Medicaid eligibility levels. In BBA 97, Congress authorized and appropriated annual funding levels totaling nearly $40 billion for FY1998-FY2007, with each state receiving access to a portion of the annual amount. Each state's portion — the original allotment — is available for three years. At the end of the three-year period of availability, states' unspent balances are redistributed to other states that have exhausted that allotment. The specific amounts redistributed to the other states are determined by the Secretary of Health and Human Services (hereafter referred to as "the Secretary").

FY2004 original allotments still unspent as of the end of FY2006 totaled $146.9 million and are available for redistribution to other states in FY2007. Based on prior actions, the Secretary would likely have used his authority to redistribute the unspent FY2004 funds to *all* the states facing shortfalls in FY2007, in proportion to their total projected shortfall (Table 1). However, in order to delay shortfalls as long as possible, the SCHIP provisions of H.R. 6164 require the Secretary to redistribute the funds "in the order in which such [shortfall] States[1] realize monthly funding shortfalls ... for fiscal year 2007."[2] According to CRS projections, as shown in table 1, five of the 14 projected shortfall states would receive redistributed FY2004 funds under H.R. 6164. These states (Illinois, Maryland, Massachusetts, New Jersey and Rhode Island) are projected to receive redistributed FY2004 funds because they are the first projected to face FY2007 shortfalls. The redistribution of FY2004 allotments specified in H.R. 6164 is projected to delay the five states' shortfalls of federal SCHIP funds to approximately the end of March 2007.

To delay shortfalls even further, the SCHIP provisions of H.R. 6164 call for an initial redistribution of up to half of unspent FY2005 original allotments as of March 31, 2007 (capped at $20 million per state) — after 2½ years of availability. For a state to forgo unspent FY2005 funds on that date, H.R. 6164 requires not only that the state have unspent FY2005 balances but that the state's *total* SCHIP balances (from the FY2005-FY2007 original allotments) as of March 31, 2007, are at least double what the state projects to spend in federal SCHIP funds in FY2007. Sixteen states are projected to have unspent FY2005 balances on March 31, 2007, according to CRS projections. Of those 16 states, three (Arkansas, New Mexico and Wyoming) would not have total available balances of at least double their FY2007 projected spending and therefore would not forgo any FY2005 funds. Table 2 shows the 13 states currently projected to forgo FY2005 funds due to the the SCHIP provisions of H.R. 6164. Four states (Florida, Tennessee, Texas, and Washington) are projected to forgo the maximum amount ($20 million) on March 31, 2007.

This redistribution of unspent FY2005 funds does not replace the regular redistribution at the end of the allotment's three-year period of availability. CRS projects that only Tennessee and Washington will forgo any additional FY2005 funds at the end of FY2007 through the regular redistribution process. The projected federal SCHIP spending in these two states is so small relative to their allotment of SCHIP funds that the SCHIP provisions of H.R. 6164 are not projected to increase the total amount of FY2005 funds forgone compared to current law; H.R. 6164 simply makes $20 million of the projected total available earlier in the year, on March 31, 2007, from these two states.

CRS projects that the redistribution of the FY2005 funds on March 31, 2007, would provide an additional $124 million to shortfall states. Again, in order to delay shortfalls as long as possible, the SCHIP provisions of H.R. 6164 require the Secretary to redistribute the funds "in the order in which such [shortfall] States realize monthly funding shortfalls ... for fiscal year 2007."[3] According to CRS projections, as shown in table 1, six of the 14 projected shortfall states would receive redistributed FY2005 funds.

* Excerpted from CRS Report RS22553, dated January 18, 2007.

The SCHIP provisions of H.R. 6164 are currently projected to delay federal SCHIP shortfalls into the first week of May, based on estimates from the CRS SCHIP Projection Model. The limitations of these projections are discussed on the last page of this report.

ADDITIONAL PROVISIONS

Redistributed FY2004 and FY2005 funds to shortfall states can only be used for covering individuals who were eligible in a state's SCHIP program as of October 1, 2006.

When paid from redistributed FY2004 or FY2005 funds, the federal matching rate for SCHIP expenditures on non-pregnant adults is the regular Federal Medical Assistance Percentage (FMAP) available in Medicaid, rather than the usual enhanced FMAP available for SCHIP child health assistance.[4]

The SCHIP provisions of H.R. 6164 authorize the Secretary to make a retrospective adjustment to the amounts of the FY2004 and FY2005 funds that are redistributed. The Secretary's initial determinations will be based on states' projections and the latest available data at the time those determinations are made. By permitting a retrospective adjustment, the Secretary may alter those initial determinations in light of states' actual FY2007 expenditure data reported by November 30, 2007. The Secretary's authority with respect to the retroactive adjustment is limited in the following ways.

- The amount of FY2005 funds forgone by a state on March 31, 2007, cannot be increased (but it can be reduced).
- Additional amounts that may be required for shortfall states because of the retrospective adjustments can only come from FY2005 original allotments still unspent at the end of FY2007 (after three years' availability).

The SCHIP provisions of H.R. 6164 also make clear that (a) the Secretary is *not* authorized to redistribute FY2006 or FY2007 original allotments in order to eliminate FY2007 federal SCHIP shortfalls, and (b) the Secretary *is* authorized to redistribute any unspent FY2005 original allotments still remaining at the end of FY2007 according to the regular redistribution process.

Any shortfall states that received redistributed FY2004 or FY2005 funds in FY2007 have access to those funds during FY2007 only. Any of the funds unspent at the end of FY2007 will not be available for another redistribution (though potentially available for retrospective adjustments by the Secretary).

In previous years, the five commonwealths and territories (Puerto Rico, Guam, the Virgin Islands, American Samoa, and the Northern Mariana Islands) have received 1.05% of the total amount available for redistribution. However, the SCHIP provisions of H.R. 6164 stipulate that only states (defined to include the District of Columbia) may receive redistributed FY2004 and FY2005 funds in FY2007.

Extending the 20% Allowance

In 2003, P.L. 108-74 created Section 2105(g) of the Social Security Act, permitting qualifying states to apply federal SCHIP funds toward the coverage of certain children already enrolled in regular Medicaid. Specifically, these federal SCHIP funds are used to pay the difference between SCHIP's enhanced FMAP and the Medicaid FMAP that the state is already receiving for these children. Subsequent legislation amending this subsection has mostly added other years of federal SCHIP funds from which 20% spending could be drawn.

Qualifying states are limited in the amount they can claim for this purpose to the lesser of the following two amounts:

- 20% of the state's applicable original allotment(s) (hence the terms "20% allowance" and "20% spending"), and
- the state's balances (calculated quarterly) of available SCHIP funds from the applicable year's funds. If there is no balance, states may not claim 20% spending.

The 20% allowance can be used by qualifying states only for Medicaid enrollees (excluding those covered by an SCHIP-funded expansion of Medicaid) who are under age 19 and whose family income exceeds 150% of poverty. The primary purpose of the 20% allowance was to enable qualifying states to receive the enhanced FMAP for certain children who likely would have been covered under SCHIP had the state not expanded their regular Medicaid coverage before SCHIP's enactment in August 1997. Eleven states qualify to claim 20% spending: Connecticut, Hawaii, Maryland, Minnesota, New Hampshire, New Mexico, Rhode Island, Tennessee, Vermont, Washington and Wisconsin. In FY2006, only three states (New Hampshire, Vermont, and Washington) reported 20% spending.

Prior to H.R. 6164, the only funds available for 20% spending in FY2007 would have been from FY2005 funds. However, the SCHIP provisions of H.R. 6164 also permit FY2006 and FY2007 funds to be used for 20% spending, increasing the total amount permitted for 20% spending. This would at least triple the maximum amount of 20% spending permitted in FY2007 among qualifying states, according to CRS estimates.

Analysis

The goal of the SCHIP provisions of H.R. 6164 is to delay as long as possible the date in FY2007 on which any state faces a shortfall. Congress may address the remaining FY2007 shortfalls as part of reauthorization that provides SCHIP with appropriations needed beginning in FY2008. H.R. 6164 delays federal SCHIP shortfalls to the first part of May 2007, according to current CRS projections. Although H.R. 6164 provides an additional $124 million for projected FY2007 shortfalls (from redistributed FY2005 funds), the shortfalls remaining for the rest of FY2007 are projected at $745 million.

Table 1. Projected Amounts of Unspent FY2004 and FY2005 Funds Redistributed to Selected Shortfall States, Their Remaining Shortfalls, and Projected SCHIP Shortfall Date in FY2007 (in millions of dollars)

State	Shortfalls without FY2004 redistribution	Pre-H.R. 6164			H.R. 6164			
		Redistribution of FY2004 funds	Remaining shortfalls	Projected SCHIP shortfall date	Redistribution of FY2004 funds	Redistribution of FY2005 funds	Remaining shortfalls	Projected SCHIP shortfall date
Alaska	$13.5	$1.9	$11.5	5/14/07		$1.0	$12.5	5/3/07
Georgia	$128.5	$18.4	$110.1	5/25/07			$128.5	5/3/07
Illinois	$365.5	$52.3	$313.2	3/17/07	$68.5	$54.4	$242.6	5/3/07
Iowa	$15.0	$2.2	$12.9	7/10/07			$15.0	6/26/07
Maine	$0.5	$0.1	$0.5	9/24/07			$0.5	9/23/07
Maryland	$79.4	$11.4	$68.1	4/19/07	$2.4	$14.7	$62.4	5/3/07
Massachusetts	$139.1	$19.9	$119.2	3/10/07	$30.8	$20.6	$87.7	5/3/07
Minnesota	$15.8	$2.3	$13.5	7/30/07			$15.8	7/19/07
Mississippi	$23.7	$3.4	$20.3	7/31/07			$23.7	7/21/07
Missouri	$3.3	$0.5	$2.9	9/20/07			$3.3	9/18/07
Nebraska	$0.1	$0.0	$0.1	9/30/07			$0.1	9/30/07
New Jersey	$178.6	$25.6	$153.0	3/20/07	$32.0	$27.3	$119.3	5/3/07
Rhode Island	$49.9	$7.1	$42.7	2/21/07	$13.2	$6.4	$30.3	5/3/07
Wisconsin	$2.8	$0.4	$2.4	9/22/07			$2.8	9/20/07
Total	$1,015.8	$145.3	$870.5		$146.9	$124.4	$744.5	

Source: CRS SCHIP Projection Model, based on data from states provided to the Centers for Medicare and Medicaid Services as of late December 2006.

Notes: Pre-H.R. 6164 assumes the Secretary of Health and Human Services would have redistributed unspent FY2004 original allotments proportionally relative to states' projected FY2007 shortfalls. Projected SCHIP shortfall dates assumes constant claiming throughout the fiscal year. Redistribution of FY2004 funds pre-H.R. 6164 reflects 1.05% of the total going to the five commonwealths and territories.

Table 2. Projected Amounts of Unspent FY2004 and FY2005 Funds Forgone in FY2007 (in millions of dollars)

State	FY2004	FY2005			
	Both pre- and with H.R. 6164	Pre-H.R. 6164	H.R. 6164		
	Forgone at end of FY06	Forgone at end of FY07	Forgone on 3/31/2007	Forgone at end of FY07	Total
Colorado			$5.0		$5.0
Connecticut	$7.5	$10.7	$11.8		$11.8
Delaware	$0.8	$0.6	$2.4		$2.4
DC			$2.0		$2.0
Florida			$20.0		$20.0
Idaho			$4.5		$4.5
Nevada	$3.7	$9.2	$12.4		$12.4
New Hampshire			$1.2		$1.2
New Mexico	$1.4				
South Carolina			$3.9		$3.9
Tennessee	$58.0	$56.0	$20.0	$36.0	$56.0
Texas	$61.5		$20.0		$20.0
Vermont		$0.4	$1.1		$1.1
Washington	$14.1	$37.7	$20.0	$17.7	$37.7
Total	$146.9	$114.6	$124.4	$53.6	$178.1

Source: CRS SCHIP Projection Model, based on data from states provided to the Centers for Medicare and Medicaid Services as of late December 2006.

LIMITATIONS OF THE PROJECTIONS

The CRS projections are based on what states provided to the Centers for Medicare and Medicaid Services (CMS) as of late December 2006. States' projections will inevitably change, not only because of the usual challenges of predicting expenditures, but because states make changes to their programs — changes that will affect how much is ultimately spent. The projections are also based on states' reported FY2006 expenditures as of late December 2006.

The pre-H.R. 6164 analysis of shortfalls shown in table 1 was based on the assumption that the Secretary would use his authority (under section 2104(f) of the Social Security Act) to redistribute the unspent FY2004 funds to shortfall states in proportion to their shortfall. However, he was not required to do so. He may instead have decided to redistribute the unspent FY2004 funds as specified in the SCHIP provisions of H.R. 6164.

The CRS projections of the amounts forgone and the amounts of monthly shortfalls assume that states' projected spending is spread evenly across the fiscal year. But states may change their claiming practices in order to affect the level of funds they receive or forgo.

REFERENCES

[1] As stated in paragraph (1)(B), a shortfall state is one whose projected FY2007 federal SCHIP expenditures exceeds its balances remaining from its FY2005 and FY2006 original allotments as well as its newly available FY2007 original allotment. For more information on SCHIP original allotments, see CRS Report RL33366, *SCHIP Original Allotments: Description and Analysis*, by Chris L. Peterson.

[2] Paragraph (1)(C). Unless noted otherwise, all legislative references in this report are to the new Section 2104(h) added by the SCHIP provisions of H.R. 6164.

[3] aragraph (2)(C).

[4] For all but Alaska, the most up-to-date FY2007 FMAPs are available at [http://aspe.hhs.gov/ health/fmap07.pdf]. For Alaska, the information is available at [http://aspe.hhs.gov/health/ fmap07a.pdf].

In: State Children's Health Insurance Program (SCHIP) ISBN: 978-1-60456-333-7
Editor: Mary T. Ewing, pp. 167-174

Chapter 7

FY2008 SCHIP ALLOTMENTS*

Chris L. Peterson

ABSTRACT

The President vetoed legislation (H.R. 976) that would have provided new federal funding for the State Children's Health Insurance Program (SCHIP) in FY2008 through FY2012. On September 29, 2007, the President signed a continuing resolution that contains a temporary FY2008 appropriation for allotments for SCHIP (H.J.Res. 52, P.L. 110-92). Under this extension, SCHIP is appropriated the same amount for FY2008 that was appropriated for FY2007 ($5 billion), with the current-law formula used to allot these funds among the states and territories. The current continuing resolution makes the FY2008 allotments available only through November 16, 2007. The FY2008 allotments can be available past November 16 only if new legislation is enacted. Based on states' projections, if the current FY2008 allotments were available through the end of FY2008, 21 states would exhaust all available federal SCHIP funds during the fiscal year, with the first states experiencing shortfalls in March 2008. This report provides projections of those states' shortfalls as well as projections of states' FY2008 allotments as would occur under the vetoed H.R. 976 and new SCHIP legislation approved by the House, H.R. 3963, which is identical to the vetoed H.R. 976 in terms of the appropriations and formulas for SCHIP allotments.

A continuing resolution (H.J.Res. 52, P.L. 110-92, referred to hereinafter as the CR) appropriated $5 billion for federal SCHIP allotments in FY2008. The CR made no changes to the statutory formula for determining states' allotments. The amount of states' FY2008 federal SCHIP allotments is shown in Column F of table 1. The CR makes the FY2008 allotments available only through November 16, 2007.

In FY2008, states may also use unspent FY2006 and FY2007 allotments, with states' projected available balances shown in Column B of table 1. In addition, certain states will receive funds from the redistribution of other states' unspent FY2005 allotments, projected to total $108.8 million. The CR stipulates that the unspent FY2005 funds be redistributed to shortfall states (that is, states that will exhaust all other federal SCHIP funds) on a monthly

* Excerpted from CRS Report RS22739, dated October 25, 2007.

basis in the order in which states experience shortfalls. States' projected receipt of redistributed FY2005 funds is shown in Column C of table 1.

Column E of table 1 shows that, in the absence of an FY2008 allotment, approximately $4.5 billion would have been required to ensure no state faced a shortfall. Fourteen states and the District of Columbia (shown as having no amounts in Column E) are projected to have enough prior-year funding that the entirety of their projected FY2008 federal SCHIP spending could be covered without an FY2008 allotment. As shown in Column G of table 1, the CR's $5 billion for FY2008 as allotted, even if available for the entirety of FY2008, is projected to be insufficient for 21 states to cover their projected SCHIP spending. The current projected shortfalls for FY2008 (assuming the FY2008 allotments are available for the entire year) total $1.6 billion.[1] Column H of table 1 shows estimates of the month in which states would face shortfalls if the FY2008 allotment were available for the entire year, with the earliest states likely to experience shortfalls beginning in March 2008.

PROJECTED FY2008 ALLOTMENTS UNDER H.R. 976 AND H.R. 3963

H.R. 976, as vetoed by the President, and H.R. 3963, as recently approved by the House, would appropriate $9.125 billion for the states and territories in FY2008. As shown in table 2, the FY2008 allotment for a given state under both bills would be 110% of the largest of four numbers: (1) the state's FY2007 federal SCHIP *spending* multiplied by the annual adjustment;[2] (2) the state's FY2007 federal SCHIP *allotment* multiplied by the annual adjustment; (3) for states that receive extra federal SCHIP funds in FY2007 because of their shortfalls, or states that were projected to be in shortfall based on their November 2006 submission of projected expenditures, the state's FY2007 projected federal spending as of November 2006 (or as of May 2006, for North Carolina) multiplied by the annual adjustment; and (4) the state's FY2008 federal SCHIP projected spending as of August 2007 and certified by the state not later than September 30, 2007.[3]

With the projected FY2008 allotments that would occur under both bills (shown in Column F of table 2), there would be no federal SCHIP shortfalls in FY2008. Column G of table 2 shows how much larger the FY2008 allotments would be under both bills compared to the current law FY2008 allotments to states.

Table 1. FY2008 SCHIP Allotments Under Current Law and Projected Federal SCHIP Financing If Allotments Were Available Through the End of FY2008, by State (dollars in millions)

State	Available unspent FY2006 and FY2007 balances	Redistribution of other states' unspent FY2005 allotments	States' own projected FY2008 federal SCHIP spending	Additional amounts necessary to eliminate shortfalls	States' FY2008 Federal SCHIP allotments	Projected FY2008 shortfalls (assuming FY2008 allotment available for entire year)	Projected FY2008 shortfall month (assuming FY2008 allotment available for entire year)
A	B	C	D	E = D - C - B	F	G = E - F	H
Alabama	$44.8		$112.5	$67.8	$72.3		
Alaska		$0.05	$23.0	$23.0	$11.2	$11.8	March 2008
Arizona	$35.5		$138.4	$102.9	$143.0		
Arkansas	$53.0		$117.2	$64.2	$47.5	$16.6	August 2008
California	$94.6		$1,226.3	$1,131.7	$789.2	$342.5	June 2008
Colorado	$102.4		$70.7		$71.5		
Connecticut	$74.4		$35.7		$38.8		
Delaware	$17.3		$10.2		$12.8		
DC	$18.0		$9.6		$12.1		
Florida	$448.6		$259.7		$301.7		
Georgia		$2.6	$370.4	$367.8	$167.9	$199.9	March 2008
Hawaii	$13.9		$19.9	$6.1	$15.2		
Idaho	$36.8		$31.1		$23.8		
Illinois		$3.6	$465.2	$461.5	$208.3	$253.2	March 2008
Indiana	$118.4		$98.7		$97.4		March 2008
Iowa		$0.2	$69.2	$69.0	$33.2	$35.8	March 2008
Kansas	$18.4		$51.4	$33.0	$36.6		
Kentucky	$65.3		$83.0	$17.8	$68.2		
Louisiana	$43.0		$131.0	$88.0	$84.1	$3.9	September 2008
Maine		$0.2	$32.9	$32.8	$15.4	$17.3	March 2008
Maryland		$1.3	$162.4	$161.1	$72.4	$88.7	March 2008
Massachusetts		$44.4	$275.1	$230.7	$73.3	$157.3	March 2008
Michigan	$36.1		$182.5	$146.3	$147.1		
Minnesota			$90.3	$90.3	$48.6	$41.6	April 2008
Mississippi			$116.8	$116.8	$61.0	$55.8	April 2008

Table 1. (Continued).

State	Available unspent FY2006 and FY2007 balances	Redistribution of other states' unspent FY2005 allotments	States' own projected FY2008 federal SCHIP spending	Additional amounts necessary to eliminate shortfalls	States' FY2008 Federal SCHIP allotments	Projected FY2008 shortfalls (assuming FY2008 allotment available for entire year)	Projected FY2008 shortfall month (assuming FY2008 allotment available for entire year)
Nebraska			$35.5	$35.5	$21.4	$14.1	May 2008
Nevada	$89.6		$37.9		$51.1		
New Hampshire	$14.9		$13.3		$10.7		
New Jersey		$37.5	$334.0	$296.6	$105.5	$191.1	March 2008
New Mexico	$78.2		$106.0	$27.7	$52.0		
New York	$437.3		$412.1		$328.7		
North Carolina	$9.0		$194.7	$185.6	$136.1	$49.5	June 2008
North Dakota	$0.7		$13.5	$12.8	$7.9	$4.9	May 2008
Ohio	$59.0		$228.8	$169.8	$157.9	$11.9	September 2008
Oklahoma	$32.0		$124.4	$92.4	$70.8	$21.5	July 2008
Oregon	$61.0		$105.2	$44.1	$60.1		
Pennsylvania	$154.4		$230.1	$75.7	$168.8		
Rhode Island		$19.0	$77.0	$58.0	$14.0	$44.1	March 2008
South Carolina	$117.2		$120.9	$3.6	$71.0		
South Dakota	$2.8		$14.0	$11.2	$10.5	$0.7	September 2008
Tennessee	$177.9		$66.4		$99.8		
Texas	$1,012.7		$800.3		$556.2		
Utah	$34.8		$56.1	$21.3	$41.3		
Vermont	$9.8		$4.4		$5.6		
Virginia	$65.9		$124.6	$58.7	$90.3		
Washington	$144.6		$30.1		$79.9		
West Virginia	$23.3		$41.3	$18.1	$25.7		
Wisconsin	$6.5		$73.7	$67.2	$69.6		
Wyoming	$9.8		$9.1		$6.4		
State total	$3,780.3	$108.8	$7,586.8	$4,521.0	$4,987.5	$1,606.5	

Source: CRS analysis of data provided by the Centers for Medicare and Medicaid Services (CMS).

Note: The current continuing resolution (H.J.Res. 52, P.L. 110-92) makes the FY2008 allotments available only through November 16, 2007. However, states' available FY2005, FY2006 and FY2007 funds would remain available after November 16, even without additional legislation.

Table 2. Projected FY2008 Allotments That Would Occur Under H.R. 976 and H.R. 3963, With Comparison to FY2008 SCHIP Allotments Under Current Law, by State (dollars in millions)

State	(1) Based on FY2007 federal SCHIP spending	(2) Based on FY2007 federal SCHIP allotment	(3) Based on FY2007 shortfall states' projections provided in May or November 2006	(4) Based on states' projections of FY2008 federal SCHIP spending as of 9/30/07	Projected FY2008 allotments under H.R. 976 and H.R. 3963 (110% of the largest of the preceding numbers)	FY2008 projected allotments under H.R. 976 and H.R. 3963: Percentage difference vis-a-vis current-law FY2008 allotments
A	B	C	D	E	F	G = (F in Table 2 ÷F in Table 1) - 1
Alabama	$102.9	$79.4		$112.5	$123.8	71% larger
Alaska	$19.1	$12.4	$32.4	$23.0	$35.6	218% larger
Arizona	$125.9	$139.7		$138.4	$153.7	7% larger
Arkansas	$77.8	$53.0		$117.2	$128.9	171% larger
California	$1,269.3	$849.0		$1,226.3	$1,396.2	77% larger
Colorado	$68.1	$77.1		$70.7	$84.9	19% larger
Connecticut	$25.3	$42.5		$35.7	$46.8	21% larger
Delaware	$10.0	$11.9		$10.2	$13.1	3% larger
DC	$10.2	$12.5		$9.6	$13.8	14% larger
Florida	$288.4	$320.8		$259.7	$352.9	17% larger
Georgia	$361.5	$179.9	$338.5	$370.4	$407.5	143% larger
Hawaii	$20.3	$16.5		$19.9	$22.3	46% larger
Idaho	$29.6	$26.3		$31.1	$34.2	44% larger
Illinois	$455.4	$224.5	$619.0	$465.2	$680.9	227% larger
Indiana	$95.4	$100.2		$98.7	$110.3	13% larger
Iowa	$58.8	$38.7	$60.7	$69.2	$76.1	129% larger
Kansas	$49.4	$39.1		$51.4	$56.6	54% larger
Kentucky	$84.5	$75.2		$83.0	$92.9	36% larger
Louisiana	$121.7	$95.8		$131.0	$144.1	71% larger

Table 2. (Continued).

State	(1) Based on FY2007 federal SCHIP spending	(2) Based on FY2007 federal SCHIP allotment	(3) Based on FY2007 shortfall states' projections provided in May or November 2006	(4) Based on states' projections of FY2008 federal SCHIP spending as of 9/30/07	Projected FY2008 allotments under H.R. 976 and H.R. 3963 (110% of the largest of the preceding numbers)	FY2008 projected allotments under H.R. 976 and H.R. 3963: Percentage difference vis-a-vis current-law FY2008 allotments
A	B	C	D	E	F	G = (F in Table 2 ÷F in Table 1) - 1
Maine	$36.2	$16.1	$26.6	$32.9	$39.8	158% larger
Maryland	$159.2	$72.0	$162.5	$162.4	$178.8	147% larger
Massachusetts	$245.1	$78.2	$229.5	$275.1	$302.6	313% larger
Michigan	$191.3	$159.5		$182.5	$210.4	43% larger
Minnesota	$74.3	$52.2	$84.5	$90.3	$99.3	104% larger
Mississippi	$122.3	$64.7	$128.9	$116.8	$141.8	133% larger
Missouri	$97.5	$77.3	$105.7	$126.2	$138.9	79% larger
Montana	$19.5	$16.8		$24.3	$26.7	68% larger
Nebraska	$36.2	$23.5	$36.1	$35.5	$39.8	86% larger
Nevada	$34.1	$57.1		$37.9	$62.8	23% larger
New Hampshire	$11.8	$11.5		$13.3	$14.7	38% larger
New Jersey	$306.6	$112.6	$306.6	$334.0	$367.4	248% larger
New Mexico	$49.4	$55.6		$106.0	$116.5	124% larger
New York	$355.4	$362.6		$412.1	$453.3	38% larger
North Carolina	$187.9	$147.5	$287.5	$194.7	$316.3	132% larger
North Dakota	$12.4	$8.2		$13.5	$14.8	88% larger
Ohio	$203.0	$168.5		$228.8	$251.7	59% larger
Oklahoma	$105.4	$76.0		$124.4	$136.8	93% larger
Oregon	$74.8	$61.1		$105.2	$115.7	92% larger
Pennsylvania	$196.8	$184.8		$230.1	$253.1	50% larger
Rhode Island	$81.1	$14.9	$75.1	$77.0	$89.2	539% larger
South Carolina	$39.3	$75.7		$120.9	$133.0	87% larg

Table 2. (Continued).

State	(1) Based on FY2007 federal SCHIP spending	(2) Based on FY2007 federal SCHIP allotment	(3) Based on FY2007 shortfall states' projections provided in May or November 2006	(4) Based on states' projections of FY2008 federal SCHIP spending as of 9/30/07	Projected FY2008 allotments under H.R. 976 and H.R. 3963 (110% of the largest of the preceding numbers)	FY2008 projected allotments under H.R. 976 and H.R. 3963: Percentage difference vis-a-vis current-law FY2008 allotments
A	B	C	D	E	F	G = (F in Table 2 ÷F in Table 1) - 1
South Dakota	$13.8	$11.1		$14.0	$15.3	46% larger
Tennessee	$27.5	$104.9		$66.4	$115.4	16% larger
Texas	$405.6	$606.6		$800.3	$880.3	58% larger
Utah	$48.2	$43.9		$56.1	$61.7	49% larger
Vermont	$3.8	$6.1		$4.4	$6.7	19% larger
Virginia	$118.8	$101.4		$124.6	$137.1	52% larger
Washington	$28.7	$85.6		$30.1	$94.2	18% larger
West Virginia	$37.9	$29.4		$41.3	$45.4	77% larger
Wisconsin	$96.0	$74.4	$106.0	$73.7	$116.6	68% larger
Wyoming	$8.2	$7.4		$9.1	$10.0	57% larger
State total	$6,701.5	$5,362.0	$2,599.7	$7,586.8	$8,960.4	80% larger

Source: CRS analysis of H.R. 976 and of data provided by the Centers for Medicare and Medicaid Services (CMS).

Notes: Shaded cells denote which of the four values is the largest. For more information about H.R. 976, see CRS Report RL34129, *Medicaid and SCHIP Provisions in H.R. 3162, S. 1893/H.R. 976, and Agreement*, by Evelyne P. Baumrucker et al., available at [http://www.congress.gov/erp/rl/pdf/RL34129.pdf].

References

[1] Legislation has been introduced (H.R. 3584, Mr. Barton; S. 2086, Sen. Lott) that would, among other things, provide $5 billion for FY2008 allotments as under current law, but with an additional $1.5 billion appropriation for shortfalls. The legislation also provides $2.5 billion for the first six months of FY2009, to be allotted to states based on the current law formula, with $1.1 billion provided for shortfalls in that period.

[2] The annual adjustment under H.R. 976 would be the product of (1) the per capita health care growth factor, and (2) the child population growth factor. The per capita health care growth factor would be 1 plus the percentage increase in the projected per capita amount of National Health Expenditures over the prior year's. The child population growth factor would be 1.01 plus the percentage increase (if any) in the population of children under 19 years of age in the state, based on the most recent published estimates from the Census Bureau.

[3] Under H.R. 976, if the state allotments as calculated exceed the available national allotment, states' allotments would be reduced proportionally. Based on the projections in this report, the available national allotments appear to be adequate to cover projected FY2008 allotments under H.R. 976. For more information about the legislation, see CRS Report RL34129, *Medicaid and SCHIP Provisions in H.R. 3162, S. 1893/H.R. 976, and Agreement*, by Evelyne P. Baumrucker et al., available at [http://www.congress.gov/erp/rl/pdf/RL34129.pdf].

In: State Children's Health Insurance Program (SCHIP) ISBN: 978-1-60456-333-7
Editor: Mary T. Ewing, pp. 175-178

Chapter 8

COVERAGE OF THE TANF POPULATION UNDER MEDICAID AND SCHIP*

Elicia J. Herz

ABSTRACT

Health insurance is an important support for individuals receiving, leaving or diverted from the Temporary Assistance for Needy Families (TANF) welfare or cash assistance program for low-income families. Medicaid and SCHIP (State Children's Health Insurance Program) are key vehicles for providing such coverage. While there is no formal link between TANF and either Medicaid or SCHIP, some TANF-eligibles, especially children, are likely to qualify for one of these programs. But state eligibility rules can be complex and often differ for parents versus children, leaving some parents, in particular, without coverage. Finally, six to 12 months of transitional medical assistance (TMA) for families losing Medicaid coverage for work-related reasons expired on December 31, 2005, but was reinstated retroactively to this date, and extended through 2006 under the Deficit Reduction Act of 2005 (P.L. 109-171).

BACKGROUND

Medicaid provided access to medical services for approximately 55.4 million people in FY2003 (the latest official enrollment figure). To qualify, applicants' income and resources (also called assets) must be within program *financial standards*. These standards vary considerably among states, and different standards apply to different population groups within a state. Medicaid eligibility is also subject to *categorical restrictions* — generally, it is available only to low-income persons who are aged, blind, disabled, members of families with dependent children, and certain other pregnant women and children.

The Temporary Assistance for Needy Families (TANF) program provided cash assistance to 2.2 million families in FY2003. TANF is structured as a flexible block grant to states, and

---

* Excerpted from CRS Report RS22035, dated March 8, 2006.

it was the centerpiece of the 1996 welfare reform law, replacing previous entitlements to cash assistance. Under TANF, eligibility thresholds and benefit levels are established by states, but federal law imposes work requirements and time limits on benefits.

Prior to TANF, families qualifying for cash assistance under the former Aid to Families with Dependent Children (AFDC) program were automatically eligible for, and in most states, automatically enrolled in, Medicaid. In contrast, there is no direct link between eligibility for TANF and eligibility for Medicaid. Although TANF eligibility does not confer automatic Medicaid eligibility, Medicaid entitlement was retained for those individuals who meet the requirements of the former AFDC program as in effect on July 16, 1996. These old state-specific AFDC-related income standards are typically well below the federal poverty level (FPL). However, states may modify (i.e., liberalize or further restrict) these criteria for determining Medicaid eligibility for low-income families like those receiving TANF. Anecdotal evidence suggests that some states have chosen to align income rules for TANF and Medicaid, thus facilitating Medicaid coverage for some TANF recipients. While some states also provide Medicaid to higher-income adults under waivers of program rules, the AFDC-related rules are the main pathway into Medicaid for low-income, working parents.

Transitional medical assistance (TMA) is available for families who lose Medicaid due to increased hours of work, earnings, or child support payments. There are two separate TMA provisions in Medicaid law — one that permanently requires four months of coverage and another that requires six to 12 months of coverage, but is subject to a sunset rule. Under the latter provision, qualifying families receive an initial six months of TMA. A second six months of TMA is provided to those families who were covered during the entire first six-month period and whose earnings are below 185% of the poverty level. The six- to 12-month TMA provision expired on December 31, 2005, but was reinstated retroactively to this date, and extended through 2006 under the Deficit Reduction Act of 2005 (P.L. 109-171).

TMA can be particularly important for low-income parents, since there are few other ways through which such adults can maintain Medicaid coverage or private health insurance. However, over the years, Congress has created several other mandatory and optional coverage categories for children that are tied to income levels at or above the poverty line (up to 185% of the FPL for infants at state option).

Another pathway for low-income children in particular is the SCHIP. Established in 1997, SCHIP builds on Medicaid by providing health insurance to uninsured children in families with income above applicable Medicaid income standards. TANF children ineligible for Medicaid due to income are likely to qualify for SCHIP if they meet other eligibility rules. Each state defines the group of children who may enroll in SCHIP using factors such as geography, age, income and resources, residency, disability status, access to other health insurance, and duration of SCHIP eligibility. As of October 2004, 39 states covered at least some groups of children in families with income at or above 200% FPL. States provide SCHIP children with health insurance that meets specific standards for benefits and cost-sharing, or through their Medicaid programs, or through a combination of both.

Coverage for adults under SCHIP is restricted to special circumstances. As of May 2005, nine states (Arizona, California, Colorado, Illinois, Minnesota, New Jersey, Oregon, Rhode Island, and Wisconsin) had been granted approval specifically to enroll one or more categories of adults with children, typically parents of Medicaid/SCHIP children, caretaker relatives, legal guardians, and/or pregnant women; three states also covered childless adults.

Parents may also be covered through SCHIP programs providing premium assistance with employer-sponsored health insurance for eligible SCHIP children.

Concerns about under-utilization of SCHIP were raised early in the program and are still voiced by some today. But enrollment is growing. In FY2004, the number of children ever enrolled in SCHIP during that year reached nearly 6.2 million. During that same year, about 646,000 adults were enrolled in the program.

The Medicaid picture is more complicated. Analyses of program administrative data show that, between 1995 and 1998 — during the early years of the newly established TANF program — the number of able-bodied adults and children on Medicaid fell, while the number of aged beneficiaries stayed roughly constant, and the number of persons of all ages with disabilities rose slightly. For adults and children, reductions were greatest among those eligible for Medicaid via AFDC-related pathways, perhaps due to confusion about the relationship between TANF and Medicaid eligibility. These losses were only partially offset by enrollment gains through other eligibility routes, especially among children. In the late 1990s, enrollment declines were also affected by a strong economy, high employment rates, and rising income; lack of awareness of continuing eligibility; cultural/language barriers and immigration issues (e.g., five-year ban on Medicaid enrollment for certain aliens entering the U.S. after August 22, 1996); Medicaid's historical ties to welfare and its associated stigma; the often arduous enrollment process itself; and agency errors.

A different Medicaid enrollment picture emerged at the beginning of the 2000 decade. Program administrative data for the FY2000-FY2003 period show increases in enrollment in Medicaid overall and for all types of beneficiaries, with the largest enrollment gains for adults and children. In FY2003, the number of adults and children ever enrolled in Medicaid during that year reached 14.4 million and 27.4 million, respectively. Reasons for the increased enrollment among children and adults include the economic downturn that began in 2001, a drop in employer-sponsored insurance, and new or expanded Medicaid eligibility pathways through waivers and liberalization of income requirements for the AFDC-related group.

FUTURE CONSIDERATIONS

Both Medicaid and SCHIP have eligibility rules that leave some members of low-income families without coverage, most notably parents. Reinstatement and extension (through 2006) of six to 12 months of TMA for TANF recipients who move from welfare to work was included in the recently passed Deficit Reduction Act of 2005 (P.L. 109-171).

Some states have used waiver authority to cover childless adults and parents under Medicaid and SCHIP. However, P.L. 109-171 bars coverage of non-pregnant, childless adults through new waivers using SCHIP funds.

In general, further simplification of Medicaid and SCHIP program rules, streamlining of enrollment processes, and additional outreach have been deemed necessary for improving coverage rates for TANF eligibles and other groups. Even though states received some fiscal relief from the federal government in FY2003 and FY2004 to help offset Medicaid and other shortfalls, expanded coverage of the TANF population under both Medicaid and SCHIP may be affected by continuing federal and state budget constraints that have surfaced recently.

For More Information

CRS Report RL31698, Transitional Medical Assistance (TMA) Under Medicaid, by April Grady.

CRS Report RL33202, Medicaid: A Primer, by Elicia J. Herz.

CRS Report RL30473, State Children's Health Insurance Program (SCHIP): A Brief Overview, by Elicia Herz, Bernadette Fernandez, and Chris Peterson.

INDEX

A

B

G

H

I

J

L

M

N

O

P

Q

R

S

T